T0329990

Evolution and Economic Complexity

Evolution and Economic Complexity

Edited by

J. Stanley Metcalfe

Stanley Jevons Professor of Political Economy and Cobden Lecturer and Co-Director, ESRC Centre for Research on Innovation and Competition, University of Manchester, UK

and

John Foster

Professor of Economics and Head of the School of Economics, University of Queensland, Australia

Edward Elgar

Cheltenham, UK • Northampton, MA, USA

© J. Stanley Metcalfe and John Foster, 2004

All rights reserved. No part of this publication may be reproduced, stored in a retrieval system or transmitted in any form or by any means, electronic, mechanical or photocopying, recording, or otherwise without the prior permission of the publisher.

Published by
Edward Elgar Publishing Limited
Glensanda House
Montpellier Parade
Cheltenham
Glos GL50 1UA
UK

Edward Elgar Publishing, Inc.
136 West Street
Suite 202
Northampton
Massachusetts 01060
USA

A catalogue record for this book
is available from the British Library

Library of Congress Cataloguing in Publication Data

Evolution and economic complexity / edited by J. Stanley Metcalfe and John Foster.
    p. cm.
    1. Evolutionary economics. 2. Complexity (Philosophy). I. Foster, John, 1947 . II. Metcalfe, J.S. (J. Stanley).

HB97.3.E8858   2004
330.1—dc22   2004047788

ISBN 1 84376 526 8 (cased)

Printed and bound in Great Britain by MPG Books Ltd, Bodmin, Cornwall

Contents

Contributors

Professor Peter M. Allen Director of the Economic and Social Research Council (ESRC) Sustainable Complex Systems Network (NEXSUS), Director of the Complex Systems Management Centre, School of Management, Cranfield University, Bedford, UK.

Professor Esben Sloth Andersen IKE Group and the Danish Research Unit for Industrial Dynamics (DRUID), Aalborg University, Denmark.

Professor Uwe Cantner Department of Economics, Friedrich-Schiller University, Jena, Germany.

Professor Kurt Dopfer Department of Economics, University of St Gallen, Switzerland.

Bernd Ebersberger Department of Economics, University of Augsburg, Germany.

Professor John Foster Head, School of Economics, University of Queensland, Brisbane, Australia.

Professor Peter Hall University of New South Wales, Sydney, Australia.

Professor Horst Hanusch Department of Economics, University of Augsburg, Germany.

Jens J. Krüger Department of Economics, Friedrich-Schiller University, Jena, Germany.

Dr Francisco Louçã Unit for Research in Economic Complexity, Faculty of Economics and Management, University of Lisbon, Portugal.

Professor J. Stanley Metcalfe Stanley Jevons Professor of Political Economy and Cobden Lecturer and Co-Director of the ESRC Centre for Research on Innovation and Competition, University of Manchester, UK.

Paul Ormerod   Volterra Consulting, London, UK.

Dr Jason Potts   School of Economics, University of Queensland, Brisbane, Australia.

Professor Andreas Pyka   Department of Economics, University of Augsburg, Germany.

Dr Paolo Ramazzotti   Department of Economics, University of Macerata, Italy.

Bridget Rosewell   Volterra Consulting, London, UK.

Introduction and overview

J. Stanley Metcalfe and John Foster

This volume is dedicated to the goal of developing evolutionary economic analysis and associated sets of empirical tools to provide a coherent scientific approach that can deal with the real world of continual change in the economic system. Following on from Foster and Metcalfe (2001), we cast such endeavours in terms of complexity science, as applied in the context of complex adaptive systems in the economic domain. Two key themes can be discerned. First, a complex system is a network structure that contains elements and connections. These connections constitute knowledge and understanding. Thus, a theme throughout the volume is the fact that knowledge is core to economic systems and the source of economic value. Therefore, a clear appreciation of the nature of knowledge in a complex system setting is fundamental to analytical developments in evolutionary economic analysis. Second, selection mechanisms, captured in replicator dynamics, are viewed from a complex system perspective. This brings into clear relief the fact that replicator dynamics do not describe a tendency towards an equilibrium state or, from an empirical standpoint, regression to the mean. Looking at selection mechanisms in this way both emphasizes their relevance and, at the same time, highlights the fact that the variety they operate upon is of prior importance in economic systems because it arises from forms of knowledge that are much less prevalent in the biological domain.

As in Foster and Metcalfe (2001), this volume is expansive in its scope, embracing: quite abstract discussion of ontology, analysis and theory; discussions of how we can operationalize notions such as 'capabilities' from what we understand as 'knowledge'; the use of simulation techniques; and empirical case studies. Such a mix is quite deliberate. We believe that any attempt to separate theory from empirical inquiry is both false and likely to lead to confusion and misunderstandings. Only through the constant interplay of theoretical speculation, the development of methodologies and related analytical techniques and the careful observation of complex reality can robust scientific inquiry emerge in the socioeconomic domain. As economics has become more specialized, so these aspects of scientific inquiry have become separated and often incompatible with one another. Complex systems thinking leads easily to the conclusion that such a separation is untenable while, at the same time, because such systems display both order and organization, it is feasible to argue that reintegration is possible. In a sense, there is nothing new in this – it is what Adam Smith and many others did in the past with considerable intuitive skill. However, for decades, economists have sought to employ the increasing logical and calculative power at their disposal to replace intuition in the style of classical physics. Today, we are in the early stages of a quiet revolution in which economic complexity can be addressed directly with the powerful computational tools at our disposal instead of being cut into lifeless pieces. What is to follow in this volume is, we hope, a small contribution to this revolution in economic science.

Chapter 1 sets a challenging agenda both for the other contributors to the volume and to evolutionary economists generally. Kurt Dopfer and Jason Potts set down the foundations that they feel are necessary for the construction of evolutionary economic analysis. They ask the question 'What is meant by claiming that an economy is a complex system?', and set out the three principles – modularity, openness and hierarchic depth – that provide the answer. The fundamental point they make is that evolutionary thought cannot be 'bolted on' to mainstream thinking; it requires its own categories and concepts expressed in terms of these three principles. Their aim is to lay bare the relationship between complex system thinking and evolutionary thinking, as it turns out through the two quintessentially Marshallian notions, order and organization. Indeed, in the analysis of evolving knowledge-based systems, notions of order and organization, both of which are based on pattern formation, are primitive. They are also emergent and level dependent and neither entails any idea of general equilibrium.

Complex systems evolve because their components and subcomponents change at different velocities and because these velocities are mutually determining. To develop these ideas, Dopfer and Potts claim that it is essential to apply a more discriminating ontology, namely, one that is not 'flat', that is, permitting anything to exist at any level in a system. From the perspective of evolutionary science, this is related to the old and enduring question of being clear about the units of selection, the forces of selection, and the processes that result in ontological variation. This is an ambitious undertaking in that ideas of organization are far less well developed than ideas of order, and their argument cannot fairly be summarized without damage to the subtlety of its interconnections. Yet much of what they say is reflected in the ensuing chapters, albeit in a fragmented way and, although what Dopfer and Potts offers us is still very much 'work in progress', it is clear that they have made large strides towards their goal of offering a coherent analytical framework for evolutionary economists to work with.

The elements of an economy, set within an organizational structure, are agents. Rules provide the connective dimension of such structure and, as such, rule systems embody and articulate the knowledge contained in the system. Agents are the carriers of rules, they are the generators of rules, and they are the interactors, creating order and organization based upon the rules that they follow, so what evolves are rule systems or knowledges in particular (the plural is deliberate, as in Andersen – Chapter 6). Evolution is about making and reforming the connections between agents. This results in rule modification and entails variety and experimentation subject to the constraint that the manner of evolution must not compromise the viability of the rule-generating system. Since knowledge is always carried by individual agents and since economic action depends on cooperation, it follows that the knowledge of individual agents must be correlated, they must come to a common understanding to the requisite degree at the appropriate levels. Consequently, knowledge cannot be treated solely as a micro-agent property; rather it is a property of populations defined at meso levels for this is where correlation, the growth of common understanding, takes place. This is the meso level of analysis and it is the independent generator of all the micro and macro phenomena in the system.

Dopfer and Potts's analysis is sketched out at three interconnected levels to explore the idea of trajectories of evolving rules and, to this end, they replace 'methodological individualism' with 'methodological cyborgism', the necessarily statistical analysis of evolving rule systems. To make these ideas more concrete, they develop several analyses of how the transition between the micro and the macro is articulated via the concept of a meso trajectory, that is to say, an ordered pattern of change in rules and knowledge, which incorporates the familiar concepts of innovation, imitation and diffusion expressed as the emergence, spread and stabilization of new rules with modification. Among the many interesting points made, we note the significance of slack within such systems, the fact that disappearance of rules is just as significant as the creation of rules, and the fact that aggregates are ensembles that must be treated statistically and cannot be interpreted as uniform wholes. Taken together this is a powerful, albeit preliminary, statement of the nature of what Dopfer and Potts refer to as 'evolutionary realism'.

In Chapter 2, Paul Ormerod and Bridget Rosewell begin by observing that agent-based models of the kind to which the Dopfer/Potts reasoning, and other chapters in this volume, leads is bound to appear strange to most economists. The predictive power of the agent-based approach appears limited, results are often not transparent and the heterogeneity of agents militates against straightforward, elemental description. However, this is not in practice a weakness but rather a necessary step to come to terms with a complex world. What is at stake in this chapter are the terms under which it is agreed that models can be validated. They suggest three criteria: the plausibility of the presumed rules of behaviour, a clear understanding of the range of facts to be explained, and the precision of predictions across the range of facts. They show how two very simple agent-based models of the business cycle and the process of competition in deregulated industries perform better than widely accepted mainstream models of these phenomena. These different models lead to different insights. In particular, that it is not necessary to base the business cycle on the propagation of exogenous shocks and that competition is not realizable as a static structure. The normative policy implications of this approach are, as they conclude, rather profound.

Within the body of evolutionary thinking in economics there is an increasing recognition of the role of the growth of knowledge as a co-evolutionary process. In some of the more managerially oriented literature this is reflected in a discussion of the capabilities theory of the firm. This is the theme taken up in Chapter 3 by Paolo Ramazzotti and in Chapter 4 by Peter Hall. Ramazzotti explores the connections between managerial strategy, learning processes and the division of labour starting from G.B. Richardson's widely accepted notion of capabilities as 'knowledge, experience and skills'. His central theme is that the structure of capabilities co-evolves with the structure of the division of labour, and that managerial decisions over the form of the latter necessarily impinge in a fundamental way on the development of the former. This follows because the division of labour, read the organization of the firm, is the context in which problems emerge and knowledge grows. A central feature of this exposition is the emphasis on potential conflict within the firm that may arise when management and workers, or any other internal coalitions for that matter, may have different cognitive, motivating frameworks. This may be reflected in conflicts over distribution of value added or more generally in power struggles that undermine the very operation of the firm. Thus, Ramazzotti points to the importance of leadership and loyalty as conflict-containing and -resolving elements in the internal coherence of the firm and, indeed, as elements of needed capability in themselves.

This leads the author into an interesting discussion of the two-way relation between capabilities and the boundary of the firm, the significance of the choice of the division of labour (external as well as internal) for the evolution of capabilities, the distribution of power and incentives to cooperate, and alternative strategies for enhancing competitive performance. One may conclude here that, in a fundamental sense, strategy has to reflect the opportunities generally available for enhancing capabilities. When these are limited, and learning is more or less a redundant issue, it is perhaps more likely that management will seek competitive advantage through cost-cutting distribution-based policies, and organize the division of labour to minimize the ability of workers to deploy their knowledge through the imposition of tightly specified template routines. Conversely, where learning opportunities are rich, competition may depend more on product innovation and enhancement and require a more collegial approach to the organization of the division of labour.

In placing knowledge at the centre of the analysis of firm performance, any writer faces formidable obstacles and these are the focus of Peter Hall's detailed investigation into some of the theory and empirics that struggle to make sense of the notion and significance of tacit knowledge. If it is accepted that only human minds can know, in the ways relevant for social and economic action, then one immediately faces a different problem, namely, the idea that a firm can be said to know at all. Clearly, if any team is to function, the knowledge of its members must be sufficiently correlated to permit complementary, purposeful action. How this correlation is established is a fundamental issue in the organization of the firm and, as Hall points out, it is made vastly more complicated by the existence of substantial tacit elements in what can be correlated. All this matters because of the link between the differential performance of firms and the claim that these enduring differences are related to differential knowledge in general and differential tacit knowledge in particular.

More problematic still, any evolutionary theory of firm performance is intrinsically dynamic and accepts that changes in the external environment are part and parcel of the competitive process. If a firm is to survive it must adapt and if it is to adapt it must possess the necessary dynamic capabilities that enable its members to know more and to organize the correlation of that new knowledge. Thus, the central question becomes the empirical status of the mapping between dynamic capabilities and changes in firm performance. In Hall's account this requires two issues at least to be addressed, the identification of knowledge that yields strategic advantage, and the translation of knowledge into capabilities that can be articulated. This leads to some interesting conundrums, for example, the attributes of tacitness that protect knowledge from external, competitive scrutiny also make it difficult to communicate that knowledge within the firm to the degree required for effective correlation and the growth of understanding. To the extent that knowledge is easy to correlate within, then why does it remain difficult to correlate without?

Whether one is concerned with knowledge growth in-house or the external acquisition of knowledge in networks or other collaborative arrangements, the empirical difficulties are formidable, and are so by the very nature of tacit knowledge as an object of enquiry. Perhaps in part this is because what a firm knows is as much to do with its constituent 'knowers' as it is the nature of what it is they are claimed to know. Hall is quite correct in saying that optimizing models of the firm may give strategic insights into the formation of dynamic capabilities independently of issues centred on the nature of knowledge. Yet here one must be careful; evolutionary theory is quite compatible with the optimizing firm, as it is with any theory of the purposeful firm, rather what matters is not the optimality of behaviours but the variation of behaviours within the competing population, so bringing us back to his initial concern, namely, 'why do firms differ?'. A careful reading of Hall's chapter should help those who seek to undertake further empirical investigation of these issues.

In the following two chapters, we turn to more formal approaches to understanding an evolving economy.[1] They have at their core the essential role of diversity, but the way diversity is levered differs substantially across the two contributions. In Chapter 5, Peter Allen uses computer engineering techniques to explore the economic significance of complexity, interpreted in terms of the qualitative as well as the quantitative adaptation of a model system. As with all evolutionary systems the drive comes from diversity, as Dopfer and Potts stress 'flat' systems are dead systems. In turn, diversity is related to the ongoing division of labour and the consequent distribution of knowledge. In a complex economy, human expertise is localized and the wisdom of the system only applies collectively, at most. By virtue of our specialisms we are largely ignorant of the wider world, and as Friedrich von Hayek and others have argued it is precisely this attribute of human society that makes the case for the market economy as a discovery process, a process that capitalizes on local knowledge and general ignorance.

The force of Allen's chapter lies in the identification of the unexpected properties of knowledge-based and market-incentive-based discovery processes. His key insight is the realization that the expansion of a system into new conceptual spaces and dimensions, the *sine qua non* of development, is the dual to the growth of knowledge. The economic system is restless precisely because its existing configurations are always being challenged in a dialogue with new possibilities, the latent potential of which is always unknown and, necessarily, conjectured. Those innovations that 'take off' change the future system irreversibly and necessarily modify the conditions under which subsequent innovations will be tried and tested.

These ideas are worked out in the context of two different simulation models of an economy and of a manufacturing system based on core principles of selection and experimentation. In both models, fitness surfaces evolve over time and, as with all algorithmic processes that are good at 'hill climbing', they risk entrapment in suboptimal regions of the economic space. To escape requires experimentation, innovation, but at a price: the future is not predictable, nor can the present be uniquely explained in terms of the past. Observed life is one of many possible histories; it is mere contingency that we are where we are and, if the tape could ever be run again, the world would be quite different. Consequently, it is futile to talk of the optimality of arrangements at any stage in history; all we can note is that history makes itself. The question 'do we live in the best of all possible worlds?' can only invoke the response 'who knows?'.

The real force of this conclusion is that continued progress depends on wasteful experimentation; it is not our careful calculations that have produced the modern world but our imagination, and this means that mistakes will be made and these are, with the benefit of hindsight, the broken signposts of progress. To this degree, optimality, the search for accountability, is the enemy of ongoing development. Agent-based modelling suggests another powerful conclusion. Our world occupies an increasingly rich and dimensional space of possibilities but it never occupies more than a small proportion of the possible alternatives. There is always unfulfilled evolutionary potential. Thus, the emergent structural attractors of the system are always incomplete representations of what might have been. Those who link economic development with economic freedom and the capability to change, such as Amartya Sen, are clearly on the right track. However, in making this connection, they cannot say what development will mean in terms of future structures and relationships. That is the Faustian bargain that the complexity perspective presents.

Chapter 6 by Esben Andersen is a thorough evaluation of the challenges faced in developing a more general evolutionary account of the economy as distinct from the partial evolutionary representations of processes that are the stock in trade of the first generation of work since the pathbreaking study of Nelson and Winter (1982). As with Allen's chapter, there is a strong emphasis on the evolution of knowledge as the fundamental driver of economic evolution, with practical knowledge in focus precisely because it is this kind of knowledge that generates connecting principles between economic phenomena and noumena. Similarly, there is a dominant concern to incorporate the principles of the division of labour in the analysis, reflecting the theme so powerfully sketched by Allyn Young, that increasing returns, associated with the growth of knowledge, applies between as well as within specialized activities.

As Andersen makes clear, evolutionary theory is growth theory or rather theory of the differential growth of particular interconnected entities. The central principle here is that economic variety drives economic change, a principle first enunciated with precision by R.A. Fisher but amplified with telling effect by the evolutionary biologist G.R. Price. Andersen shows how Price's formula can always be deployed to decompose the growth of some focal variable into a 'selection effect' and an 'innovation effect' with the respective moments, variances and covariances of the joint population distributions being the measures of the evolutionary forces at work. This is a theorem of great power and generality that applies both within and between industries at as many levels of aggregation as one cares to specify. As with all evolutionary theory based on selectionist principles, how the economic world changes depends on how its various attributes are correlated. Thus, the search for an evolutionary theory of economic growth is a search for the relevant theories of the causes of economic correlation. We know that this necessarily involves dealing with markets and innovation analytically, but clearly there is more at stake.

This is a formidable intellectual challenge, made particularly difficult, as it is in Peter Allen's chapter, by the qualitative variation associated with the addition of new economic activities and the deletion of existing ones. Andersen sketches how these challenges can be confronted: by including endogenous research activity, by decomposing activities into subactivities and by introducing specialized intermediate goods into the analysis. He also demonstrates, along with Allen, how simulation techniques can be used to stretch our understanding of analytical results, reinforcing the significance of computer engineering in the evolutionist's tool kit. This is a rich agenda made particularly promising because the Price formula provides an opportunity to bridge directly between advanced work in evolutionary biology and evolutionary economics. Further work of this nature is likely to be crucial in determining the empirical agenda for the evolutionary economic research programme.

The final three chapters are more empirical in tone, while picking up on the evolutionary themes of their predecessors. In Chapter 7, Francisco Louçã explores the theme of statistical error in the historical development of economics, a theme of particular importance in the context of the competing claims of chance and necessity in the evolution of economies. He demonstrates how the idea of 'error' has passed through at least three incarnations: beginning with the notion of a mistake in measurement, developing into the idea as the deviation from average, predicted behaviour which is a property of a model not the real world, and finally, transmuting into the notion of an additive non-interacting disturbance to some system that is in equilibrium. He explores the conflicts between the early econometricians on this matter, pointing to the very wide range of (incompatible) meanings attached to the error term in modern economics. His conclusion is one that fits closely with the other chapters in this volume, namely that a biological notion of error as mutation opens up the scope for path-dependence and the impossibility of arbitrarily separating a model structure from the forces of error. We note in passing that the Fisher/Price methodology explored by Andersen is precisely a framework of this nature, as indeed is Allen's discussion of complexity.

Louçã demonstrates that in dealing with complex systems in economics, how we deal with something as seemingly innocuous as statistical error turns out to have fundamental implications for how we conduct statistical modelling exercises in economics. These implications are vast in that they challenge the validity of a very large proportion of empirical findings in academic journals of good standing and call for new ways of modelling that take explicit account of the evolutionary character of economic processes. Although we can be inspired in this quest by modelling strategies adopted by biologists, the higher order of complexity that we observe in socioeconomic systems will require more sophisticated modelling methodologies that grow out of the way we conceive of knowledge and associated understandings in such systems. It is in this regard that the insights offered by Dopfer and Potts (Chapter 1) can be of great assistance.

A central aspect of any evolutionary model is that the relative position of different competing entities changes over time, that is to say we expect to find mobility in relative positions with regard to variables of evolutionary significance. This is a difficult empirical domain in which to work, since its elucidation depends on having available data at a sufficiently disaggregated level over a sufficient period of time; the latter to wash out the less systematic forces, the former to ensure that evolution's signature is not erased by aggregation effects. In Chapter 8, Uwe Cantner and Jens Krüger explore this problem in an assessment of the amount of interfirm mobility in relation to productivity performance and relative market position across 11 German manufacturing industries over the 1981–93 period. In contrast to other approaches, they make imaginative use of two measures, the so-called Salter curves and Markov chain mobility indices, to unpack their data. They demonstrate that there are significant differences in mobility across industries and reach the general finding that mobility with regard to rates of productivity growth is always greater than mobility in terms of market shares; a finding they summarize in the notion that the technological sphere is more turbulent than the economic sphere. These results are also relevant to the issues raised by Paolo Ramazzotti and Peter Hall in that they imply a link between dynamic capabilities and their translation into competitive performance. As the authors point out, the elucidation of theoretical models that connect the different dimensions of turbulence provides a promising avenue for further evolutionary research, picking up issues in earlier chapters.

In Chapter 9 by Andreas Pyka, Bernd Ebersberger and Horst Hanusch, many of the threads contained in the previous chapters are drawn together into a discussion of ways in which a market, the energy market in their case, can be explored and modelled using evolutionary concepts and methodologies. The problem they pose is how development can be understood in terms of economies transforming themselves over time, quantitatively and qualitatively, through structural changes, broadly conceived. The answer they provide is that agent-based modelling is the preferred evolutionary method, as suggested by Paul Ormerod and Bridget Rosewell, Peter Allen and Esben Andersen. Such a framework enables variety to be represented formally and its dynamic consequences to be modelled in rigorous fashion. Crucially, it opens up the possibility of vicarious economic experiments; this is exactly the claim that is made for these techniques in computer engineering. From a policy point of view this is of crucial importance, since it allows for the experimental design of any degree of complexity and is capable of uncovering stable relationships that are beyond analytic representation. The authors go on to catalogue the requirements for an agent-based model of the energy market that is capable of addressing key policy questions, such as the balance between renewables and non-renewables or the implications for CO_2 emissions, as well as the nature of past major energy transitions.

Taken together the chapters, originally presented at the second Brisbane Club conference in Manchester, 5–7 July 2002, provided a sharpening of our focus on the relationship between economic evolution and economic complexity. Needless to add, the meeting raised more questions than it answered, particularly in relation to the notion of complexity and the growth of knowledge. We anticipate that this will be one of the themes of the next Brisbane Club meeting.

Finally, it remains to thank the many contributions of our colleagues who helped to organize the workshop. In particular, we thank Sharon Hammond and colleagues in the ESRC Centre for Research on Innovation and Competition for their assistance together with the ESRC for its financial support. We also thank Sharon Dalton for the very considerable contribution she made editing the chapters and turning the manuscript into a finished product. We thank them all and hope we can call on their services again.

NOTE

1. A companion paper by J.S. Metcalfe, J. Foster and R. Ramlogan, 'Adaptive Economic Growth', analysed modern capitalism as a self-transforming process, tracing the relationship between micro diversity and emergent macro structure in the presence of enterprise and the coordinating role of markets. This paper is to appear in the *Cambridge Journal of Economics*.

REFERENCES

Foster, J. and J.S. Metcalfe (eds) (2001), *Frontiers of Evolutionary Economics: Competition, Self-Organization and Innovation Policy*, Cheltenham, UK and Northampton, MA, USA: Edward Elgar.

Nelson, R.R. and S. Winter (1982), *An Evolutionary Theory of Economic Change*, Cambridge, MA: Harvard University Press.

PART I

Theoretical Perspectives

1. Evolutionary foundations of economics

Kurt Dopfer and Jason Potts

ON ECONOMICS, COMPLEXITY AND EVOLUTION

All ordered systems resemble one another, but each complex system is complex in its own way. The economy is a complex system, and so we might ask what, then, are the specific properties that make it complex? We say this: the complexity of the economic system is due to its *modularity*, *openness* and *hierarchic depth*. The economic system is modular in the sense of being made up of a large number of functionally specific parts. It is open in the sense that these parts interact with degrees of freedom. And it is deep in the sense that each module is itself a complex system: every part is a whole and every whole is a part. The economic system is modular, open and deep, and because there are many ways for a system to be like this, complexity is inherently emergent. Each complex component of the economic system tends to be complex in its own way.

Yet there are overarching insights, and models of economic evolution nowadays incorporate many of these aspects of complexity (see, for example, Arthur et al. 1997; Foster and Metcalfe 2001). These refinements and additions have brought many improvements in the range and quality of evolutionary economic analysis. The problem, however, is that complexity is not really something that just bolts-on to an extant analytical framework to add a 'complexity perspective' over and above a 'mainstream perspective'. For example, it has become commonplace now to see 'evolutionary models' or 'complex systems' analysis claimed as such because replicator dynamics or statistical selection were used somewhere in the argument. These misrepresent what complexity means in relation to economic evolution. Complexity is a way of viewing the economic system in terms of what it really is. It is modular, in the sense that it is made up of functional systems that are connected to other systems. It is open, in the sense that these connections can change. And it is deep, in the sense that the modules are closed self-generating (autocatalytic) processes. In our view, what this means is that at the core of evolutionary economics must lie a distinction between the two classes of structure represented by these dimensions of complexity: order and organization. The purpose of this chapter is to show how ontological abstraction about the meaning of the complexity of economic systems leads us naturally into a micro–meso–macro structure for evolutionary economic analysis.

Order, in general, appears in the form of a pattern. A pattern is a stable set of interactions, spatial or temporal. The interactions between electrons in a crystal lattice and between agents in a regular market, although on very different time scales, are both instances of order. In general, where patterns of interaction repeat, we say there exists order. Organization is a special type of order. Organization is order that suggests design because of the property of functional closure about a cycle of work processes (for example, Collier and Hooker 1998; Kauffman 1998). Organization is more than order because an organization also does something functional. Order and organization are structures of interactions or connections variously in space and time. An ordered pattern may continue in time by a process of regeneration (for example, a standing wave) or self-replication (for example, a cellular automata: CA). When order is driven externally (as in the case of the standing wave), or does not essentially require interaction and exchange with its environment (as in the case of a CA), then it is order and not yet organization. Organization is the self-containment of a repli-cation process (and therefore is more than the general replication of order). Organization refers to a functionally closed system interacting with its environment, in part to maintain the organization, in part to develop it. The elements of an economic system are units of organization, or rules.

The problem is that most received economic theory is not actually about organization at all, but rather entirely about order (see Coricelli and Dosi 1988; Mirowski 1989; Potts 2000). Most economic theory is based on the idea that when dealing with an economic system, we are dealing with an ordered system. Mechanics and the analysis of equilibria in closed systems are examples of theories of order. These and associated techniques under-pin the methods of inference, analysis and control that support the great-est part of theoretical and applied science. Order is a concept accompanied by a significant body of general scientific understanding, which is, perhaps, why economics has traditionally offered such feeble resistance to the idea that the economic system is made up of *nothing but* order (for example, ordered preferences, ordered technologies, order as choice, order as equi-libria). The fact of the matter is that there are many theories of order, but few theories of organization. There are no general theories of organization to rival the general theories of order – classical, statistical and quantum mechanics – in refinement and scope. Given that the economy is complex and complexity is a property of organization, economics will ultimately require a theory of organization.

We do not accept theories of mechanism design or transaction cost economics as general theories of organization. These deal with objects that are organizations (firms) or objects that are designed (market mechanisms), but they are analysed as ordered systems that simply react to external stimuli and do not essentially require *interaction* to exist. They ultimately fail to distinguish between order and organization.

Indeed, the only serious contender to a general theory of organization is the theory of evolution. But, for this to be so, evolution must be interpreted simultaneously as a theory of design (Simon [1968] 1981; Dennett 1995), a theory of self-organization and complexity (Prigogine 1976; Kauffman 1993), and a theory of rule-systems (von Neumann 1966; Holland 1975; Mirowski 2002). Organization, as an emergent form (for example, life, consciousness, agent), is a process of autocatalytic closure in an open system maintained through ongoing exchange with the local environment (*pace* Arrow 1974). Hooker and Christensen (2000) propose organization as a kind of metabolic process about the maintenance (or self-making) of knowledge. But despite these and other such advances, most evolutionary theory is still about ordered processes: there is, as yet, no general evolutionary theory of organization. We do well to remain mindful of this distinction (as did Hayek 1991) because an evolutionary theory of the origin of order interpreted as the origin of organization is all we have at the moment to explain complex processes of change in open systems (see Kauffman 1998, p. 72).

That said, what are the units of organization in an economic system? Primarily, the economy is made up of *agents*. Agents include humans, firms, households, governments, industries, nation states and other such organized coalitions. The self-generation of order, as the concept of organization, is essential to the concept of agency. The concept of an agent is, in this sense, congruent with the concept of a mechanism, which also enforces an order (see Potts 2001). But an agent is more than a self-generating order. An agent also interacts intentionally with the environment to maintain this order, and organization therefore extends to making order in the external environment of the agent. An agent is a bounded entity – an organized rule system – that interacts with an environment to sustain its internal order and organization.

The economy is complex and this complexity is manifest in both order and organization. Agents and rules are the basic units of organization. The economic system is the emergent order between organizations. Evolutionary foundations for economics require an entirely new ontological approach defined in terms of evolution, agency and complex systems. This is what we propose in evolutionary realism and its central concept: the meso rule, the element of both micro organization and macro order.

EVOLUTIONARY REALISM AND THE MESO

Beyond Flatland: On the Need for an Evolutionary Ontology

A new ontology is necessary to advance evolutionary analysis in economics. This is because of a basic problem with the received ontology in economics: in short, it is too flat. Specifically, the problem is that everything that exists in a flat ontology exists everywhere at once and all on the same level. There is no essential modularity, openness or depth in this conception of the economic object, and there is a growing appreciation that the underlying analytical problem is ultimately ontological in nature (see Dopfer 2001; Mäki 2001). Evolutionary theory demands a clear identification of the units of replication, variation, interaction and selection, but a flat ontology can make no sense of this. It is quite meaningless to search for units of organization or to map interaction networks when theorists are just as happy with agents that are infinitely small or economies that are infinitely large (see Potts 2000: ch. 2 on the geometry of economic space).

So, what is the alternative to a flat ontology? What is a complex economic system actually made up of? Consider the pragmatic empiricist posture, in which the economic system comprises agents, resources, preferences, technologies, institutions, behaviours and, indeed, all sorts of things. The problem is that all of these existences are ontologically dissimilar. Some are observable and denumerable, some are statistical constructions, and some are processes: theoretical elegance hides ontological incommensurability. But does this really matter? What consequences will arise if we continue to ignore this ontological muddle?

In our view, the basic problem when ontology is flat is that effectively anything can exist. In a flat ontology, for example, it is perfectly alright to refer to phenomena such as 'social capital' or 'stocks of ideas' without ever actually specifying what must be true in order for such implied things to exist. This sort of highly permissive ontological posture, although inordinately useful for subject domain assimilation, ultimately serves to weaken economic theory because it renders it all but impossible to actually test – what, for example, are the units in which one measures a stock of ideas or a unit of social capital? The overarching methodological implication of ontological flatness is that theories become displaced only by other theories and rarely by evidence. A flat ontology makes it very difficult to scientifically analyse processes of change and evolution in the social domain.

Ontological flatness is each existential dimension orthogonal to every other, so that each existence is in effect ontologically equivalent to every other. Ontological flatness is the sometimes-convenient absence of a theory of what actually exists. But, as our pragmatic empiricist list indicates, we do, of course, innately distinguish between the different categories of things that constitute the economic system. As Nelson and Winter (1982) perceptively pointed out, the appreciative ontology of economic analysis is rather different from the formal ontology upon which theories are based (see also Vromen 1995; Clower and Howitt 1997; Lawson 1997; Potts 2000; Mäki 2001). But if a flat ontology can be accommodated in this subtle way, does it really matter?

Consider the costs and benefits of a flat ontology. There should be no doubt as to the benefit. Ontological flatness improves the import of technology, the general use of powerful analytical methods such as comparative statics, real fields, equilibria-based solution concepts and the like, and the analytical results (that is, proofs) they bring. Ontological flatness has the massive benefit of high rates of technical adoption. But it is rather light on the meaning of these, and herein lie the costs. The basic cost of ontological flatness is the loss of 'dynamical-only' concepts, as all evolutionary concepts are. Emergence, organization and novelty cannot occur in a flat ontology. One can never talk sensibly about properties that are emergent at different levels of interaction in a flat ontology because *there are no different levels of interaction*. Certainly, some may be faster or slower than others (as in economic dynamics) but nothing can be said about the openness of interaction and the emergence of new forms of order and organization. The problem with ontological flatness is that you cannot analyse open-system processes – and that is problematic, because the economic system is almost a paradigmatic example of an open-system process.

So let us be clear about these costs and benefits. If analysis is essentially about comparative statics or closed-system dynamical processes, then ontological flatness has many more benefits than costs. But for analysis of open-system dynamics the order is reversed. Here, ontological flatness is problematic for the simple reason that without the analytical approximations afforded by ontological flatness – equilibrium methodology, field theory and so forth – then analytical foundations must instead come from a clear statement of what specifically exists and how. What is the proper identity of the unit of selection/variation/interaction/replication? What actually changes in a process of change? What is the role of interactions in building organization? Where specifically is the complexity in a complex system? Dynamics, and especially evolutionary dynamics, requires a more

structured ontology than closed-system statics because of the need to constrain the possible transformations of the system while still allowing for
openness, variety, interaction and emergence.

The central idea in our framework of evolutionary realism is that an economic system is made up of knowledge in the form of meso rules. Rules are
the elements of knowledge in the form of a structure and a process. The
rule ontology of knowledge extends across many economic concepts. Rules,
for example, are carried by agents and therefore must be accessed, adopted
and adapted by agents (preferences and technologies are knowledge). The
learning of a rule is the micro growth of knowledge. An institution, as we
define it, is a consequence of the population of a rule. Statistical aspects of
rule adoption are part of the macro growth of knowledge. Behaviours are
rule processes, and so are outcomes; rules are objects and rules are
processes: utility is a measure of a rule, and profit is another. This is to say
that rules have value. Competence is a cluster of rules, as a rule system.
Markets are rule systems, and so are firms and agents. Objects and systems
are rules. An economy is made up of knowledge, as the system of rules that
have value. But where ontologically speaking is the concept of a rule? The
building block of an economic system, in our view, is the unit of organization that makes the elements of order an open and hierarchic component
of a higher system (macro) and an open and modular subsystem into which
it fits (micro). This rule and its population is the concept of the meso. The
meso underpins and connects both the micro and macro evolutionary
domains.

The Meso

The economy is made up of meso rules. *Evolutionary realism* is an ontology
to describe this form of existence in terms of three empirical axioms: (1)
the associations between rules; (2) the processes implied by each rule; and
(3) the bimodal populations structures of each rule. Association, process
and bimodality ontologically define the meso building blocks of evolutionary economic reality.

Axiom 1: all existences are associations
This says that existences are always by association with other existences and
are never singular (existences are not *events*). Association, however, does not
imply association with all other existences, only to some. The geometry of
associations is partial and the geometry of economic space is non-integral
(Potts 2000). Existences are therefore always systems of elements and connections and it is the connectedness (or embeddedness) of reality that makes
it 'real' (in the realist sense). The building blocks of evolutionary reality are

systems of associations (and processes, by axiom 2) that we call *rules*. Rules (and their populations of matter-energy actualizations, by axiom 3) are the elementary existences of an evolving economic system.

An element is defined by the specific nature of its connections. In this way, the axiom of partial association gives the concept of information analytical meaning. Information is the measure of the quality of association between parts that 'inform' each other, by being in some form of structural relation, or correspondence or correlation, to each other. If two ideas cannot or do not associate, then there is no information (in-formation) between them. Associations, as information, are the statics of knowledge; economic evolution is the growth of knowledge. The growth of knowledge refers to the dynamics of connections. New experimental associations are created, working associations are maintained and redundant associations are destroyed (Schumpeter 1942; Loasby 1999). The dynamics of association are the dynamics of information. Connections and information are variables in the analysis of an evolving universe. Associations are not directly observable (they are not material objects) but rather must be conjectured, discovered and tested by experimental processes. This is the empirical significance of axiom 1: meso is an element in a connected system and does not exist otherwise. Knowledge is a connected system. The concept of rules as both elements and connections allows us to refer to a static structure of associations as providing the necessary ontological conditions for a computational structure of information (Hayek 1945; Potts 2001). The structure of associations is the geometry of the meso. This will refer to the learning environment in the micro, and the deep structure of the knowledge base in the macro.

Axiom 2: all existences are processes
By axiom 1 alone, existence has no temporal aspect. Axiom 1 says that information exists as associations, but it does not say *how* those associations exist. Axiom 2 says that information exists as a process. This is what we mean by *knowledge*. Knowledge is an associative rule as a process. It is both a spatial and a temporal structure. When a process ends or when a new process begins, the information content of the universe has changed. When a process continues, the information content of the universe has been maintained. Associative processes are the elements of history, and evolutionary analysis is the study of these associations as processes in time. Knowledge is a process because it is the concept of the extension of an association in time.

Axiom 3: all existences are bimodal
Axiom 3 states that a rule is both an idea and an actualization in matter-energy form. Bimodality is between the idea mode (form/information) and

its physical realization (matter-energy). Bimodality is the concept of the one and the many, with each idea having perhaps many realizations. This set of realizations is the population of the rule. A stable and significant rule population is called an institution. The dynamical path of a meso is called a trajectory (and related to the idea of an information cascade on a network).

An Economy is a Complex System of Rules

The meso refers to the existential population of a rule that satisfies the three axioms of evolutionary realism: knowledge is a structure of associations, as a process, as a population. The economic system is composed of a bimodal-associative-process structure of meso rules: the economy is a complex adaptive system of meso rules. When we conceive of an economy as an ensemble of these rules, we are doing macroeconomic analysis. When we focus on the carriers of these rules and the processes of adoption and adaptation, we are doing microeconomic analysis. And when we focus upon the evolution of a rule through a process of origination, diffusion and retention, then we are principally doing mesoeconomic analysis. The three-phase evolution of a rule, outlined later in the section 'A framework for evolutionary economics', is described as a *meso trajectory*.

An economy is a complex system of rules, and economics is the study of the coordination of these rules and how they change. Economics, when viewed from an evolutionary perspective, is not methodologically centred upon the individual agent, but rather on the individual unit of knowledge, the rule. The rule is carried by the agent, but an evolutionary description of an economic system requires focus upon the dynamics of the rule populations. Economics, then, is the study of the economy as a complex system of rules, not all of which reduces to choice theory.

Consider it this way: our rejection of methodological individualism is perhaps otherwise seen as an acceptance of 'methodological cyborgism' (Mirowski 2002). We view the concept of the meso as a step towards a machine ontology of knowledge (or 'cyborg naturalism') in which the meso element refers to any concept of a rule as a process unit (for example, habit, routine, strategy, technology, heuristic, skill, institution, competence and so on). The cyborg ontology is based about the idea that the economy is made up of rules and rule systems. This is a view that is becoming increasingly prominent. Recently, for example, experimental economists have begun to argue that markets are automata and that automata are rule systems (for example, Gode and Sunder 1997). Evolutionary economists argue that markets are rule systems (for example, Buchanan and Vanberg 1991; Kirman 1997; Mirowski and Somefun 1998; Ménard 1995; Potts 2001). This aligns with our evolutionary ontology: the economic system is made up of rules (the meso), and the subject of evolutionary economics is the structure and change of these rules. Now this is certainly not a novel idea, for economic rules viewed as a kind of self-reproducing automata is almost precisely John von Neumann's original vision for economics as a cyborg science (Mirowski 2002, p. 536; Wolfram 2002). Evolutionary realism is a cyborg naturalism in the sense of both von Neumann and Wolfram (also Stanislaw Ulam, Herbert Simon, John Holland, Stuart Kauffman et al.) to underpin a methodology of rule-following interacting agents and their emergent statistical dynamics. The meso is the plane where we acknowledge the existence of rules as associations and processes.

Evolutionary economists often say that their methods are 'process oriented' or 'dynamics first'. What they mean is that processes exist, and that static analysis mostly fails to see this. By starting with process dynamics, this limitation is avoided. But statics is not dismissed altogether, because we still need to be able to say what actually exists at a point in time in order to recognize what is actually changing. By evolutionary statics, then, we mean stable ordered patterns of interaction between elements. Evolutionary statics are the statics of processes, as stable patterns of interactions between rules. *Pace* Schumpeter's espousal of the static foundations of the Walrasian circular flow, we prefer Marshall's forests and trees, or Prigogine's dissipative systems, for our conception of statics as a structure of rules. A complex evolving economic system is always in substantial disequilibrium, but it still has a meaningful conception of statics in relation to the processes of order and organization that sustain it. Dynamics first means looking first at the statics of these dynamical processes in terms of their organization at the micro level and their order at the macro level. Both of these analytical domains are underpinned by the meso.

The Meso Foundations of Micro and Macro

Meso concepts relate to systems of rules. Micro concepts relate to agents carrying and using rules. Macro concepts are about the order of all rules (the structure of the meso). The analytical foundations of micro and macro are both meso, and therefore of the relation between evolutionary microeconomics and evolutionary macroeconomics. Evolutionary microeconomics concerns rules carried in agents and the interaction between these agents. This includes learning, search, strategic interaction, problem solving and local processes of adoption, adaptation and retention. In essence, the micro is all about the organization of the agents and the order of their interactions. Evolutionary macroeconomics connects the deep structure of the meso (the knowledge base) to the surface structure of the economy. Macro addresses market competition, industrial dynamics, increasing returns, networks, structural change, self-organization, co-evolution and growth theory. But one does not go directly from micro to macro, or vice versa. Both evolutionary micro and evolutionary macro are constructed in terms of the meso, the analytical domain in which the growth of knowledge occurs.

The Economic Problem and the Meso

The evolutionary economic problem – in the sense of a general problem for both agents and the whole, such as the allocation of scarce resources (Robbins 1935) or the distributed computation of information structures (Myerson 1999) – is the coordination of parts into emergent wholes (Dopfer 2001). Evolutionary economics is the generalized study of the coordination problem in the context of the growth of knowledge by evolutionary mechanisms (Loasby 1999). Both the allocation and the computation problem are special cases within this (see Mirowski 1989, 2002). The evolutionary economic problem is defined as a growth of knowledge problem by the concept of the meso. Evolutionary economics is the study of the order and organization in meso objects. Meso objects are rules, and rules evolve as a process of order and organization.

The principle that connects the evolutionary economic problem to theory and analysis is that of *efficacy*. Efficacy is to evolutionary economics, what the concept of efficiency is to neoclassical economics, namely a selection principle (Alchian 1950). Efficacy is the quality of rules working together. *Associations* are rules working together. *Processes* are the result. And *bimodality* is the idea that the real (compare nominal) economic system is a manifestation of a deep meso structure. There exist rules and there exist realizations of these rules. Efficacy is both a local and global selection principle for analysing the coordination and growth of knowledge in which knowledge is a bimodal process structure of associations. Evolutionary economic analysis requires an ontology for an evolving economy, and the purpose of this ontology is to provide a foundation for a theory of economic evolution. We have so far outlined in three axioms the ontology of evolutionary realism. We now outline the framework that is built upon it.

A FRAMEWORK FOR EVOLUTIONARY ECONOMICS

A Meso Trajectory

Central to the theory of economic evolution is the concept of a meso trajectory. A meso trajectory is a three-phase process of change in the knowledge base of an economic system. It consists of a change in the order and organization of the economic system, as it evolves from one state of coordination to another. A meso trajectory is the process unit of economic evolution as a growth of knowledge process.

The growth of knowledge is a process of creative destruction at many levels simultaneously. For example, the adoption and learning of a new rule by an agent is a creative process at the micro level. Yet this event is at the same time a destructive process at the macro level, as the new actions of the agent disturb the existing macro order. We conceive of both micro and macro implications of a meso trajectory as playing out simultaneously. A meso trajectory (Meso 1-2-3, for the (1) emergence, (2) diffusion and (3) retention of a rule) entrains waves of both micro and macro trajectories. This is illustrated in Figure 1.1.

Evolutionary dynamics are conceptualized in terms of a three-phase meso trajectory, from one state of coordination (organization at the micro and order at the macro) to another, with each meso phase giving rise to simultaneous micro and macro trajectories. The consequence of these processes is that each meso regime is modular, open and deep. In this way, we can proceed to theorize about the micro effects of a new rule as the layered consequences of each phase of the rule's meso trajectory. The emergence of the generic meso idea is followed by a phase of micro learning and adaptation that leads to new forms of organization and interaction: the micro is so transformed by the meso, and vice versa. We think of the macro in a similar way, as a general disturbance of an order inducing a process of re-coordination leading to the stabilization of a new order

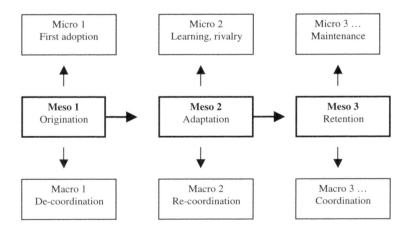

Figure 1.1   The analytical structure of a meso trajectory

of meso. A meso trajectory is both driven and constrained by micro and macro processes of change in state organization and order: the upshot is economic evolution.

In evolutionary economics, an economic system is a rule system. Economic evolution is the process by which a rule system changes, and the three-phase meso trajectory is the core description of that process. The state of a meso trajectory is measured in the frequency of the rule (the number of adoptions). The first phase of a meso trajectory is the emergence of a novel rule. The second phase is the diffusion of that rule by processes of adoption and adaptation. The third phase is the retention of that rule by the stabilization of new organization and new order.

Meso 1: Emergence as a Generative Process

A meso trajectory begins with the emergence or generation of a new rule. A new rule is a new association in the plane of knowledge. Holland (1975, ch. 7) defines emergence in terms of an extension of the concept of a mechanism to open combinations of mechanisms working as *constrained generating procedures*. Emergence is the product of new combinations of mechanisms. We wish to abstract this further, by generalizing the concept of a mechanism as a rule (see Potts 2001), in order to conceive of emergence as the generation of a new association between elements to form a new rule. At the level of the meso, emergence is the process whereby a new rule is generated by combinations of existing rules. Lane et al. (1996) refer to this as a *generative* process.

Emergence is something that is only generated in certain classes of systems. Typically, they are modular, open and deep, although not necessarily all at once. The implication is that emergence is almost by definition indefinable. It is a new concept in the realm of concepts, or a new rule in the meso plane. Kauffman (1998, p. 85) argues that novelty generation is a form of symmetry breaking in non-equilibrium systems. As a consequence of the many ways that an economy can be complex, there will be many realizations of emergence. Perhaps taxonomy is in order? It might attempt to classify the different ways a rule can be a new rule: a novel rule might be a concept, a theory, a conjecture, a product, a relationship, an inference, a design, a technology and so forth. We place no hard claims of inclusion or exclusion on meta-theoretical grounds on the exact formation of the object of emergence. We simply say that whatever it is, it might be usefully conceived of as a new association between elements, as a new combination of mechanisms, or, equivalently, a new rule.

Meso emergence has micro and macro effects. The micro process induced by meso emergence is the process of first adoption, as, for example, might refer to a firm discovering, learning about and implementing a new technology. At the macro level we observe the effect of Meso 1 when the local and then global coordination of the economic system (in terms of markets and production) is disturbed by the emergence of a new market about a monopoly position held by the first adopter. The emergence of a new rule has evolutionary significance if it affects the organization of agents, the order of their interactions, as well as the coordination of economic activities descriptive of the macro order.

What micro is
Standard microeconomics is largely a story about individual choice subject to constraints. Its central concept is efficiency. Evolutionary microeconomics, however, is largely a story about carriers adopting and adapting new rules: its central concept is efficacy. Efficacy is the quality of rules working together.

The micro agent is a carrier of knowledge and therefore has a mind which it uses to observe the outside world (institutions and behaviour) and its own inner world of ideas (cognition and rationality). By epigenetically combining these with mechanisms such as language, the mind is capable of adopting and adapting novel generic ideas. The economic agent is involved in an evolutionary process when the boundaries of the carrier change, or the interactions between the carrier and other elements in the environment change, or both. The evolutionary-relevant aspect of the agent is the organization of the agent's rules, and the order of the agent's interactions. Agents evolve by adopting and adapting new rules, including the destruction of old rules. The agent behaves in this way in order to solve problems, which is to say that the purpose of knowledge, of which the economic system is composed, is to solve problems: knowledge is for problem solving and evolution is a mechanism for ongoing problem solving. Evolutionary agents are not motivated to maximize utility, but rather to solve problems.

Thus there are two classes of analytically relevant behaviour in evolutionary microeconomics: (i) rule-related behaviour, and (ii) environment-related behaviour. Rule-related behaviour is evolutionary behaviour in relation to the processes associated with the rule, such as origination, learning, adoption, adaptation, retention, maintenance, experimentation and understanding (playing out over a three-phase process). This also includes imagination in dealing with the uncertainty and potential profits associated with an unknown rule. Environment-related behaviour deals with the interactions between carriers in relation to competition, cooperation, rivalry and coalitions, and to features of the environment such as prices and constraints. Environmental behaviour is centred about the interactions and exchanges with the environment of resources and other agents. Economic evolution is a process of making and reforming connections, and the empirically relevant sort of behaviour to explain is behaviour that results in changes in the organization of the rules agents carry and the order of the interactions between rule-carrying micro agents.

Meso 1: micro

The unit of evolutionary dynamics is a meso trajectory, and the first place we should consider this is in relation to micro processes following the first adoption of the novel rule. The frequency of the novel rule r_i goes from $0 \Rightarrow 1$ during this phase of first adoption. (This defines the micro boundary of Meso 1. Meso 2 begins with second adoption.) From the initial adoption of the rule, the micro phases of Meso 1 unfold as the carrier begins to experiment with the rule and to learn about its properties and applications. This is the phase of adaptation prior to the systematic exploitation of the rule, which often includes the expansion of the scale or scope on which it is used. By phase three, the organization of the carrier (in the sense of routines) will have stabilized. This is the first micro trajectory of a meso rule.

At the behavioural level, the carrier is driven by the perception (or discovery, or imagination, or realization) of new profit opportunities associated with the rule. Most of these evolutionary behaviours are rule-related behaviours. However, to the extent that outside knowledge is required, including partnerships and access to markets, and to the extent that finance or insurance may be required to develop and exploit the rule, then new interactions will also be inevitable.

What macro is

Standard macroeconomics is largely a story about aggregates. It sometimes has micro foundations. Evolutionary macroeconomics, on the other hand, is largely a story about complex systems and it has meso foundations. The macro is the correspondence order of associations between meso regimes. Each meso regime is the product of a meso trajectory. In relation to a meso trajectory, the micro is essentially about the agents that carry the new rule. The macro is not about carriers and organization. Rather, it is about the relation between that new rule and all other rules. The micro deals with one system, the macro with many systems (the meso, being the unit of all evolutionary systems, deals with no systems but rather refers to a distribution of actualizations of a rule). Evolutionary macroeconomics encompasses industrial dynamics, market dynamics, institutional change and the theory of growth and development. Evolutionary micro does not provide foundations to evolutionary macro, because these are provided by the meso.

Instead, micro and macro relate to each other dynamically and statistically, continually feeding back impulses and constraints over various time scales.

In our revised view, there are three orders to the macro. First, the *deep order* of relations between rules is the result of rules fitting together irrespective of meso population. The second order is a *structural order* characterized by the fit of the frequency of rules. Deep order does not imply structural order in the sense that the right elements might be present, but if they are combined in the wrong frequencies then they will not have structural order. But even if the right ideas are combined in the right frequency, there may still be problems if the *operational order* – which refers to such things as the use of resources, the maintenance of capacity, the sorting of labour and so forth – is wrong, then we still do not have macro order. Modern macroeconomics is entirely a story about operational order and tells us nothing about the deeper structural concerns of the evolutionary orders of macroeconomic systems.

Meso 1: macro
The macro aspect of Meso 1 is associated with the new market and industry structure implied by the new monopolist. The macro trajectory associated with Meso 1 consists in the new rule disturbing the order of existing rules.

The temporal relation between micro and macro along a meso trajectory is important. It might seem sensible to insist that first comes micro as a firm works on a new idea, and then later comes macro, and the consequences of that local event become global. But that would be to misunderstand macro. Macro is not just about the final aggregate consequences, but is ultimately about how the rules in the economic system fit together. By constructing meso foundations to both micro and macro, we can consider a new rule as its fits into a bounded interacting organization (micro) and as it fits into an ordered system of other rules (macro).

The macro phase associated with Meso 1 is a process of de-coordination that is simultaneously the generation of variety. The existing order and division of knowledge and labour is disturbed as the first phase of the process of creative-destruction. This may involve the signalling of a new technology, a new product, or a new market, or some other such change. A macro economy is a statistical object and the first macro phase is the introduction of variety, in some way, into the system.

The three macro phases relate to: (1) the *correspondence order* of the new rule (the viability of the monopolist in terms of rule complementarity); (2) the *structural order* of the rule (the coordination of operations); and (3) the *operational order* (the ability to access resources, and the effects this has). The immediate point to note is that in the manner of Keynes (1937), Leijonhufvud (1968) and Loasby (1991), the ability of the macro system to absorb the generic idea will be proportional to the slack in the system (the availability of finance, the institutional conditions surrounding experimental behaviour, the surplus capacity, the skill level of the labour force and so forth). Economic evolution is conditional upon the ability of the macro system to admit variety and experimentation without compromising the rest of the system.

Meso 2: Adoption and Diffusion

In Meso 1 a novel rule emergences and in Meso 2 that rule is adopted and diffused. The micro effects of this are associated with the multiplication of learning and applications of the rule, and the macro effects are associated with the processes of market and industrial change that are consequences of the adoption and diffusion of the rule.

During Meso 2, the frequency of the rule goes from 1 to n, and traces out the growth part of a logistic curve (in four-phase growth models, this is phases 2 and 3 about the inflection point). Meso 2 takes us from the one to the many, in terms of realizations of the rule. But there is still just one rule. That is the meaning of the one and the many implied in the concept of ontological bimodality. Evolutionary mechanisms of variation, replication and selection apply generally in all phases at all levels. There is selection involved in the initial micro experimentation with the rule, as well as variation (imagination) and replication (persuading others). Similarly at the macro level, there is selection about how the rule fits (the particular market the monopolist is in may not actually be the one they intended), and so forth. But this does not mean that each mechanism applies equally in all phases. As Meso 1 was principally about variation, Meso 2 is principally about replication. Replication is a process of communication of rules.

Meso 2: micro
We go from Meso 1 to Meso 2 in the micro as first one carrier adopts the rule, then others do. This phase of mass adoption introduces further variation and selection as the rule comes to interact with many other rule systems. This process may induce new meso trajectories.

As many carriers begin to experiment with the rule and learn about its properties and applications, and as expectations begin to firm as uncertainty recedes about the capabilities and potential of the new rule, product and process innovations begin to accumulate. This is the growth phase of knowledge associated with the rule. The systematic exploitation of the rule is now well under way, and experimentation of scale and scope will begin to normalize about a standard form of organization. Industry leaders will be those with leads in experience and market share; they will often be looking to consolidate or to lever this into the development of a new rule.

At the behavioural level, carriers are driven by the observed success of other carriers and drawn to learn about that rule. Formal and informal networks will emerge to share information and experience with varying measures of stability. In this turbulent environment, interactions will tend to be based upon strategic considerations.

Meso 2: macro

The macro aspect of Meso 2 is associated with the re-coordination of the industry and market structure first disturbed by the new monopolist. With micro adoption comes an increase in the number of firms and the emergence of competition in the market and rivalry in the industry. The entry and exit in the micro due to the differential replication of the rule will induce a statistical process of transformation in the macro.

The main macro event of Meso 2 is the search for the appropriate scale and order of the rule and those rules associated with it. The correspondence order of the new rule begins to adapt as the viable monopoly in terms of rule complementarity now becomes complex. The initial disturbance of the structural order has grown more pronounced, characterized by significant differential growth rates of firms occupying somewhat different regions of activity space within an industry and associated industries. This is the acceleration of the process of de-coordination and a search for the path of re-coordination. This phase is characterized by the initial order, at first only slightly disturbed, now becoming complex. It is here that entrepreneurs and finance and competition in networks are most apparent. The process of re-coordination also occurs here, as dominant designs and other forms of organization emerge from the micro to condition macro processes (for example, Metcalfe 1998).

Meso 3: Stabilization and Retention

In Meso 2 a novel rule is adopted and diffused and in Meso 3 that rule is retained and maintained so that it becomes in effect a new system. The micro effects of this are associated with the normalization of behaviours associated with the rule and its context. The macro effects are associated with the new order it implies. During Meso 3, the frequency of the rule stabilizes at n. This stability is reflected in the micro as the stabilization of firm activities and organizational forms, and in the macro in terms of a new division of labour about an industry form and market structure. Meso 3 is the phase of evolutionary stabilization, and it is also a phase of selection in well-formed markets that is well described using the standard analytical framework (in terms of the analysis of a competitive process with given rules).

Meso 3: micro

The micro trajectory associated with Meso 3 is the period of sustained but stable competitive rivalry between the adopters and the set of all agents they interact with. By and large, the micro trajectory associated with the third meso phase consists of everything that Alfred Marshall ever wrote about, except this: Meso 2 begins the process of expansion in the scale and scope of a rule, and Meso 3 begins the process of shakeout (by selection and agglomeration), which occurs as the number of realizations grows and stabilizes, the number of firms may collapse dramatically (Klepper 2002). This implies a significant change in the boundaries of firms, which, of course, also has macro aspects. After a shakeout, the boundaries of firms come to stabilize about ordered patterns of interactions. Behaviourally, the rule is well known and its immediate implications have all been made apparent. Rule-related behaviours will then tend to become institutionalized into norms of behaviour. Knowledge will begin to institutionally correlate and implicit understandings will emerge. In Meso 1 rule-related behaviours were predominant, but in Meso 3 context-related behaviours predominate.

Meso 3: macro

Stable boundaries of firms and other agencies, and ordered interactions between these carriers, makes for a stable market environment and well-defined industries. The deep structure of knowledge is manifest in the correspondence order between rules and this is the new order that is institutionally stabilized, retained and maintained in the macro trajectory associated with Meso 3. We now arrive at the full correspondence of the new rule. The market structure will be in a kind of suspended state between two possible forms. In Meso 1 it began as monopoly but by Meso 2 competition begins to flourish, as do experimental coalitions, along with the growth of the successful early entrants. Meso 3 will either tend to a shake-out to leave a small number of large stable players (as above), or, at the other extreme, towards a state of perfect competition. Little is known about the nature of this tipping point, or structural bifurcation in the division of knowledge in terms of organization.

In the macro trajectory of Meso 3 a new structural order comes to rest on a stable correspondence order. What are called 'fluctuations' in standard macroeconomics are the vibrations of operational order within an evolutionary-defined structural order. It is only here that conventional macroeconomic measures of a 'growth phase' or some such will become apparent. But in evolutionary economics, this may be the beginning of a co-evolutionary process, as the newly stabilized rule (the emergent meso regime) becomes an element that interacts with another rule to begin the process again at a higher level.

CONCLUSION

The ontology of evolutionary realism and the methodological concept of the meso provide a foundation upon which to build an analytical framework to describe economic evolution as a growth of knowledge process. The framework consists of a three-phase meso process that entrains at each phase micro and macro processes. The growth of knowledge is the emergence of a new meso regime in the knowledge base of the economic system.

We began by defining complexity in terms of the modularity, openness and depth of a system in relation to order and organization. The significance of the rule-based conception of the agent is that it has both of these properties at once. The rule is a meso concept. This unfolded analysis as respectively focused about organization (micro) and order (macro). The meso foundation of micro and macro analysis is, in our view, the central analytical concept in evolutionary economics.

REFERENCES

Alchian, A. (1950), 'Uncertainty, evolution and economic theory', *Journal of Political Economy*, **58**, 211–22.

Arrow, K. (1974), *The Limits of Organization*, New York: W.W. Norton.

Arthur, W., S. Durlauf and D. Lane (eds) (1997), *The Economy as a Complex Evolving System II*, New York: Addison-Wesley.

Buchanan, J. and V. Vanberg (1991), 'The market as a creative process', *Economics and Philosophy*, **7**, 167–86.

Clower, R. and P. Howitt (1997), 'Foundations of economics', in J. D'Autume and J. Cartelier (eds), *Is Economics Becoming a Hard Science?*, Cheltenham, UK and Lyme, USA: Edward Elgar, pp. 17–34.

Collier, J. and C.A. Hooker (1998), 'Complexly organised dynamical systems', *Open Systems & Information Dynamics*, **36**, 1–62.

Coricelli, F. and G. Dosi (1988), 'Coordination and order in economic change and the interpretive power of economic theory', in G. Dosi, C. Freeman, R. Nelson, G. Silverberg and L. Soete (eds), *Technical Change and Economic Theory*, New York: Pinter, pp. 124–47.

Dennett, D. (1995), *Darwin's Dangerous Idea: Evolution and the Meanings of Life*, New York: Simon & Schuster.

Dopfer, K. (2001), 'Evolutionary economics', in K. Dopfer (ed.), *Evolutionary Economics: Program and Scope*, Boston, MA: Kluwer, pp. 1–44.

Foster, J. and J.S. Metcalfe (eds) (2001), *Frontiers of Evolutionary Economics: Competition, Self-Organization and Innovation Policy*, Cheltenham, UK and Northampton, MA, USA: Edward Elgar.

Gode, D. and S. Sunder (1997), 'What makes markets allocationally efficient?', *Quarterly Journal of Economics*, **112**, 603–30.

Hayek, F. (1945), 'The use of knowledge in society', *American Economic Review*, **35**, 519–30.

Hayek, F. (1991), 'Spontaneous ("grown") order and organized ("made") order', in G. Thompson (ed.), *Markets, Hierarchies and Networks*, London: Sage, pp. 293–305.

Holland, J. (1975), *Adaptation in Natural and Artificial Systems: An Introductory Analysis with Applications to Biology, Control, and Artificial Intelligence*, Ann Arbor, MT: University of Michigan Press.

Hooker, C.A. and W. Christensen (2000), 'Organised interactive construction: the nature of autonomy and the emergence of intelligence', in A. Etxeberria, A. Moreno and J. Umerez (eds), *The Contribution of Artificial Life and the Sciences of Complexity to the Understanding of Autonomous Systems, Communication & Cognition*, **17**, special edn, 133–58.

Kauffman, S. (1993), *The Origins of Order: Self-organization and Selection in Evolution*, Oxford: Oxford University Press.

Kauffman, S. (1998), *Investigations*, New York: Oxford University Press.

Keynes, J. (1937), 'The general theory of employment', *Quarterly Journal of Economics*, **51**, 209–23.

Kirman, A. (1997) 'The economy as an evolving network', *Journal of Evolutionary Economics*, **7**, 339–53.

Klepper, S. (2002), 'The capabilities of new firms and the evolution of the US automobile industry', *Industrial and Corporate Change*, August, **11**(4), 645–66.

Lane, D., F. Malerba, R. Maxfield and L. Orsenigo (1996), 'Choice and action', *Journal of Evolutionary Economics*, **6**, 43–76.

Lawson, T. (1997), *Economics and Reality*, London: Routledge.

Leijonhufvud, A. (1968), *On Keynesian Economics and the Economics of Keynes*, New York: Oxford University Press.

Loasby, B. (1991), *Equilibrium and Evolution: An Exploration of Connecting Principles in Economics*, Manchester: Manchester University Press.

Loasby, B. (1999), *Knowledge, Institutions and Evolution in Economics*, London: Routledge.

Mäki, U. (ed.) (2001), *The Economic World View: Studies in the Ontology of Economics*, New York: Cambridge University Press.

Ménard, C. (1995), 'Markets as institutions versus organizations as markets?', *Journal of Economic Behaviour and Organization*, **28**, 169–82.

Metcalfe, J.S. (1998), *Evolutionary Economics and Creative Destruction*, London: Routledge.

Mirowski, P. (1989), *More Heat Than Light: Economics as Social Physics*, New York: Cambridge University Press.

Mirowski, P. (2002), *Machine Dreams: Economics Becomes a Cyborg Science*, New York: Cambridge University Press.

Mirowski, P. and K. Somefun (1998), 'Markets as evolving computational entities', *Journal of Evolutionary Economics*, **8**, 329–56.

Myerson, R. (1999), 'Nash equilibrium and the history of game theory', *Journal of Economic Literature*, **37**, 1067–82.

Nelson, R. and S. Winter (1982), *An Evolutionary Theory of Economic Change*, Cambridge, MA: Harvard University Press.

Potts, J. (2000), *The New Evolutionary Microeconomics*, Cheltenham, UK and Northampton, MA, USA: Edward Elgar.

Potts, J. (2001), 'Knowledge and markets', *Journal of Evolutionary Economics*, **11**, 413–31.

Prigogine, I. (1976), 'Order through fluctuation: Self-organization and social systems', in E. Jantsch and C.H. Waddington (eds), *Evolution and Consciousness: Human Systems in Transition*, Reading, MA: Addison-Wesley, pp. 93–133.

Robbins, L. (1935), *An Essay on the Nature & Significance of Economic Science*, London: Macmillan.

Schumpeter, J. (1942), *Capitalism, Socialism and Democracy*, London: George Allen & Unwin.

Simon, H. ([1968] 1981), *Sciences of the Artificial*, Cambridge, MA: MIT Press.

Von Neumann, J. (1966), *Theory of Self-Reproducing Automata* (edited and completed by Arthur Burks), Urbana, IL: University of Illinois Press.

Vromen, J. (1995), *Economic Evolution: An Inquiry into the Foundations of New Institutional Economics*, London: Routledge.

Wolfram, S. (2002), *A New Kind of Science*, Champaign, IL: Wolfram Media.

2. On the methodology of assessing agent-based evolutionary models in the social sciences

Paul Ormerod and Bridget Rosewell

INTRODUCTION

Agent-based evolutionary models appear strange to most economists. They offer solutions with apparently limited predictive power and where a range of outcomes is often possible. Individual agents are usually heterogeneous, defying simple, easily generalizable descriptions. Probabilistic behaviour of such agents is normally incorporated in the models. It is not surprising that there is suspicion of this modelling approach, since it looks, indeed is, so different from the deterministic models in which most economists are trained.

But both conventional economic models and agent-based evolutionary ones face a fundamental problem of validation. Because we can rarely undertake fully controlled experiments, the result of any empirical testing in social and economic science is inevitably to a degree ambiguous. No theory in economics or sociology can be justified or tested simply by reference to the data. We have only to look at the enormous efforts spent in time-series econometrics in specifying the consumption function, or at attempts to identify in cross-sectional data the elasticity of female labour supply with respect to the real wage, to realize that conventional econometric 'testing' has not taken us very far.

Moreover, predictive power is necessarily limited in a world where practical experiments are few and far between. Indirect tests are the most that can be hoped for. This is analogous to much of the current situation in theoretical physics. While the discovery of quantum mechanical rules was capable of experimental testing and refinement at each stage, the development of string theory has not been so testable. It has proceeded by theoretical insight, the ability to integrate issues previously seen as conundrums and some indirect experimental results (Greene 1999).

Such approaches have relied on the ability to stand alone in both logic and plausible realism. Social science is not in the position of Albert

Einstein who, when asked what he would think if observations failed to confirm his prediction concerning the bending of light said, 'I shall be very surprised'. But it is in the position of those who suddenly realized that string theory integrated quantum mechanics and gravity and predicted, rather than assumed, the existence of the graviton.

In any system there are three elements that need to be considered in assessing model configurations, and this seems to be general across scientific effort. The first is the rules of behaviour that the model system postulates. These rules may themselves rest on other theories and be developed in a particular context. In physics, this will refer to rules covering such elements as force, mass, energy and momentum; in biology perhaps molecules or perhaps creatures; in social science it is people, groups, firms and so on.

The second is the facts that the theory is designed to explain. In physics, very different theories are applied to macroscopic forces, visible to us in the world, and microscopic quantum fluctuations. In biology, modelling the evolution of a finch's beak will imply different models over different time scales from the models required for the development of a pharmaceutical product. In social science, we may need different theoretical constructs for the business cycle than for the evolution of industrial structure. Of course, in every case, theoreticians are always yearning for the Theory of Everything – but a partial theory of something is better than a misleading complete construct.

The third is the precision of prediction. Clearly a theory which produces a clear and refutable prediction is preferred – but not necessarily right. In considering modelling approaches, the solutions the models proffer, their testability and relevance must also be considered.

This chapter looks at each of these issues in turn. It illustrates them with reference to two particular agent-based models which have been developed by us in different contexts and to illustrate two different issues. One looks at the business cycle, and the other at the dynamic process of competition. We hope that this will help make concrete some of the issues of model assessment in social science which are currently not properly taken into account.

RULES OF BEHAVIOUR

It is important that the behavioural rules of agents in any theoretical specification of a model of a complex system should be plausible in themselves. In other words, the rules chosen within any particular model should be capable of justification in a wider context than that of the model under immediate consideration.

We cannot at this stage hope to obtain *general* rules of agent behaviour which are valid in all contexts. The rules will be specific to explaining the task in hand. This is a familiar issue in physics, for example, where different sets of rules are used to describe the behaviour of problems at the everyday level (for example, how to build a bridge which stays up) than are used to describe behaviour of particles at the quantum level. This example illustrates the extreme difficulty of obtaining completely general rules or a Theory of Everything.

Consider, for example, the neoclassical representative agent, maximizing utility under conditions of perfect information. As a behavioural rule for agents it lacks plausibility in many contexts. There is a large literature in the other social sciences on the limits to knowledge processing by individual agents. There is a rapidly growing empirical literature within economics itself on this subject (an early and important example is Loomes et al. (1991) and more recent ones are Fehr and Fischbacher (2002) and Tenorio and Cason (2002)). In the context of general equilibrium, there is the classic theoretical demonstration by Radner (1968) that existence of general equilibrium under uncertainty can only be proved provided that each agent has access to literally an infinite amount of computing capacity.

However, in limited contexts, it might not be a bad behavioural rule to use. This is particularly the case in situations in which (a) there is only a restricted set of information to process and (b) the consequences of actions taken now for the future are small, for it is the introduction of the future which complicates enormously the task of the representative agent. So, for example, in a model which contains agents choosing between brands of a particular product in a supermarket, it might be quite reasonable to assume that agents act according to the postulates of standard consumer demand theory. There is, at this stage of the purchasing process, a strictly limited amount of information to process and the choice of one brand of a fast-moving consumer product rather than another will have only marginal implications for the future well-being of the agent making the choice.

In other contexts, different rules might be more appropriate. In particular, other agents – firms, for example – need to be considered. In each case, we are seeking to postulate rules which are consistent with what has already been established to work in more limited contexts and to achieve internal plausibility for the context under investigation. To illustrate these considerations, we turn to the motivation for the rules chosen in our two model examples.

An Agent-based Model of the Business Cycle

This model addresses the issue of the business cycle in the United States. It focuses on the rate of growth of real output both of individual firms and of its aggregate (GDP). A detailed description is in Ormerod (2002). The business cycle is assumed to arise primarily in the corporate sector, so the agents in the model are taken to represent firms. Although it is not completely accurate to say that the sole reason for the business cycle is the activity of firms, it is a reasonable simplification to make (see, for example, Burns and Mitchell 1946).

Firms are assumed to operate at different scales of activity. This is well known to be the case. (As it happens, without going into the details here, this is a key reason for the existence of the business cycle.)

As a simplification, the model is populated by a limited number of agents (500). In other words, it is assumed that the business cycle arises primarily through the activities of the 500 largest firms. Again, this seems a reasonable simplification to make. Decisions by General Electric are of more immediate consequence for output in the United States than those of, say, a small retailer.

The behavioural rules
The model evolves on a step-by-step basis, and in each step, or period, each firm decides two things:

- its rate of growth of output for that period; and
- its degree of optimism or pessimism about the economic conditions in which it is operating – 'sentiment' for short.

The rate of growth of output each agent decides to have depends upon three things. First, its rate of growth in the previous period. Second, the general level of sentiment about the future (where this is the weighted sum of individual agents' sentiment). Third, uncertainty which is *specific* to each individual agent, and which varies from period to period. Agents are uncertain about the general level of sentiment (they do not have perfect information), and agents are uncertain about the implications of any given level of overall sentiment for their own decisions. Agents act in a heterogeneous way in the face of such uncertainty.

The level of sentiment each agent has also depends upon three things. First, its level in the previous period. Second, the rate of growth of overall output. Third, uncertainty which again is specific to each agent, and which varies from period to period. Agents are uncertain about the implications of any given rate of growth of overall output for their own level of sentiment. The connection between the level of sentiment of an agent and the rate of growth of overall output is consistent with Keynes's description of the 'trade cycle' in chapter 22 of the *General Theory* (1936).

Indeed, the overall theoretical perspective of the model is very Keynesian. Agents do not follow complicated behavioural rules involving multi-period optimization. In this model, they are myopic and follow simple rules of thumb. Further, uncertainty plays a key role in the behaviour of agents. Finally, agents behave in heterogeneous ways in the face of uncertainty.

The specific behavioural rules are not obtained empirically. Rather, they are set in the context of an overall theoretical approach which we believe gives a reasonable description of how firms actually behave. In economic theory, the activity of business is in principle very easy: just discover your cost and demand schedules and maximize subject to these. In practice, business is a difficult and demanding activity.

It is not necessary, in our view, to test these behavioural rules directly. Rather, they can be tested, especially against alternative rules, by investigating whether the solutions to a model incorporating such rules provides a better representation of the key features of the actual data than models which incorporate different rules.

However, in other circumstances, we might wish to be able to observe more directly the parameters of a particular behavioural rule. Our second example illustrates this.

The Evolution of Market Structure and Competition

This model addresses the dynamic evolution of market structure and competition. The specific focus is on the consequences of new entrants into a market in which there is initially a single monopoly supplier.

In the 1980s and 1990s, a wide range of industrial structures with a single, dominant firm was undermined. In part this was due to regulatory changes, such as in electricity and gas markets. In part, it arose from technological change, with the rise of the PC (personal computer) eroding IBM's position, for example. And in yet a further group of industries, such as telecommunications, both regulatory change and technology were important.

Competition policy in many countries remains fixed in the mind-set of (a) comparing static equilibria and (b) regarding perfect competition as the ideal. A model which is widely used is that of Cournot oligopoly. The fewer the number of firms in the market, the greater the price is assumed to deviate from the competitive ideal. A priori, the existence of a firm with a large market share is thought to be anti-competitive.

The behavioural rules

Initially, there is a single monopoly supplier. The model evolves on a step-by-step basis. A rule is specified for each of the following:

- an entry process for new firms;
- the process by which firms gain/lose market share;

- the process of how firms react to competition; and
- the process of how consumers choose between firms.

The entry process of new firms is stochastic. The probability of whether new firms enter the market in any given period is a parameter of the model, and the number of firms which do enter is also a parameter. Firms operate under uncertainty, and the simple rule for entry reflects this fact. In any event, the reason why firms enter markets is understood imperfectly at best (see, for example, Carroll and Hannan 2000).

Each firm offers the product at a particular price and with a particular level of quality, where both the price and quality of the product are in [0, 1]. The monopolist initially offers a price and quality of 1. The price of 0 corresponds to the lowest price at which the product can be offered, given the state of technology, and a normal profit made. Similarly, a value of 0 for the quality dimension indicates the *best* which is available.[1]

New entrants offer a price and quality both chosen at random from [0, 1]. Firms are heterogeneous, and differ both in their ability to provide the product profitably at any given price, and in their perception of what price and quality they need to offer to gain a desired level of market share.

Each firm gains access to a fixed proportion of consumers, drawn at random from [0, 1]. We mean by this that a particular proportion of consumers become aware that a given firm is making an offer in the market. By definition, the monopolist has access to all consumers. Firms may differ in the proportion of consumers which they wish to target. Further, both firms and consumers operate with imperfect information. In practice, by no means all consumers are aware of the full range of firms which operate in any given market – a point illustrated in a seminar we gave to economists in 2001, when they were challenged to name, in their role as consumers, all the firms making offers in the UK domestic electricity and gas industries. None of them could. Equally, firms may wish to gain access to a large proportion of consumers, but their marketing campaign may be more or less successful than planned.

Each consumer reviews the price and quality offered by each of the firms on his or her network, that is, the firms of which any given consumer is aware. Consumers are heterogeneous in their preferences between price and quality, and each consumer is assigned a weight, w_i, in [0, 1] and calculates the utility of the product offered by the jth firm by $w_i p_j + (1 - w_i)q_j$. The consumer switches to the lowest value of this on offer (remembering that low values of p and q are better than high values). However, each consumer does so with a fixed probability, drawn at the outset from [0, 1]. This reflects a further dimension of the heterogeneous nature of consumers. They differ in their sensitivity to price and quality, and they differ in the benefits they derive from a switch compared to the costs of switching.

Firms can react to the offers of competitors. Firms do not have complete information on the preferences of consumers, and calculate at each step of the model for all of the other firms $\omega p_j + (1 - \omega)q_j$, where ω is the average of the w_i across the consumers. They are able, in principle, to match immediately this (p, q) offer. However, each firm is allocated a 'flexibility' factor, drawn at the outset from $[0, 1]$. This gives the probability of a firm being able to match this (p, q) in any given step of the model. In practice, firms differ in their 'X-efficiency', and this rule reflects this fact.

The model allows both firms and consumers to react to price and quality, as in conventional economic theory. However, the model allows for:

- heterogeneity of agents;
- uncertainty; and
- imperfect information.

The rules of behaviour described here are in some ways less general than in the business cycle example. In that case, an individual firm's growth depended on its own past and growth and its expectation of the system's future growth. In this case, firms and consumers are given individual characteristics which vary – and how they vary will affect the solutions of the model.

For example, the degree of customer loyalty or the flexibility of individual firms in matching price and quality will have a marked impact on how the market structure evolves in practice. In this context, external data about these parameters can be used to refine the way in which the rules operate. This does not affect the rules of behaviour as such but would certainly result in greater precision of solution.

It might be the case that market research data were available on the willingness of consumers to consider switching product – this would inform the distribution on which the 'loyalty' parameter could be based. And of course, such willingness might well vary from industry to industry – to the 'classical' position where all consumers are always willing to switch with a probability of one.

In the case of this model, then, we cannot test the model simply from its solutions. We will also need to test the parameters.

THE FACTS TO BE EXPLAINED

A key part of the empirical assessment of the model needs to be made with reference to the ability of the model to reproduce the key facts of the issue which is being modelled. Often these are referred to in social science as 'stylized facts' – themselves simplified versions of the more complex facts of the real world. This, in itself, suggests that the stylized fact is a fact which may not always be true. We shall return to this point in our section on the explanatory/predictive power of a model. If a fact is not always true, does it matter if your model does not predict it?

Picking the key facts that require explanation is a central issue and has a major impact on the kinds of model approach chosen. If your theory suggests that perfect competition is an ideal, then you will wish to explain deviations from its predictions. When your model makes no such assumption, the facts that you wish to explain may look rather different. Our examples illustrate the debate that can be caused by which facts are taken as key.

An Agent-based Model of the Business Cycle

Business cycle theory is one area where there is disagreement about what constitutes the key facts to be explained. The time-series properties of real GDP growth in the United States are:

1. positive but weakly determined low-order autocorrelation, with other terms in the autocorrelation function being insignificant; and
2. a weak concentration of the power spectrum at frequencies associated with those of the business cycle.

In general, real business cycle (RBC) models are unable to replicate such features, leading Eichenbaum (1995), for example, to state that these models suffer from 'first-order failure'. RBC enthusiasts ignore these aspects of business cycle data and concentrate instead on the so-called 'method of moments', attempting to reproduce the relative variances and cross-correlations of different segments of GDP. We should say in passing, however, that the methodology of validation adopted by RBC theorists has much in common with that of agent-based evolutionary models. Unlike the trivial curve-fitting exercises of time-series econometrics, the RBC approach does not attempt to replicate any particular series of past data which we actually observe, but to replicate certain underlying properties of such data. Where we part company with the RBC approach is on the questions of agent homogeneity and perfect information.

The key facts
The key facts of output growth are identified to be the following:

- positive but weakly determined low-order autocorrelation, with other terms in the autocorrelation function being insignificant;

- a weak concentration of the power spectrum at frequencies associated with those of the business cycle;
- in general, positive correlations between the growth rates of individual agents over the course of the business cycle; and
- a particular statistical distribution of the duration of recessions.

Given the first two points above, economists have been required to consider to what extent it is meaningful to speak of a business 'cycle' at all. Lucas (1977) noted that output changes across broadly defined sectors of the economy tend to move together over time, and argued that with respect to the qualitative behaviour of co-movements among [sectors], business cycles are all alike. The agents in our model are not aggregated into sectors, and the correlations between their individual growth rates will be lower than that observed at the sector level, because of competition between agents within sectors. But we still expect, a priori, positive correlations. This is widely recognized to be a central feature of the business cycle.

The fourth point above is discussed in Ormerod and Mounfield (2001), where the duration of recessions in capitalist economies is shown to be approximated by a power law. The observation of power-law distributions – fractal behaviour – in a system's macroscopically observable quantities is a characteristic property of many-body systems representing the effects of complex interactions among the constituents of the system.

The Evolution of Market Structure and Competition

The model of the business cycle seeks to describe the evolution of a particular time series, in terms of the components of which it is composed. In the case of this model, it seeks to describe an evolution in a number of features of a market and to position such changes in time. Since the rules of behaviour are specified in a general context, the process of the evolution under examination is also taken as a general one at the outset. Thus the model is not attempting to explain a particular set of facts, but a set which has been generalized – 'stylized' – from a variety of experiences.

In the case of this model, we therefore identified a set of potential outcomes, which we wished the model to explain, as follows.

The key facts
We have observed a number of features in the relevant industries:

- reductions in market price, both relative to the general price level, and in many cases, in absolute terms;
- improvements in the quality of the offer;

- the original incumbent retains a large market share;
- a relatively small number of competitors succeeds in establishing itself in the market; and
- most new entrants fail and withdraw from the market.

A further point is that competition and market structure evolve dynamically in time. We rarely, if ever, observe a static equilibrium.

These are rather different 'facts' from those usually taken to be the key elements in describing an industry. First, industry models do not generally look at dynamics at all, preferring to explain a particular snapshot. This means that the failure of entrants through time would not be considered at all.

Second, this would also imply that considerable emphasis is put on the number of firms in an industry and their combined and several shares. Indicators such as the Herfindahl index become key facts, rather than individual firm behaviour.

Finally, if models cannot cope with individual behaviour by agents, industry studies (particularly in the context of competition policy) pay immense attention to the boundary problem – who is in and who is out, which products substitute for which others and which markets which firm operates in. With individual behaviour, these become problems rather of deciding on a distribution of tastes, loyalty and market access and do not require such hard and fast judgements.

Thus far we have considered some of the issues in choosing and testing the behavioural rules of a model, and in selecting the facts that it is designed to explain. Finally, we turn to perhaps the central issue – how to judge success.

PREDICTIVE POWER

The aim in any model-building exercise is to develop a model which:

- fits into a theoretical context;
- has plausible rules of agent behaviour; and
- is able to replicate the relevant (stylized) facts.

Even if a model has all three of these properties, it does not mean that it is therefore *the* model of the problem being addressed. But it is in a stronger position than models which do not possess these properties.

Nor does it mean that it will have predictive power. Much of the criticism levelled at evolutionary and agent-based models (whether separately or together) is that they fail to provide precise predictions. By contrast, it has been argued, traditional profit-maximizing agents can provide models of, for example, auction processes which can successfully be used to guide action and policy in the real world.

Let us look at the solutions of the models under discussion to review the testability of their predictions and whether this is a relevant criticism.

An Agent-based Model of the Business Cycle

We have already argued that many models of the business cycle do not provide a full enough description of the key facts – if this model is capable of explaining both the 'usual' facts and the 'missing' facts it will clearly have predictive power that is missing from standard models and ought therefore to be preferred.

This model is able to replicate the key stylized facts of the US business cycle summarized above.

It implies that the business cycle is generated *endogenously* and, although external shocks can be added to the model, it is not necessary to posit the existence of exogenous shocks to generate the cycle. The three key reasons for the existence of the business cycle are: (a) the existence of uncertainty, (b) the heterogeneous reactions of firms to such uncertainty and (c) the fact that different firms operate at different levels of output. A specific prediction which arises from this last point is that the amplitude of the business cycle will be lower, the less concentrated is production among a small number of very large firms. Since around 1960, smaller firms have become more important in the US economy and the amplitude of the cycle has indeed dampened, so the prediction is consistent with this outcome.

Despite the scientific power of the model and its clear grounding in economic theory, it has been met by a mixture of hostility and incomprehension among most economists who have seen it. One such group is simply unable to grasp that scientific testing extends far beyond the simple curve fitting of time-series econometrics, an exercise which, as a matter of interest, is *not* considered to be 'modelling' at all in other sciences. For another, smaller, group, it is as if macroeconomics consisted solely of an exegetical account of the writings of Keynes, and any attempt to improve or extend them is heresy. Finally, and most generally, most economists reject the model purely because agents in it do not carry out maximizing behaviour.

It is perhaps useful to consider why the model has attracted the attention of physicists and is being published in the world's leading journal of statistical physics. The main reason is as follows. Statistical physics is concerned with the interactions between individual agents (or particles) and the behaviour of the system as a whole which emerges from such interactions. Many such systems exhibit power law, or fractal, behaviour at the aggregate level. Evidence is growing for the existence of power law behaviour within economic systems – for example, the duration of capitalist recessions (Ormerod and Mounfield 2001), the size distribution of firms (Axtel 2001), the extinction patterns of firms (Cook and Ormerod 2002) and the distribution of growth rates among firms (Amaral et al. 1998).

A widespread explanation for the existence of power laws is that of self-organized criticality. However, as Amaral et al. (1998) comment on the existence of power law behaviour in social and biological systems, it is difficult to imagine that for all these diverse systems, the parameters controlling the dynamics spontaneously self-tune to their critical values. In a study of the distribution of the growth of firms in the United States, they propose an alternative mechanism based on (a) the complex evolving structure of the units making up individual firms and (b) an evolution of these units according to a random process. The business cycle model offers an account of the existence of power law behaviour of the system as a whole (the duration of recessions) which also arises from similar principles. In other words, it is grounded in the micro behaviour of the agents which comprise the system, rather than arising by mere serendipity.

The Evolution of Market Structure and Competition

This model is general in two senses. First, its rules of behaviour do not describe any particular industry or product situation. Second, its rules are probabilistic – every time the model runs there is a different outcome. Multiple runs can be used to determine both an average and a range of solutions.

On average, the model shows, for a certain choice of behavioural parameters, the speed with which price and quality might adjust and the number of entrants that might succeed. It also shows the range of potential outcomes – how many times the incumbent might either disappear or indeed see off all competition. These solutions are predictions of how often these outcomes might be observed in practice.

The model is able to reproduce the key stylized facts which are observed in the dynamic evolution of competition. A further stage of validation can also be carried out, although so far we have not had access to any relevant data set. The model described contains parameters which are not calibrated against any particular set of empirical evidence. A specific industry is likely to have a particular configuration of consumers with a particular distribution of loyalty parameters, for example. In order to test the model more widely, the outcomes need to be tested against specific information on a variety of different observed behaviours. The model, if broadly true, will provide predicted outcomes which then fit a relatively wide range of behaviours, and, in particular, the model will be able to show it provides for a wider range of real-world outcomes than the standard model.

A problem which economists appear to have with this model is a normative criticism. Many economists believe that they can analyse an optimum solution – the best from the point of view of welfare. A description of the outcomes of a set of rules carries no such weight. It simply is. If the sort of model of behaviour described here is accepted, then there is little basis for all the policy prescriptions beloved of competition authorities. We suspect that this will mean continued suspicion of the results.

CONCLUSION

All models are simplifications and there should be a presumption to keep any model as simple as possible, in terms both of the description of the rules which are used and the number of such rules. It is important to be able to understand *why* a model of a complex system gives particular results, and this rapidly becomes very difficult in complicated models.

The question is whether the right simplifications are chosen and this is a theoretical as well as an empirical question. We have suggested a number of criteria on both counts.

First, we should choose clear rules of behaviour for agents which are relevant to the context in which they are being applied. They should be as general as possible and should be capable of testing whether their parameters might vary in particular circumstances.

Second, the facts that the model is attempting to explain should be both carefully defined and clearly set out. In some cases, these may be stylized facts – a simplified or generalized description of the real world. Ideally, if facts are to be ignored, we should explain why – though perhaps it is more realistic to suggest that critics should search for such facts!

Third, the power of such models needs to be judged by its ability to provide solutions which match the key facts under investigation. Probabilistic models may also explain outlying solutions that might occur. Application of the model parameters to a number of cases and adjustment of the parameters to different choice situations is a good way of testing models which are formulated in a general framework. Indeed, the more general the framework which can be shown to be robust to a number of situations, the more acceptable it should be.

NOTE

1. Obviously, it makes no difference whether the best quality is defined as being a value of 1 or a value of 0.

REFERENCES

Amaral, L.A.N., S.V. Buldyrev, S. Havlin, M.A. Salinger and H.E. Stanley (1998), 'Power law scaling for a system of interacting units with complex internal structure', *Physics Review Letters*, **80**, 1385–8.

Axtell, R.L. (2001), 'Zipf distribution of US firm sizes', *Science*, **293**, 1818–20.

Burns, A.F. and W.C. Mitchell (1946), *Measuring Business Cycles*, Chicago: National Bureau of Economic Research.

Carroll, G.R. and M.T. Hannan (2000), *The Demography of Corporations and Industries*, Princeton, NJ: Princeton University Press.

Cook, W. and P. Ormerod (2002), 'Power law distribution of the frequency of demises of US firms', mimeo, Volterra Consulting.

Eichenbaum, M. (1995), 'Some comments on the role of econometrics in economic theory', *Economic Journal*, **105**, 1609–21.

Fehr, E. and U. Fischbacher (2002), 'Why social preferences matter – the impact of non-selfish motives on competition, co-operation and incentives', *Economic Journal*, **112**, C1–C33.

Greene, B. (1999), *The Elegant Universe*, New York: W.W. Norton.

Keynes, J.M. (1936), *The General Theory of Employment*, Basingstoke: Macmillan.

Loomes, G., C. Starmer and R. Sugden (1991), 'Observing violations of transitivity by experimental methods', *Econometrica*, **59**, 425–39.

Lucas, R.E. (1977), 'Understanding business cycles', in K. Brunner and A.H. Meltzer (eds), *Stabilisation of the Domestic and International Economy*, Carnegie-Rochester Conference Series on Public Policy 5, Amsterdam: North-Holland, pp. 7–29.

Ormerod, P. (2002), 'The US business cycle: power law scaling for interacting units with complex internal structure', *Physica*, **A**, **314**, 774–85.

Ormerod, P. and C. Mounfield (2001), 'Power law distribution of duration and magnitude of recessions in capitalist economies: breakdown of scaling', *Physica*, **A**, **293**, 573–82.

Radner, R. (1968), 'Competitive equilibrium under uncertainty', *Econometrica*, **36**, 31–58.

Tenorio, R. and T.N. Cason (2002), 'To spin or not to spin? Natural and laboratory experiments from *The Price is Right*', *Economic Journal*, **112**, 170–95.

3. What do firms learn? Capabilities, distribution and the division of labour[1]

Paolo Ramazzotti

INTRODUCTION

The aim of this chapter is to investigate the relation between the learning processes of firms and their industrial specialization.[2] Its point of departure is recent research in the theory of the firm – namely the capabilities- (or competence-) based approach[3] – which has stressed how codified and tacit knowledge jointly account for the existence of differences in individual and organizational capabilities within and among firms. Following this approach, the variety of capabilities accounts for inter- and intra-firm division of labour so that specialization – the activities that a firm becomes fit to carry out – would seem to be an almost natural outcome.

The capabilities approach raises a range of issues, which will be discussed in the sections that follow. First, despite the many insights that the approach has provided, there still are some problems in defining and appropriately accounting for the origin of capabilities as well as in understanding the key features of the division of labour. Capabilities are often assumed to exist a priori or they are claimed to be part of an ongoing, yet not adequately outlined, process. As for the division of labour, it is treated as a technical issue rather than as a strategic variable. The chapter contends that this approach is unsatisfactory and it stresses that capabilities depend on the division of labour that management devises (see: 'Whence capabilities?', below).

A related set of issues focuses on the function that the division of labour may have. The chapter argues that it may be devised in order to achieve cost-effectiveness, to enhance and direct learning processes and to affect bargaining power among the parties concerned. Which function is given priority depends on the strategic outlook of management, thus on how management positions the firm on the market and how it organizes the available capabilities and arranges the required learning processes. In this regard, the chapter discusses the manifold nature and the requirements that knowledge – thus the capabilities – of the workers has to meet in order to be consistent with management's strategic outlook. Two major problems may arise. First, misperception of management's strategic outlook may prevent workers from effectively taking part in the overall problem-solving activity of the firm. Second, inconsistent values – for example, different views concerning distribution – may give rise to cognitive dissonance and undermine the firm as an organization. While the first problem may require an extension of the knowledge workers have access to, the second one may require a restriction of that knowledge. In the latter case, the relevance of the division of labour, from the point of view of management, is that it affects the bargaining power of workers (see: 'Capabilities and knowledge creation', below).

The division of labour and the resulting capabilities affect the pattern of specialization of the firm, which feeds back on the strategy pursued. Two alternative patterns may be envisaged. If, for whatever circumstance, management focuses on qualitative competitiveness and leaves distribution – within the firm or within the industry's value chain – unaffected, then the parties concerned are more likely to share the firm's strategic outlook. A division of labour may be devised to solve problems associated with qualitative competitiveness and, in so far as such a goal is achieved, the value added accruing to the firm – and to the value chain – will rise and distribution will remain a minor issue. Alternatively, if management focuses on distribution, conflicts of interest may force it to devise a division of labour that assures loyalty at the expense of problem solving. Under these circumstances, value added may not grow much, thereby leading to cost stripping as the only way to ensure short-run profitability (see: 'Distribution, learning and specialization', below).

The self-reinforcing patterns here outlined may help to provide an account for actual divergences in the patterns of specialization at the regional and country – as well as firm – levels. Because of the implications this may have for overall growth patterns, the conclusive remarks point to a few policy-related issues.

WHENCE CAPABILITIES?

Capabilities and the Division of Labour

In a famous paper, Richardson defined capabilities as 'knowledge, experience and skills' (Richardson [1972] 1990, p. 231). He acknowledged: 'The notion of capability is somewhat vague, but no more so perhaps than that of, say, liquidity and, I believe, no less useful' (ibid.). Although the notion has been elaborated upon by subsequent research, it does remain 'somewhat vague'.[4] There are two reasons for this. The first one is that it is fairly common for scholars who investigate an emerging field of inquiry to label the same concepts in different ways, thereby leading to a somewhat fuzzy situation.[5] The second reason is that, much like in the case of liquidity, there is something in the notion of capability that is irreducible to a regularity. Capabilities are what is required to solve problems as they arise. Depending on the nature of the problem, a solution may be sought by resorting to logical deduction or to heuristics, to 'know that' or to 'know how', to tacit knowledge or to codified knowledge. Independently of how it is sought, a solution to a problem implies a learning process. Thus, the difficulties in appropriately defining capabilities presumably arise because of the manifold nature of problem-solving activities (Dosi and Egidi 1991). In this section, I shall elaborate on this issue by arguing that capabilities co-evolve with those activities by means of the division of labour.

We do know that each individual has distinct knowledge, experience and skills (Minsky 1985). This means that he/she has distinct capabilities, which differ from those that others have. Furthermore, bounded rationality and incomplete and scattered information imply that no single individual can solve all problems. A single problem may be too large to tackle by a single individual, so that it has to be split up into subproblems, each one of which will be assigned to distinct individuals.

The nature of the problems that agents have to cope with varies. It may consist in executing a detailed procedure,[6] in learning how to do something, in learning how to learn. A learning process generally occurs even when the most trivial tasks have to be carried out. When Adam Smith stressed the importance of the division of labour, he focused on how specialization in pin manufacturing would favour the identification, and possible introduction, of improvements in fairly trivial tasks.

The division of labour within a firm consists in the assignment of a set of tasks to individuals who presumably have the capabilities to carry them out. It therefore defines the subproblems each individual will have to cope with, thus also the boundaries of the environment he/she will have to focus on. This entails that each individual knows only a part of what is required to solve the problem, while the team as a whole has the knowledge required for the solution (Nelson and Winter 1982; Egidi 1992). The division of labour is, in this sense, the link between individual and organizational capabilities. In a more dynamic perspective, the above boundaries define the knowledge required to carry out the task but also guidelines for future learning processes.[7] Consequently, individual capabilities at any given moment result from the evolution of original individual capabilities and the

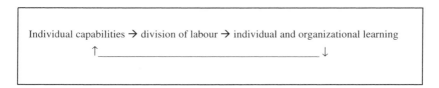

Figure 3.1   The division of labour and learning

nature of that evolution depends on the learning potential that the division of labour assigned to each individual. Organizational capabilities reflect these circumstances. The feedback process outlined is summarized by Figure 3.1.

Just as tasks may be assigned to individuals within a firm, they may be assigned to distinct firms within an industry, or to distinct industries. I introduce this topic in the subsection that follows. Subsequently, I shall discuss who determines the division of labour and on what grounds.

Coordination and the Division of Labour

By definition, the division of labour implies complementarities between distinct tasks, or activities. In turn, complementarities require some sort of coordination. Richardson ([1972] 1990) investigated distinct forms of coordination – direction, cooperation and market transactions – in relation to the technical characteristics of activities, namely similarity and the degree of complementarity. In particular, he argued that activities are 'similar' when they require the same capabilities; they are 'closely complementary' when they belong to different phases of a given production process so that they require *ex ante* interaction between the parties involved. Consequently, capabilities have to be shared either when activities are similar or when they are dissimilar but they interlock tightly. What this leads to is that the coordination issue deals with the inter-firm division of labour, that is, whether tasks are carried out within a firm or are left for other agents to carry out, and it depends on the technical characteristics of capabilities. This conclusion is clearly pointed out by Langlois and Foss: 'Richardson's insight is a simple but extremely profound one. For it suggests that – as a quite general matter – capabilities are determinants of the boundaries of the firm' (Langlois and Foss 1999, p. 209).

The above conclusion raises a range of important issues. First, is it exhaustive? Capabilities may exist that are not profitable. In such a case it would be pointless to claim that they determine the boundaries of the firm. It is therefore appropriate to refer to a more specific bundle of capabilities:

those that are consistent with an expected rate of profit. The capabilities in this bundle determine what Teece (1988) names 'core business'.[8] However, as Dosi et al. (1992) and Dosi (1994) argue, a given set of core capabilities may be compatible with different boundaries. While a minimum bundle of capabilities is required for a firm to exist, the bundle that actually exists within a firm may well be larger, including a range of additional capabilities that favour complementary activities. Under these circumstances it is not clear that 'capabilities are determinants of the boundaries of the firm'. Core capabilities are more likely to be mere constraints. At the very least some co-determinants must be identified. This is precisely what Dosi et al. (1992) do. We shall return to them shortly.

The second issue concerns the causal relation between capabilities and coordination. The claim that coordination (the boundaries of the firm) depends on capabilities needs to be qualified. If capabilities are assumed to be exogenous, the claim is consistent. While this may be the case, to some extent, for individual capabilities, it is not when organizational capabilities are taken into account. The latter result from a division of labour within organizations/firms, which, in turn, arises only if and when the coordination problem is solved, that is, when the boundaries of the firms are appropriately defined.

A more appropriate way to explain the relation between capabilities and coordination is to assume the following recursive process. Consider an initial situation where employers resort to individual capabilities and determine a division of labour within their firms. This situation allows organizational capabilities to arise, whereby firms learn to cope with problems they could not tackle before. This means that firms learn how to deal with complementarities, including how to change them. As a result, new capabilities, both individual and organizational, determine a reassessment of the coordination problem. The (new) boundaries of the firms allow a new internal division of labour to be determined. The process is depicted in Figure 3.2. What it suggests is that boundaries are determinants of the capabilities of the firm just as 'capabilities are determinants of the boundaries of the firm'.

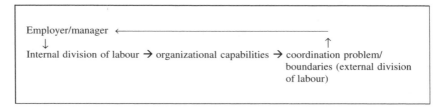

Figure 3.2   Coordination and organizational capabilities

The account Dosi et al. (1992) provide of 'coherent' boundaries seems to imply the existence of such a recursive process. Furthermore, they explain what determines the boundaries of firms by introducing a range of co-determinants of the firm's learning process: path-dependence, the technological environment, selection and so on. What they do not seem to be concerned with is what employers/managers pursue, thus the degrees of freedom that firms have and how these may affect the process depicted in Figure 3.2. The behaviour of a firm apparently consists in passive adaptation to the requirements of a given external environment. This restrictive view is criticized by Nelson, who comments:[9] 'Absent a reasonably coherent and accepted strategy . . . [t]here is no real guidance regarding the capabilities a firm needs to protect, enhance, or add in order to be effective in the next round of innovative competition' (Nelson 1991, p. 69).[10]

The notion of strategy as mere adaptation is extremely restrictive in a world where, owing to incomplete and scattered information and bounded rationality, agents have to procedurally choose how to carry out their activities (Simon 1976; Dosi and Egidi 1991). Under these circumstances they have to make some sense of the environment they act in and choose a set of actions that, in their view, will consistently achieve the pursued goal. Depending on how and what they learn about what is going on, they will identify one out of many possible strategies. The third issue qualifies the previous one in that it is concerned with how the (internal) division of labour[11] is devised. Teece's notion of core competences entails a hierarchy of capabilities in terms of a firm's competitiveness. Egidi argues that the 'process of problem solving by division into independent sub-problems seems to suggest that the existence of hierarchies in organizations may be intrinsic to the method of solving problems' (Egidi 1992, p. 168). In Egidi's framework, the capabilities of the agent who decomposes the main problem presumably lie at the top. What remains to be assessed is how he/she decomposes the problem, thereby arranging all the other capabilities available: what is at issue is how tasks and routines are devised.

This issue would be irrelevant if only one division of labour were available. This is not the general case, however. As Egidi (1992, p.168) argues, 'it should be emphasized that there is usually more than one way of decomposing a problem, and that there are therefore an equal number of possible hierarchies'. In other terms, different types of division of labour are possible. Under these circumstances, the division of labour turns out to be a co-determinant of – rather than a mere technological constraint to – the boundaries of the firm.

Following the above discussion, capabilities result from a process originated by the division of labour. Thus, they can be understood only through an inquiry into what determines the choice among different types of division of labour. This implies the discussion of three issues. The first one is who decides what division of labour is required. The second is what rationale underlies the decisions. The third is whether and how distinct capabilities and activities are likely to be consistent with that rationale.

In a decentralized economy decisions about what activity to carry out are taken by single firms. Thus, as far as the first issue is concerned, I assume that the specific agent who decides is a firm's management. In particular, I conceive of management as the (collective) agent who: conjectures an appropriate decomposition of a broadly defined economic problem (for example, making profits); identifies the capabilities to cope with each sub-problem; and, combines them in order to achieve a solution.[12] In order to focus on the specific issues I pointed out above, I shall assume that no conflicts exist within the management of a firm.[13]

In the section that follows I shall focus on the second issue. In particular, I shall discuss the functions that the division of labour may have in relation to the strategic outlook of management. I shall stress why knowledge is a key issue in this regard, and then point to the division of labour as a knowledge-creating device.

CAPABILITIES AND KNOWLEDGE CREATION

Profits, the Division of Labour and Strategy

In order to understand what underlies the behaviour of a firm's management, it is important to identify the goal the latter pursues. In the above section I pointed out that capabilities may be hierarchically arranged in terms of the goals pursued and I mentioned two possible goals. The first one concerns problem solving. Its generality is such that it may be applied to basically any kind of problem, economic or not. Precisely because it is so general, there is a risk that any inconsistency between, say, technical and economic problems may be missed or inadequately appreciated. The second goal, on the contrary, is competitiveness. It is much more specific, so much so that it need not even be the prime goal a firm pursues: the claim that profitability is impossible without competitiveness may be open to debate, whereas it is fairly clear that competitiveness would be pointless if it did not achieve profitability.

Following a widespread tradition that goes back to Karl Marx, Thorstein Veblen, Joseph Schumpeter and John Maynard Keynes, I assume that the main goal that management pursues – thus the main problem it has to face – is (money) profitability. Profits may be made in a variety of ways and production of real output is only one of them.[14] As I shall contend in this and the next section ('Distribution, learning and specialization'), this implies that not all the parties involved in the profit-seeking process need gain from it. In some instances such a process may resemble a zero-sum or even a negative-sum game. Management has to decompose the profit goal/problem into a range of subgoals/problems, which may be further decomposed into second-, third- and so on, order subgoals/problems. Each department or individual involved in this problem-solving hierarchical arrangement will end up pursuing the solution to a specific subproblem. Depending on the priorities assigned, thus to what problems are in the higher tiers of the hierarchy, a specific intra- and inter-firm division of labour will ensue.

Leaving aside the influence of external factors, three elements are crucial in the choice of the appropriate division of labour. The first one is cost-effectiveness: assuming a given type of product, unit costs will depend on how production is organized. At any given moment this may be viewed as a problem of static efficiency. As Leijonhufvud points out, however, these elements should be viewed in terms of an evolutionary process. Drawing on Adam Smith and Marx, he stresses that: 'As one subdivides the process of production vertically into a greater and greater number of simpler and simpler tasks, some of these tasks become so simple that a *machine* could do them' (Leijonhufvud 1986, p. 215; emphasis in the original). Thus, the enactment of a division of labour eventually determines a reshuffling or reassessment of the capabilities required by the firm (see Figure 3.2).

The second element, which also draws on Smith, is learning. The relative importance assigned to a capability by a given division of labour implies that it will be greatly resorted to and that learning specifically associated to its use will be enhanced (Levitt and March 1988; Loasby 1991, 1999). Consequently, the division of labour, by determining a specific hierarchy among capabilities, affects the nature and the availability of future capabilities. It determines the weight each single capability has in the learning process depicted by Figure 3.1.[15]

This leads us to the third element: bargaining power. The existence of hierarchies in the capabilities used implies that a relatively more important capability increases the influence of the agent who possesses it (Marglin 1974). While this may lead to an efficient outcome – *in terms of the subgoal* pursued – it may also determine what is commonly known as an incentive compatibility problem, that is, an inefficient outcome *in terms of the main goal*. The actual availability of capabilities and the related hold-up problems may eventually lead to a reassessment of the coordination issue, as in Figure 3.2.

Before I discuss bargaining power any further, let us consider the first two elements. Cost-effectiveness and learning may influence profitability in different ways, depending on what the specific circumstances are. Cost-effectiveness is a fairly straightforward concept in a static context. When learning is involved, it is rather less intuitive. Costs may be curbed following the acquisition of relevant knowledge, which usually requires a (costly) learning process. Whether it is convenient to undergo such a learning process depends on expectations concerning the future.

It is, however, doubtful that cost-effectiveness is the key variable for profitability: product quality also has a fairly important role, especially in wealthier economies.[16] 'Good' products may be more profitable than 'cheap' ones even though they are more expensive. Here, too, the convenience of the learning process to achieve product quality depends on expectations about what the market is going to be like – what it is going to deem a 'good' product – as well as on expectations about the cost structure and relative prices. Under these circumstances a strategy involves the pursuit of competitiveness within a scenario that management deems likely to occur. Learning therefore consists in identifying both the means to achieve competitiveness and the relevant scenario.

Up to this point of my analysis, learning allows the firm to identify the most appropriate ways to compete with other agents in the market. The behaviour of the firm is not exclusively outward looking, however. In a learning environment, the cost and quality of output also depend on how capabilities are put to use within the organization. In a new institutionalist setting this occurs through incentive compatible arrangements that make agents behave so as to meet the management's requirements. While this may be plausible when the fulfilment of a task can be somehow assessed, it hardly works when learning is involved: the achievement of a cognitive goal may not be assessable because, *ex ante*, it may not be possible to identify the goal (future knowledge) in the first place. The problem is not quite that a principal will be unable to control his/her agent. It is that the agent him-/herself needs to know what he/she has to look for, that is, what problem he/she has to solve. In general the agent will be able to identify and solve a problem only if he/she appreciates its relevance, that is, if he/she is able to situate it in a strategic setting. This means that the agent must have a strategic setting in mind and it must be consistent with his/her management's strategy.

Owing to the idiosyncratic features of learning – which depend not only on personal characteristics but also on the specific tasks individuals focus on – workers need not view the firm's environment in the same way as management. A common view, however, is essential if the firm is to pursue a consistent strategy. Workers not only need to have specific skills, they must also view things according to management's strategic perspective.

When – following Richardson ([1972] 1990, p. 231) – we refer to capabilities as 'knowledge, experience and skills', there is more to knowledge than just know-how: an all-encompassing cognitive frame is also involved.[17] This leads Witt to stress the role of involvement. He argues that workers cannot share their management's strategic outlook 'on the basis of a mere instruction process or by devising organizational and administrative routines. It is socialization in informal communication processes within the firm that is crucial for inducing people to adopt those conceptions' (Witt 1998, p. 167). In Witt's view, management does not just tell workers what to do. By providing them with a shared cognitive frame, it teaches them to look at things from a specific perspective. This frame isolates that part of the environment that is deemed relevant and identifies the priorities according to which it has to be analysed. In other terms, management provides workers with a common 'cognitive context'.[18]

Witt is correct when he points out the restrictive view that new institutionalists have of the activities within a firm. Nonetheless, he does not actually deal with possible conflicts of interest. He acknowledges that asymmetrical information may be relevant, but only because management – the entrepreneur, in Witt's terms – may fail to involve its workers. He therefore conflates inconsistent strategic views with conflicts of interest. In what follows I shall contend that this is not appropriate. Management has to deal both with the creation of a common cognitive context and with the existence of conflicting views associated to distribution. The former requires 'persuasion'; the latter requires 'bargaining' or 'politics' (March and Simon 1958). This is where bargaining power comes into the picture. The division of labour has an important role to play as a 'political' tool. It determines what single agents need to know, thus also their bargaining power. Before I discuss this issue any further, I must elaborate on the importance of knowledge in relation to capabilities. This is the subject of the subsection that follows.

Capabilities and Knowledge

A worker's (or a department's) capability is not just any collection of 'knowledge, experience and skills'. That collection must be relevant to the strategic outlook of management and it also has to be functionally oriented, that is, it must enable the agent to identify, and cope with, the specific problems that the pursuit of the firm's strategy raises. As for the capability of an entrepreneur, it does not merely consist in the ability to match exogenous competitiveness requirements with the capabilities that are available at some given moment. Rather, it consists in the ability to conceive a cognitive image that will functionally orient the capabilities of the firm.

Capabilities include, in this perspective, a broad notion of knowledge, defined as a structured belief system about the way things are and the way things should be (Stein 1997).[19] Emphasis is, here, on beliefs about 'the way things should be'. It is this feature of knowledge – a perspective, which in our case includes the main goal of the firm, profitability, as well as a range of subgoals that are deemed functional to the former – that the strategic outlook and the individuals working in the firm must share.[20] Both in the case of the worker and in the case of management, capabilities involve learning how to use previous knowledge – about how things are – in order to obtain what is believed the way things should be. In this sense, learning does not consist in adding newly processed information to a pre-existing stock of knowledge; it is the process whereby previous knowledge is viewed in a new perspective.[21] Knowledge in a community includes various belief systems, that is, various outlooks on reality and on how things should be. Only part of this knowledge is required to achieve a business goal: this is why a strategic outlook need not be intuitive to workers.

Three aspects of this manifold nature of knowledge should be outlined. The first one is *relevance*. Some skills may be useless (irrelevant) in terms of the goal pursued: a caring parent may wish to learn about the best possible way to bring up a child but this may be of little help to a firm's activities when, say, lathing is required. The second one is *orientation*. Although a skill may be appropriate, it may be inadequately used (misoriented): a researcher with an academic background may be proficient but his/her previous experience may make him/her incapable of complying with the relatively more stringent time constraints that an R&D (research and development) department has.

The third aspect of knowledge is *consistency*: some of its elements may or may not conflict with others. A very important case consists in conflicting (inconsistent) goals associated to the absence of a shared view as to what the common good is.[22] This may be determined by a *misperception* of a superior common interest, as when knowledge of what is best for a single individual or a single department apparently conflicts with what is best for the company as a whole. Such a situation may occur either because the agent who pursues the local goal is not capable of understanding the firm's overall goals or because he/she was not appropriately involved by management and did not fully understand that a convergence of interests is possible.

An inconsistency of greater significance occurs when a common good is not identified and is believed not to exist. This *value inconsistency* may occur when knowledge as an overall view of life conflicts with the specific knowledge required by a firm's activity. The pursuit of local goals, contrary to the above example of misperception, may be determined by the intentional refusal to subsume one's personal interests to the organization's interests. Thus, on grounds of social equity, workers may claim a proportion of value added which contrasts with the profit goal underlying their employer's strategy.[23]

It may be worth emphasizing that the main consequence of knowledge inconsistency within a firm does not lie in the potential outcome of the conflict, for example, lower profit than expected, or in the greater importance that informational asymmetries – for example, moral hazard – may have. It consists in the absence of a common strategic view. If some or all of the workers use a cognitive frame that is not compatible with the one provided by management, cognitive dissonance may ensue, leading to a potential collapse of the firm as an organization (Loasby 1999).

In the light of the above features of knowledge it is possible to delve into how management shapes the learning process within a firm. Assuming a strategic outlook exists, three types of purposeful action are possible so far. *Capability selection* occurs when an employer selects (hires) those individuals whose capabilities are potentially functional to the company's strategy. *Capability shaping* occurs by involving the workers of a firm in its strategy. *Internal knowledge selection* consists in selecting the knowledge that results from the ongoing learning process within the firm: misoriented knowledge has to be reoriented, relevant knowledge has to be enhanced, irrelevant knowledge has to be neutralized and inconsistent knowledge has to be discarded or somehow neutralized.

The above discussion was centred on knowledge within firms. It can be extended to knowledge within the value chain. From a firm's point of view, the knowledge of the firms it interacts with may be irrelevant, misoriented or inconsistent with respect to its profit goal. The relations it establishes with them – much like those with single workers – need not merely acknowledge the existence of these differences: it may attempt to act upon them. Thus, it will not only select firms with the appropriate knowledge; it will also try to shape their capabilities and enhance convergence in learning processes.

If the firm has a dominant role in the value chain, that is, its market power is such that client firms can only adapt to its strategy, it may succeed by devising a division of labour that will eventually favour such a convergence. Independently of ownership, it will then treat those firms just as if they were single departments or workers. Conversely, when no firm has the bargaining power to prevail over the others, this strategy will not be possible: the strategic outlooks of the firms may still converge, but only if at least one of the firms provides a cognitive frame that takes into account the interests of the others.

What the above discussion leads to is that a parallel may be traced between inter-firm relations within the value chain and intra-firm relations.

This issue will be discussed in greater detail in the section on 'Distribution, learning and specialization'.

The Division of Labour and Knowledge Creation

The first subsection in 'Capabilities and knowledge creation' stressed that the cognitive context provided by management must be consistent with the overall profit goal of the firm. The second one pointed out what this requirement implies for the learning processes of workers and client firms. Let us now return to the involvement issue.

Independently of a management's efforts to involve workers, two circumstances may prevent them from learning according to the former's cognitive frame. First, 'misperception' may easily occur when the cognitive frame provided by the management is not related to what a worker does. A problem/goal is usually identified in so far as it falls within the range of problems/goals one usually tackles. When the range of assigned tasks is narrow, the problems a worker is able to appreciate are very specific. As the range becomes more extensive, the degree of generality of the problems may rise as well. Thus, the tasks assigned to someone provide him/her with a specific standpoint. From that standpoint, the firm's general goals may be too abstract in relation to those of the single department or of the single individual. In other words, when a worker is only expected to execute a menial procedure, it is most likely that he/she will not be able to appreciate the subtleties of a new technology. This is a case where 'workers do not know enough'. Skills are that part of capabilities that is strictly associated with assigned tasks. If the division of labour does not provide a worker with the skills to identify extensive ameliorations, sharing a strategic outlook may be of little help.

Second, the overall knowledge of the workers may determine what I defined above as 'value inconsistency'. In other words, owing to their political, religious or ethical values, workers may choose not to meet all the requirements that the firm's goals imply. A typical case is when they do not accept the management's views on distribution; another case may occur when workers claim better working conditions, albeit at the expense of profit. Under these circumstances, workers may actually put forward a 'structured belief system', which contrasts the management's cognitive frame and puts forward alternative actions. This latter case may be one where 'workers know too much' relative to the management's requirements.

Let us focus on the relevance of these two circumstances. The first one suggests that Witt's view, whereby communication is the only channel that provides workers with an appropriate knowledge context, is misleading: the division of labour also plays an important role. Moreover, the division of labour may purposefully be chosen in order to achieve the knowledge context decided by management. Management may decompose strategy-related problems – that is, choose tasks – so as to provide guidelines to the learning processes of the workers.

The second circumstance points precisely to what learning processes are required. When workers have an extensive knowledge of the activities carried out by the firm, they are more likely to share their management's strategic outlook and to learn to solve problems they are confronted with. Especially when competitiveness requires widespread problem solving, it is therefore suitable to extend the range of tasks that workers are assigned. On the other hand, when a value inconsistency exists, the knowledge workers have may increase their bargaining power at the expense of the goals pursued by management. Thus, although extensive knowledge may be convenient in terms of problem solving, when workers are not involved it may also preclude profitability.

An appropriate learning process by the workers is fairly easy to identify if loyalty prevails. When this is not the case and loyalty[24] must be reinstated, such an identification may be problematic. A division of labour may be devised so as to restrict the range of tasks single workers carry out, thus also their learning potential. This determines a shift in the balance of knowledge within the firm, thereby leading workers to accept strategies that forsake their interests. It also prevents them from taking part in the overall problem-solving process that the firm is involved in. Thus loyalty (and short-run profitability) may be reinstated at the expense of the firm's competitiveness and (long-term) profitability.

The above discussion allows us to reassess the role and origin of capabilities and the division of labour in terms of the overall strategy a management pursues. The way capabilities are created depends on the involvement and loyalty of workers. When involvement is not possible, the division of labour must ensure the achievement of loyalty by acting on the knowledge that workers can gain access to. In so doing, the division of labour affects present profitability but it also acts upon the learning processes – thus the creation of new capabilities – within the firm. The loyalty required for short-run profitability may be achieved through a division of labour that is incompatible with the learning processes required for long-run profitability. Consequently, competency traps[25] may ensue.

In the section that follows, I shall point to possible inconsistencies among the subgoals that firms pursue. The aim is to show how a division of labour that is functional to short-term profitability may undermine long-term profitability.

DISTRIBUTION, LEARNING AND SPECIALIZATION

Production and Distribution

The previous sections discussed the role of problem solving and strategy. Within this framework a strategy was claimed to involve a range of subgoals, which eventually ought to allow the achievement of the main goal. What needs to be assessed is whether the subgoals are mutually consistent, thereby converging towards the main goal. The aim of what follows is to argue that inconsistencies are possible and that the outcomes they lead to may be far from desirable from the firm's – and society's – point of view.

Let us consider the following identity, referred to a single firm:

$$P = \frac{P}{VA} * \frac{VA}{O} * O$$

where P is profit, VA is value added and O is output.[26] The identity may be read as follows. Profit results from:

- the share of profit in value added, that is, distribution within the firm;
- the proportion of value added over output, that is, the degree of vertical integration of the firm; and
- sales.

What the decomposition suggests is that a firm may pursue its profit by acting on three distinct fields of action: the good's market, where producers of the same good operate; the (external) value-added chain, where firms linked by upstream or downstream relations operate; and the activities within the firm.[27] These fields of action are interdependent but it is appropriate, in the first instance, to examine them separately.

A firm may act upon the product's market by increasing its sales (O) for any given degree of vertical integration (VA/O). Assuming the level of aggregate demand is given, a rise in sales is possible by redefining the composition of demand, at the inter- or intra-industry level.[28]

The second field of action consists in the relations the entrepreneur establishes within the firm. Given the total amount of the firm's value added, profit may be increased only by increasing the profit share (P/VA) at the expense of the value added that goes to workers. This goal may be achieved with or without the consent of the workers. The first case occurs when workers believe that a superior common goal exists and may be pursued.[29] This usually happens when workers are involved in the entrepreneur's strategic outlook. The second case is more troublesome because it implies conflicting beliefs about the nature and/or existence of a common goal.

The third field of action consists in inter-firm relations within the value-added chain. The goal, here, is to raise the firm's proportion of value added over output VA/O. Two situations are possible. When control of the phases of production does not change, the share of value added rises if the firm's prices rise in relation to those of other firms in the value chain. The second situation occurs when, all other things given, the firm gains access to the most profitable phases of production.[30]

In all three cases a distributive conflict emerges between two (groups of) parties. A successful strategy would imply that these conflicts are dealt with so as not to disrupt economic activity. This may be done either through involvement – in Witt's sense – or through loyalty – in Simon's sense.[31] When the former is not possible and the latter must be resorted to, a possible strategy is to devise a division of labour that reduces the negative consequences of the conflict by creating an appropriate knowledge context. In the subsection that follows I shall discuss the implications that such a response may lead to under two opposite sets of circumstances. The aim is not to provide a fully fledged model but to point out what seems to be a crucial issue: the division of labour may foster distinct – possibly inconsistent – types of capabilities and patterns of specialization.

Distribution and Learning

Suppose that a firm has a competitive edge, so that its output and value added rise. Redistributive action within the company or within the value chain is not necessary and a cooperative environment in these two fields of action can be achieved. Management may therefore carry out a long-term strategy to foster quality competitiveness. This consists in devising products and production processes that define appropriate market boundaries for the products of the firm: the ideal outcome is to qualify and differentiate one's products to the point that a monopoly ensues; a less stringent outcome is to create a well-defined market niche.

A quality-centred strategy requires the enhancement of capabilities that favour qualitative improvements. In so far as this strategy is successful, value added within the firm and within the value chain is going to grow so that distributive tensions will not be strong and cooperation will be easier to accomplish. The ensuing learning process is depicted in Figure 3.3.

An alternative process is one where redistributive action is required. Suppose that competition on the product market is very fierce and that the company's market share is likely to fall.[32] The only way to offset the ensuing drop in profitability is to act on the two remaining fields of action. Let us

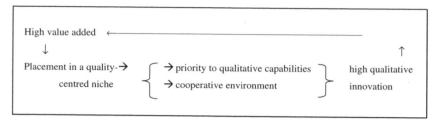

Figure 3.3   The learning process in a quality competitive strategy

focus on relations within the company. If value added drops and profit must remain constant, P/VA must rise and the wage bill must drop. This may imply lower wages and/or higher productivity followed by – or associated with – layoffs. Alternatively, the fall in value added may be offset by acting on inter-firm relations within the value chain. Here VA/O must rise, which requires that, given the boundaries of the firms, suppliers cut prices and/or (non-final market) buyers suffer price rises.[33]

The above strategies accentuate the underlying distributive conflict between management and the other parties involved, be they workers or firms. This is likely to prevent a common cognitive frame from being accepted by the parties. Thus, the company's management will have to focus its learning activity on the best ways to check possible reactions as well as on how to cut costs. Note that the client firms involved in such a strategy will most likely behave in a similar fashion. Given the demand constraint, they will try to maintain profitability by cutting costs. This will determine a redistribution of income both among firms and between wages and profit.

Under these circumstances, relations among the parties involved recall those depicted by the new institutionalist theory: the absence of a common view increases contractual hazards so that the key issue is to devise contracts with appropriate safeguards (Williamson 2000). The real problem, however, is to achieve the bargaining power that will allow those contracts to be accepted: workers might well go on strike; client firms might look for new partners.

When loyalty is undermined, the key strategic issue that management must tackle is to prevent the parties affected by redistribution from having any critical control (knowledge) over the core activities of the firm or the value chain. The capability to seek alternatives depends on how much the parties know. When 'workers know too much', management may assign tasks – it may devise a division of labour – so that the core capabilities are in the hands of the management or of those who remain involved in its strategy.[34] In a similar fashion and with the same intentions, management may redefine the inter-firm division of labour within the value chain. Gaining access to a key resource, especially a knowledge-based one, is a typical way to devise what tasks need to be carried out within the firm and what tasks are of minor importance.[35]

Let us focus on the learning behaviour all this leads to. In so far as this strategy is successful, profitability is achieved in the short run. Under special circumstances – associated with the price elasticity of demand for the goods it produces – the company may even achieve price-based competitiveness. Since low costs are pursued, management will resort to the capabilities that enhance this subgoal. Other capabilities, which would enhance quality-based competitiveness, will be relatively neglected. Furthermore, owing to the lack of cohesion these policies lead to, cooperation to improve quality is most likely to fade away. The final outcome is that the learning process depicted in Figure 3.1 will favour a specialization in the market niche where prices are valued more than quality. Ultimately, since the division of labour devised to keep workers and client firms under control affects the nature of future capabilities, the consequence is that the pursuit of an appropriate bargaining power today precludes a whole range of learning processes that would enhance quality competitiveness on the product market tomorrow.[36] The process is summarized by Figure 3.4.

The two processes depicted in Figure 3.4 are characterized by self-reinforcing learning processes. Firms learn to solve the problems they need to cope with. They focus on some activities at the expense of others, so they end up specializing in those specific activities. This occurs both within and among firms belonging to the same value chain. Similarly, since strategies depend on the capabilities available at any given moment, they tend to be self-reinforcing as well. The nature of the competitiveness pursued – specialization – tends to persist over time.

Self-reinforcement occurs within industries as well. Interaction among firms is associated with productive links. It also depends on learning processes under uncertainty. Bounded rationality and the absence of a general solution to their problems forces economic agents

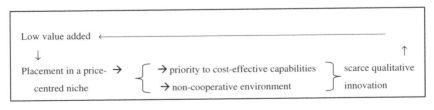

Figure 3.4   The learning process in a price competitive strategy

to resort to 'ready-made anchors of sense, ways of partitioning the space of representations, premises for decisions, and bounds within which [they] can be rational – or imaginative' (Loasby 1999, p. 46). These anchors of sense derive from common patterns of behaviour but they also determine them. It is therefore most likely that firms will converge, at least to some extent, towards a common conception of competitiveness. The implication is that the above processes may provide some insights on the patterns of industrial and, given sectoral interdependence, regional specialization.

The above conclusions require a few qualifications. The processes here outlined need not be as clear-cut as they appear. First, cost-cutting and quality-enhancing strategies were assumed to be mutually inconsistent. This need not always be the case, as when quality enhancing occurs on the shop floor and does not require time-demanding efforts to create the appropriate capabilities and to acquire the relevant technical knowledge. Under these circumstances the creation of capabilities that favour cost competitiveness might coexist with the creation of capabilities that favour quality competitiveness. The second element concerns the nature of the learning process. Stein (1997) notes that *realized* learning includes both *intended* and *emergent* – or spontaneous – learning. Thus, when management determines a division of labour functional to a specific learning process, the final outcome may differ owing to emergent learning.

Two circumstances may accentuate the depicted processes, however. The first one is bounded rationality: it is easier to focus on a single goal rather than on two, possibly inconsistent, ones. The second is the stringency of profitability: a quick rise in interest rates, for instance, is likely to turn a firm's main goal into a particularly stringent constraint, thereby forcing it to act on a quick cost-stripping basis, at the expense of long-term improvements in the qualitative nature of its output (Perlman 1996).

CONCLUDING REMARKS

The general conclusion of the chapter is that firms learn what management deems appropriate. Profit-seeking management may focus on either the production or the distribution of value added. It consequently devises a division of labour that reflects the chosen priority. The ensuing capabilities and pattern of specialization are likely to re-enforce the original strategic outlook. In some instances, the pursuit of short-run profitability may forsake long-run profitability.

A theoretical implication of the above analysis is that it provides a possible account for differing growth rates. Its emphasis is not on circumstances that merely constrain business behaviour (North 1990); rather, it suggests that managerial strategies play a major role in determining capabilities, learning processes and business behaviour itself.

The policy implication is that the ensuing patterns of specialization and growth can change only if the learning processes within firms are changed. Measures that focus on the immediate reactions of firms but disregard effects on learning processes may lead to undesired outcomes. Restrictive monetary policies, for instance, may favour cost-effectiveness but they may also enhance a process such as the one depicted in Figure 3.4. Similarly, policies that lay emphasis on labour flexibility and wage cutting favour profitability through distributional measures, thereby providing few incentives to the enhancement of qualitative competitiveness.

In so far as public policy has to take into account how firms learn, it cannot rely on a mechanistic stimulus-reaction framework: craftsmanship needs to prevail over technique. Nonetheless, general points of reference exist. Price- and quality-based strategies, for instance, may be favoured or contrasted by the time range the firm has: in terms of expected profitability, a quality-based strategy usually requires more time than a cost-based one. Although both strategies require that capabilities be identified and created, the latter may act upon existing products and processes whereas the former usually requires the identification and introduction of new products and/or processes. The conclusion is that a price-based policy is going to be more likely if the timing of returns on investment is short. A typical circumstance that may act upon this timing is the rate of interest, that is, monetary policy.

NOTES

1. I wish to thank Marco Rangone for his comments. The usual disclaimer applies. Financial help from CNR (Consiglio Nazionale delle Ricerche, Italy's National Research Council) (contract n.98.01492.CT10) is gratefully acknowledged.
2. Does a firm learn? Typically, one might answer that this expression is metaphorical, since only individuals can actually learn. Although the chapter is not inconsistent with this view, it may be worthwhile to 'Consider the meaning of an action to an individual undertaking it. It depends in part on how it is received by other agents. But the reception by other agents will only correspond to the meaning which the individual gives to the action if all agents share the same understanding of the action. In other words, it seems that each individual, if they are to achieve understanding, must relinquish some part of their idiosyncratic interpretation of their actions. This is something social, as distinct from individual, but where does it come from? There are only individuals attempting to understand their actions and consequently it seems again that we can understand neither the whole nor the parts in isolation: the individual and society are mutually constituted' (Hargreaves Heap 2000, p. 158).
3. The section 'Whence capabilities?' provides a definition of capabilities and references that help to clarify some of the nominal ambiguities in the literature. Suffice it to say here, that

the term 'capabilities' will be used throughout the chapter not only in relation to organizations but to individuals as well.

4. Carlsson and Eliasson remark: 'competence which is difficult to articulate at the individual level may not be recognized or even recognizable in a different environment or organizational structure operating under a different set of assumptions or rules. Research on business competence thus borders on the unsearchable' (Carlsson and Eliasson 1994, p. 694).

5. Dosi et al. (2002) provide a useful survey of the literature where they attempt to distinguish conceptual from nominal differences in the terms used.

6. Apparently the execution of a procedure requires no problem solving because a rigid routine has been set up already. Understanding instructions and applying them, however, remains a problem that the agent needs to solve, even though a great many other people may have already solved it before him/her (Egidi 1992).

7. It is therefore possible to extend Egidi's remark whereby 'the conjectural division of problem solving is a process which gives rise to a division of knowledge' (Egidi 1992, p. 166) to the division of labour in general.

8. '[A] set of production/manufacturing activities are typically implied by a particular research focus, a firm's "core business" . . . by which is meant the set of competences which define its distinctive advantage' (Teece 1988, p. 265).

9. Nelson's comment refers to an earlier version of Dosi et al. (1992).

10. The degrees of freedom Nelson posits in his definition are denied in the rather deterministic statement Teece makes with regard to the same issue: 'Except by entering the market for corporate control, profit seeking firms have limited abilities to change products and technologies' (Teece 1988, p. 266). Similarly, Teece and Pisano argue: 'The strategic posture of a firm is determined not only by its learning processes and by the coherence of its internal and external processes and incentives, but also by its location at any point in time with respect to its business assets' (Teece and Pisano 1998, p. 201).

11. Unless otherwise specified, in the rest of the chapter the division of labour is intended to be the internal division of labour.

12. In an uncertain environment a range of outlooks is possible. Through existing capabilities in the firm, management collects the relevant information and interprets it. Capabilities as such, however, do not provide a unique and consistent strategic outlook. It is the management's task to select relevant issues and identify the appropriate strategy.

13. I shall also leave out of my discussion possible conflicts between ownership and management.

14. 'The business man's place in the economy of nature is to "make money", not to produce goods' (Veblen [1919] 1964, p. 92).

15. This affects what Iansiti and Clark define as 'technology integration', that is, 'the capacity to link the evolving base of technical knowledge . . . to the existing base of capability within the organization' (Iansiti and Clark 1994, p. 570). The relevance of the issue is stressed, with special reference to large firms based in OECD countries, by Pavitt who states that 'lack of technological knowledge is rarely the cause of innovation failure . . . The main problems arise in organization' (Pavitt 1998, pp. 434–5) and subsequently argues that 'This can best be understood if more attention is paid to what Adam Smith said about the division of labour, and less to what Schumpeter said about creative destruction' (ibid., p. 435).

16. In standard microeconomics, cost-effectiveness is reflected in the shape of the cost curve, while quality affects the shape of the demand curve.

17. This issue is accentuated by the fact that '[t]he key characteristic of detailed management control is increasingly bounded and impaired as a result of the growing complexity of the production process' (Hodgson 1999, p. 197).

18. 'We use the term context for its meaning in the phrase, "the meaning of information depends on context"' (Imai 1990, p. 188). An analogy is possible with a research programme or a scientific paradigm (Loasby 1991) but the role of codified and systematized knowledge and analytical rigour in a knowledge context is obviously less important.

19. The definitions adopted here do not coincide with those provided by Stein (1997) but, in my view, they are consistent with the overall framework he adopts.
20. Obviously this implies that a great number of beliefs on 'how things are' must be shared as well.
21. From this point of view, cognitive structures co-evolve with the strategies pursued (Nooteboom 2000).
22. Such an inconsistency may occur both at the individual level (Sen 1982; Hirschman 1984) and at the level of an organization (March and Simon 1958; Loasby 1991).
23. This latter kind of inconsistency generally leads to March and Simon's (1958) notion of 'bargaining' and 'political' conflicts within an organization.
24. Following Simon (1997), two types of loyalty are possible: motivational and cognitive. In the first case, workers rely on the management's decisions because they believe they cannot properly assess what the relevant circumstances are. In the second case, the activities they carry out force them to concentrate their learning on those very activities, thereby losing track of what is going on at a more general level.
25. 'A competency trap can occur when favourable performance with an inferior procedure leads an organization to accumulate more experience with it, thus keeping experience with a superior procedure inadequate to make it rewarding to use' (Levitt and March 1988, p. 322).
26. In what follows, sales are assumed to match output.
27. The above variables do not depend on the action of firms alone. Distribution affects relative prices and sales, and output depends on aggregate demand. For simplicity's sake these circumstances will be ignored. Government intervention, especially in terms of income distribution, will also be assumed away.
28. In the first case, the firms that belong to an industry pursue a common goal: to expand the industry's market share – thus their overall value added – at the expense of other industries. In the second case a conflict arises among those same firms: given the total amount of value added in the industry, the value added of a firm may rise only at the expense of another firm. What is at stake is intra-industry distribution.
29. This is typically the case when workers believe that higher profits are required for investment and that investment increases employment and improves the competitiveness of the firm, thus future available value added.
30. The distinction provided here is only conceptual. Mergers and acquisitions may allow a firm not only to acquire the most profitable phases but also relevant resources and/or knowledge that will eventually allow favourable changes in the relative prices within the value chain.
31. Note that these goals are not inconsistent. Cognitive loyalty is likely to favour motivational loyalty. Since loyalty implies that workers hardly perceive possible alternatives, this circumstance may eventually make involvement easier.
32. This is a case where the firms in the market have inappropriate business conceptions and the company under inquiry fears it may have to forsake its goals to the advantage of its competitors.
33. A third strategy crosses the two fields of action. It consists in delocalizing production (outsourcing). A special case occurs when former workers set up firms that will carry out some of the activities previously carried out by the company.
34. Braverman (1974) stressed how this occurred under the Taylorist organization of production. Coriat and Dosi (1998) make similar considerations for Toyotism.
35. Some authors would refer to this as the creation of a competitive advantage through internalization.
36. A priori, this strategy could be just as profitable as the quality-centred one. In Western economies this is less straightforward, owing to competition from the Third World and low price elasticities. Indeed, a 'paradox of competition' may occur: 'Intense local price competition can reduce global competitiveness . . . by limiting the capacity of the sector to invest in its future; the result is a diminished capacity to compete against rival sectors located elsewhere' (Best 1990, p. 18).

REFERENCES

Best, M.H. (1990), *The New Competition. Institutions of Industrial Restructuring*, Cambridge: Polity.

Braverman, H. (1974), *Labor and Monopoly Capital*, New York: Monthly Review Press.

Carlsson, B. and G. Eliasson (1994), 'The nature and importance of economic competence', *Industrial and Corporate Change*, **3**, 687–711.

Coriat, B. and G. Dosi (1998), 'Learning how to govern and learning how to solve problems: on the co-evolution of competences, conflicts and organizational routines', in A. Chandler, P. Hagstrom and O. Solvell (eds), *The Dynamic Firm: The Role of Technology, Strategy, Organization, and Regions*, Oxford: Oxford University Press, pp. 103–33.

Dosi, G. (1994), 'Firms, Boundaries of the', in G.M. Hodgson, M.R. Tool and W.J. Samuels (eds), *The Elgar Companion to Institutional and Evolutionary Economics*, Aldershot, UK and Brookfield, US: Edward Elgar, pp. 229–37.

Dosi, G. and M. Egidi (1991), 'Substantial and procedural uncertainty', *Journal of Evolutionary Economics*, **1**, 145–68.

Dosi, G., R. Nelson and S. Winter (2002), 'Introduction', in *The Nature and Dynamics of Organizational Capabilities*, Oxford: Oxford University Press.

Dosi, G., D.J. Teece and S. Winter (1992), 'Towards a theory of corporate coherence: preliminary remarks', in G. Dosi, R. Giannetti and P.A. Toninelli (eds), *Technology and Enterprise in a Historical Perspective*, Oxford: Oxford University Press, pp. 185–211.

Egidi, M. (1992), 'Organizational learning, problem solving and the division of labour', in M. Egidi and R. Marris (eds), *Economics, Bounded Rationality and the Cognitive Revolution*, Aldershot, UK and Brookfield, US: Edward Elgar, pp. 148–73.

Hargreaves Heap, S.P. (2000), 'How far can we get with hermeneutics', in P.E. Earl and S.F. Frowen (eds), *Economics as an Art of Thought: Essays in Memory of G.L.S. Shackle*, London: Routledge, pp. 149–72.

Hirschman, A.O. (1984), 'Against parsimony: three easy ways of complicating some categories of economic discourse', *The American Economic Review*, **74** (2), 89–97.

Hodgson, G.M. (1999), *Economics and Utopia: Why the Learning Economy is Not the End of History*, London: Routledge.

Iansiti, M. and K.B. Clark (1994), 'Integration and dynamic capability: evidence from product development in automobiles and mainframe computers', *Industrial and Corporate Change*, **3** (3), 557–605.

Imai, K. (1990), 'Patterns of innovation and entrepreneurship in Japan', in A. Heertje and M. Perlman (eds), *Evolving Technology and Market Structure: Studies in Schumpeterian Economics*, Ann Arbor, MI: University of Michigan Press, pp. 187–201.

Langlois, R.N. and N.J. Foss (1999), 'Capabilities and governance: the rebirth of production in the theory of economic organization', *Kyklos*, **2**, 201–18.

Leijonhufvud, A. (1986), 'Capitalism and the factory system', in R.N. Langlois (ed.), *Economics as a Process*, Cambridge: Cambridge University Press, pp. 203–24.

Levitt, B. and J.G. March (1988), 'Organizational learning', *Annual Review of Sociology*, **14**, 319–40.

Loasby, B.J. (1991), *Equilibrium and Evolution. An Exploration of Connecting Principles in Economics*, Manchester: Manchester University Press.

Loasby, B.J. (1999), *Knowledge, Institutions and Evolution in Economics*, London: Routledge.

March, J.G. and H.A. Simon (1958), *Organizations*, New York: John Wiley & Sons.

Marglin, S.A. (1974), 'What do bosses do? The origins and functions of hierarchy in capitalist production', *Review of Radical Political Economics*, **6**, 60–102.

Minsky, M. (1985), *The Society of Mind*, London: Heinemann.

Nelson, R.R. (1991), 'Why do firms differ, and how does it matter?', *Strategic Management Journal*, **12**, Special Issue, Winter, 61–74.

Nelson, R.R. and S. Winter (1982), *An Evolutionary Theory of Economic Change*, Cambridge, MA: Harvard University Press.

Nooteboom, B. (2000), *Learning and Innovation in Organisations and Economies*, Oxford: Oxford University Press.

North, D.C. (1990), *Institutions, Institutional Change and Economic Performance*, Cambridge: Cambridge University Press.

Pavitt, K. (1998), 'Technologies, products and organization in the innovating firm: what Adam Smith tells us and Joseph Schumpeter doesn't', *Industrial and Corporate Change*, September, **7** (3), 433–52.

Perlman, M. (1996), *The Pathology of the US Economy. The Costs of a Low-Wage System*, London: Macmillan.

Richardson, G.B. ([1972] 1990), 'The organization of industry', *Economic Journal*, September, reprinted in Richardson, *Information and Investment*, Oxford: Clarendon Press, 1990, pp. 224–42.

Sen, A. (1982), 'Rational fools: a critique of the behavioural foundations of economic theory', in A. Sen, *Choice, Welfare and Measurement*, Oxford: Basil Blackwell, pp. 84–106.

Simon, H.A. (1976), 'From substantive to procedural rationality', in S.J. Latsis (ed.), *Method and Appraisal in Economics*, Cambridge: Cambridge University Press, pp. 129–48.

Simon, H.A. (1997), *An Empirically Based Microeconomics*, Cambridge: Cambridge University Press.

Stein, J. (1997), 'How institutions learn: a socio-cognitive perspective', *Journal of Economic Issues*, **3**, 729–40.

Teece, D.J. (1988), 'Technological change and the nature of the firm', in G. Dosi, C. Freeman, R. Nelson, G. Silverberg and L. Soete (eds), *Technical Change and Economic Theory*, London: Pinter, pp. 256–81.

Teece, D.J. and G. Pisano (1998), 'The dynamic capabilities of firms: an introduction', in G. Dosi, D.J. Teece and J. Chytry (eds), *Technology, Organization, and Competitiveness: Perspectives on Industrial and Corporate Change*, Oxford: Oxford University Press, pp. 193–212.

Veblen, T. ([1919] 1964), 'The vested interests', in *The Vested Interest and the Common Man (The Modern Point of View and the New Order)*, New York: Kelley, pp. 85–113.

Williamson, O.E. (2000), 'The new institutional economics: taking stock, looking ahead', *Journal of Economic Literature*, September, 595–613.

Witt, U. (1998), 'Imagination and leadership – the neglected dimension of an (evolutionary) theory of the firm', *Journal of Economic Behavior and Organization*, **35** (2), 161–77.

4. Dynamic capabilities, tacit knowledge and absorption

Peter Hall[1]

INTRODUCTION

The primitive assumptions that distinguish firms in an evolutionary model of competition are that:

1. they are inherently different from one another;
2. differences among them persist through time;
3. they adapt to a changing competitive environment; and
4. they influence the competitive environment by their own innovations.

Assumption 1 is the basis for the heterogeneity essential for selection processes to have a variety of 'experiments' to work on. Assumption 2 implies some inheritance or inertia characteristic that allows the differences to persist for long enough for selection processes to operate. Assumptions 3 and 4 reflect the operation of firm-level behaviours designed to promote survival and growth in an environment of continual change engendered by:

- changes in scientific and technological knowledge;
- changes in consumers' tastes, preferences and levels of awareness and understanding; and
- other firms' decisions, whether elsewhere in the supply chain or in direct competition.

The core behavioural assumption is that firms act to survive and, with varying degrees of commitment, to do well (that is, to earn above-average returns).[2] Firms are more or less successful, depending on what they know and what they do with what they know, period by period and over time, in the changing environment they confront. The common feature of all evolutionary accounts of the firm that draws these assumptions together and provides the key concept for tests of evolutionary theory at the firm level is *dynamic capabilities*:[3] 'the capacity to sense opportunities and to reconfigure knowledge assets, competences and complementary assets and technologies to achieve sustainable competitive advantage' (Teece 1998, p. 73).

The notion of dynamic capabilities is complex and multidimensional, and in this chapter we first deconstruct it to extract essential elements that are potentially testable and have been tested. Then we ask whether the tests necessarily show the operation of evolutionary behaviour and whether other explanations might serve equally well.

KNOWLEDGE AND CAPABILITY

An evolutionary account of how firms compete with one another might be summarized as follows (with due acknowledgement to Nelson and Winter (1982) and those who have subsequently emphasized the strategic centrality of technological knowledge to an understanding of dynamic competition).

Firms exist to produce and production involves the transformation of inputs into outputs. What makes firms different from one another (Assumption 1) is what their people know about how to achieve such transformations, knowledge reflecting what they brought to the firm with them and what they have since learned. These differences persist (Assumption 2) because initially differentiated knowledge is remembered from period to period and individuals and organizations learn (discard and reshape their knowledge from period to period) in different ways. Part of how firms learn is through imitation: they observe the behaviour of other firms (competitors or otherwise) and if they perceive success or benefit flowing from such behaviour, they may seek to adapt their own behaviour (Assumption 3) in order to keep up and survive. Because no two firms have identical knowledge and learning mechanisms, imitation always implies some element of innovation: an imitator both adapts its own production behaviour as it imitates and adapts the knowledge it is absorbing. Such adaptation complements innovation originating within the firm (Assumption 4). Innovation may be the almost automatic result of learning by doing or the deliberate and intentional outcome of purposeful investment in new knowledge creation through research and development (R&D). In either case, new knowledge reshapes the way the firm transforms inputs into outputs, often changing the outputs themselves. Innovation may be necessary to survive, either because tastes and preferences have changed or because technological opportunities exist which offer the potential for competitive advantage to successful innovators but extinction to laggards. Successful innovation may bring growth as well as above-normal returns.

In brief, firms are producing entities, and firm-specific differences in knowledge are at the heart of understanding what makes them more or less competitive (that is, more or less able to survive and grow), and how they compete. Demonstrating that firms know different things and build knowledge in different ways, however, is hardly a convincing test of the evolutionary credentials of a theory of the firm or inter-firm competition. While very simple neoclassical theories assume that all firms are perfectly and equally well informed about production, standard models of monopolistic competition and oligopoly at least imply differences in knowledge and in many cases explore the implications of differential rates of investment in new knowledge. Evolutionary economists need to show that specifiable differences in firms' knowledge bases and knowledge-investment activities make (on average) predictable impacts on the competitive success of firms and the dominance and diffusion of products and processes. They also need to show that when relationships between knowledge and performance are observed, they can be explained by invoking mechanisms that require us only to presuppose that firms are doing what they believe will (in some sense) 'work', not what they know will happen. The contrast is with models of the firm that assume that observed outcomes at the system level can be explained by the successful application of *ex ante* optimizing behaviours at the level of the individual decision-making unit.

To offer a theory that patterns the links between differential knowledge and differential performance, evolutionary scholars need to say why the specific knowledge of some firms may be potentially advantageous relative to that of other firms, and how that potential is translated into action and results. This calls for an understanding of how some sorts of knowledge are of particular strategic value, and how firms use such knowledge. The first task leads us towards the distinction between tacit and explicit knowledge, the second towards capabilities.

TACIT AND EXPLICIT KNOWLEDGE

As is now widely appreciated (Polanyi 1967; Nelson and Winter 1982; Howells 1996), tacit knowledge is characterized by difficulty in codification and communicability, and its origins in action (learning by doing). Because it is hard to articulate, communicate and codify, it is also hard to trade in any way independently of the human 'knower' of the tacit knowledge. Because it is generated by the actions of an individual, or a group, it is also uniquely related to the specific experiences of that individual or group. By contrast, explicit knowledge either is or relatively readily can be codified and communicated and has its origins in abstract principles and/or observable facts. Building on Nelson and Winter (1982, pp. 78–80), Cowan et al. (2000) emphasize that the extent to which knowledge is articulated and becomes codified depends importantly on the net benefit of performing the codification. Tacitness is thus not so much an intrinsic characteristic of knowledge as an economic attribute.

The importance of the distinction for firms is that tacitness in essential bodies of knowledge about production renders such knowledge costly (perhaps sometimes even impossible) for others to imitate. Even if tacitness may be viewed as an economic attribute of knowledge (as argued by Cowan et al.), Johnson et al. (2002) point to the 'numerous failures of codification projects' (p. 256) and the vast underestimates of costs and time that have been associated with attempts to codify tacit knowledge. If such knowledge supports the creation and production of products valued in the market, its firm-specific uniqueness and non-imitability is clearly of strategic value to the firm that possesses it. This has been a keystone of reasoning in the resource-based theory of the firm which Foss (1993) has argued fits well within the broader evolutionary approach.

On the other hand, if a firm's tacit knowledge contributes to its competitive advantage, it will want that knowledge to be as widely available in the organization as is necessary to maximize the impact of using the knowledge. Processes that focus on diffusing tacit knowledge within the organization and purposefully generating new tacit knowledge to sustain competitive advantage are discussed by Nonaka and Takeuchi (1995), Von Krogh et al. (2000) and Nonaka et al. (2001).

Finally, it is also recognized that, despite the difficulties of transferring tacit knowledge, firms engage in activities aimed at complementing their knowledge base by implicit trade (Von Hippel 1988), in-house R&D to assist in understanding and absorbing the tacit knowledge of others (Cohen and Levinthal 1989), formal research collaborations (Hagedoorn et al. 2000) and informal networking – especially with knowledge-generating institutions.

Ongoing work continues to build on the seminal work of Nelson and Winter, of which Spender (1996) says:

> For Nelson and Winter, the firm is a production function made up of decision rules, a set of production rules in the sense that this term is used by expert systems designers, or a script . . . The boundary between the explicit tacit types of knowledge is both porous and flexible, so there is a traffic between the domains. Nelson and Winter move towards a theory of the firm by assuming that the firm provides a special context in which the implicit and explicit bodies of knowledge are both selected by interaction with the external economic reality and then stored in the routines available to future generations of employees. Over time, the quality of the interaction of the explicit and evolving implicit types of knowledge may lead to further improvements and, thence, to superior firm performance. (p. 50)

Drawing on work in the Nonaka tradition, we would argue that a necessary condition for survival in evolutionary competition is the pursuit of a spiral of learning. To maintain a competitive edge, firms must continue to generate new elements of tacit knowledge even as existing elements become more exposed or prone to imitation as the result of in-house 'socialization' and 'externalization' and interorganizational exchanges, alliances and collaborations. In strategic terms, knowledge *transfer* processes internal to the firm principally support *survival* and must be supplemented by knowledge *creation* processes to promote *advancement* or growth (Von Krogh et al. 2000).

What this implies is that tests of evolutionary theory have to be tests that can link learning spirals to success or failure; differentiate among firms in terms of their learning experience; and predict success or failure of a firm, product or process on the basis of the learning experience undertaken.

CAPABILITY

In its earliest uses, the notion of capability was used to describe 'appropriate knowledge, experience and skills' (Richardson 1972). Little distinction is thus made between the production knowledge discussed above and a capacity to use it. Adapting a more recent definition and discussion of the concept by Zander and Kogut (1995), we would argue that a capability is an organization's *ability to accomplish a given set of production-related activities* – and that this is underpinned by two qualitatively different sorts of thing. First, an understanding of the knowledge related to those activities is required, in turn derived (at least in part) from experience in performing those activities. Second, there must be a mechanism (principle of organization) by which the underlying efforts and understandings of individuals are structured and coordinated to convert knowledge into successful activity on a repeated basis.[4] Clearly, firms may not only vary in what they know, they may also differ in how they structure, coordinate and organize what they know. Adequate tests of evolutionary theory need to reflect this.

What is understood in our definition by 'a given set of production-related activities' importantly determines, however, how we view the empirical work that has so far been done. In general discussion, Zander and Kogut (1995, p. 77), for example, offer as examples of capabilities just-in-time (JIT) manufacturing, designing for manufacturability, and decreasing time to market. As we shall see later, however, their tests relate to more specific capabilities – the ability to manufacture product innovations including drugs, explosives, ball bearings and a lawn-mower. To us, the first sort of capability seems *generic* with respect to product and the latter *product-specific*. Neither, furthermore, seems to us to be a good description of *dynamic* capabilities.

Dynamic capabilities are conceptualized as a 'coordinative management process' (Teece et al. 1997); 'the capacity to sense opportunities and to reconfigure knowledge assets, competences and complementary assets and technologies to achieve sustainable competitive advantage' (Teece 1998, p. 73); 'the capacity of an organization to consistently nurture, adapt, and regenerate its knowledge base, and to develop and retain the organizational capabilities that translate that knowledge base into useful actions' (Iansiti and Clark 1994, p. 563). In terms of the distinctions made above, it would seem to us that the notion of dynamic capabilities reflects either the capacity to shift to new product-specific capabilities, or the capacity to adopt a different or further generic capability, or both together. In either case, the sort of organization envisaged has a 'high-flex' character.

Dynamic capabilities clearly imply the operation of a learning spiral, described earlier. Since they also involve sensing, sense-making (Weick 1995) in relation to and building on opportunities, they imply cross-boundary interaction with other organizations and *their* tacit knowledge. This fits nicely with the thinking that the operation of the spiral is 'a dynamic process, starting at the individual level and expanding as it moves through communities of interaction that transcend sectional, departmental, divisional and even organizational boundaries' (Nonaka et al. 2001, p. 20). Essential to an understanding of dynamic capabilities is thus an appreciation of the mechanisms used to *absorb* external knowledge (scientific, technological and market-related, both explicit and tacit), and to interact with external knowers.

TACIT KNOWLEDGE AND THE HIERARCHY OF CAPABILITIES

We have made a distinction between capabilities which achieve outcomes by organizing and coordinating knowledge and knowers, and the knowledge itself. The organizing principles, however, are clearly knowledge in themselves (written down as codes of practice, or known by those who implement them). For each level at which knowledge and knowers are coordinated, there is a higher level of knowledge about how the coordination should proceed. At the highest level, there is knowledge about the overall strategy of the organization and how to choose and change it. Within such bodies of knowledge there are tacit elements as much as there are in product-specific production knowledge.

Empirical work which addresses evolutionary theory through the lens of dynamic capabilities thus needs to have regard to the tacit elements of each type of knowledge as much as just product-specific knowledge.

EMPIRICAL WORK: TWO FOCI

Analysis of the investment decisions of firms could, in principle, focus either on their *internal* acquisitions of physical, human and knowledge-related assets or on their *external* asset-building arrangements through alliances, collaborations and other cooperative relationships. A fully rounded analysis of the firm's investment decisions would also examine complementarities and strategic relationships between the two. Such work would highlight the tension between the benefits of sharing, for example, the costs of R&D and the strategic advantage of developing closely held knowledge valuable in the competitive environment.

In what follows, we take a highly selective look at some of the empirical work that has been done to incorporate tacit knowledge-building into the analysis of competition. First, we look at analysis focused on in-house capability-building. Second, we look at networks spanning firms and other knowledge-producing organizations.

IN-HOUSE TACIT KNOWLEDGE AND DYNAMIC CAPABILITIES: EMPIRICS

Analysis that takes as its perspective the generation of capabilities from tacit knowledge sourced in-house focuses on two modes of knowledge conversion: 'socialization' or tacit-to-tacit, and 'externalization' or tacit-to-explicit (Nonaka and Takeuchi 1995, ch. 3). Since it abstracts from co-investment activity with other organizations (dealt with in the next section), it necessarily also abstracts from several aspects of knowledge-building itself. Socialization may involve the interorganizational mobilization of tacit knowledge. Following through with the Nonaka–Takeuchi schema, agencies external to the organization may also be, and often are, involved as sources of explicit knowledge in two other types of knowledge-building. When externally sourced explicit knowledge becomes explicit knowledge of the organization, 'combination' is said to have occurred. When externally sourced explicit knowledge is converted into the organization's tacit knowledge, 'internalization' occurs.

Work which explicitly aims to examine empirically the influence of tacit knowledge on firms' performance is, as yet, quite scarce. There is a good reason for this: tacit knowledge, by definition, is hard or impossible to observe and, as a consequence, difficult to measure. On the other hand, while 'tacitness' *per se* may not have obvious metrics, either absolutely or in terms of proportion to a given body of knowledge, interesting work is available which identifies central constructs by which to characterize knowledge – and which yield something very close to a measure of tacitness.

Building on the taxonomies of Rogers (1980) and Winter (1987), Zander and Kogut (1995) adopt as constructs 'codifiability', 'teachability', 'complexity', 'system dependence' and 'product observability'.[5] Using the first four of these constructs, they then test the following proposition:

The more easily a capability can be communicated and understood, the shorter the times to transfer or imitation.

'Transfer' relates to *intra*-firm diffusion, 'imitation' to *inter*-firm diffusion. The idea is to show that the harder knowledge is to codify and teach, the more difficult it is to transfer that knowledge or imitate it – and hence the more slowly the capabilities founded on such knowledge will diffuse. Zander and Kogut argue that it is 'nonsensical to believe that there is a single dimension called tacitness' (p. 79) but it seems that is what they are testing:

It makes sense that the competitive pressures of imitators create an incentive for the innovator to expand rapidly by speeding the voluntary transfer of what is commonly called technology . . . The ability to transform *tacit capabilities* into a comprehensible code, understood by large numbers of people, is derived from the collective experiences of members (of) a firm organized by persisting rules of coordination and cooperation. (p. 78) (added emphasis)

Of even greater interest for our purposes is that Zander and Kogut claim for their findings a wider implication – that transferring and recombining organizational capabilities are the 'foundation of an evolutionary theory of the firm' (p. 76). What they describe as 'non-optimal rules of coordinated action' may, they argue, yield an evolutionary advantage when the pressure of competition places a premium on timely and speedy decision-making and intra-firm diffusion. What they say they mean by this is that firms come to rely on routinized behaviours

because they are efficient ways of doing things given what they already know how to do . . . [so] . . . it is not surprising that given the difficulty of arriving at optimal solutions for relatively simple tasks, the pressure of competition forces behaviour toward the reiteration of learned behaviours that have been successful in the past and that speed the coordination among individuals. (pp. 78–9).

What, then, do Zander and Kogut actually do and find, and how can we interpret their results? In particular, do their findings necessarily reflect the evolutionary firm at work?

Zander and Kogut's sample comprises 35 successful manufacturing innovations (from a rather smaller number of separate firms). Respondents (the original innovator, or a closely associated manufacturing or product manager) provided information on time taken to transfer or before imitation, and on the characteristics of manufacturing capabilities, that is, the nature of the firm's *manufacturing* of the innovation. In relation to the latter, constructs representing characteristics (such as codifiability) were derived from responses to questions marked on a seven-interval scale. Zander and Kogut use the constructs in a likelihood estimation procedure to judge the effects of the five dimensions of tacit knowledge on transfer and imitation rates. When expressed as the probability of transfer or imitation conditional on no previous event, these rates may be defined as hazard rates.

What they find is that their constructs of codifiability and teachability are statistically significant in their effects on the hazard of transfer: 'the more codifiable and teachable a capability is, the higher the "risk" of rapid transfer' (p. 85). By contrast, there is no statistically significant relationship between measured variation in the dimensions of knowledge tacitness and rates of imitation. Instead, variations in the imitation rate seem best explained (in terms of the variables tested) by a measure of the publicness of knowledge of the capability (labour turnover having a positive influence) and the extent to which the innovators build on their current capabilities (an impeding effect on imitation).

These results are interesting. But what do they say?

First, it might be argued that the results are compromised by focusing only on *successful* innovations. (This is rather like survivor bias in studies of the success or failure of first-to-market firms.) By focusing on successful innovations, Zander and Kogut put slow transfer down to high levels of tacitness in underlying knowledge when analysis of more and less successful innovations might have revealed that the transfer rate had other determinants – such as expected success. Contrary to the inference drawn from the paper, some innovations which are *easy* to communicate and teach may diffuse slowly – simply because they are perceived to be unpromising.

Evolutionary analysis, as much as any other, requires an appropriate sample frame. Zander and Kogut want to understand the relationship between ease of communicating a capability and the speed of its transfer or imitation. But they confine their investigation to capabilities associated only with successful, not with all innovations. The relationship they address applies across all innovations, successful or otherwise, so we are seeing only part of the story. One candidate model to address the experience of *all* firms might focus on a comparison of benefits from expected success with expected costs of implementation or adjustment – a model which *could* take an optimizing form.

Second, if capabilities are highly tacit, one would expect the *costs* of in-house socialization and externalization also to be relatively high (see our earlier remarks derived from Cowan et al. 2000). It might well then be possible to 'explain' the relatively slow diffusion of knowledge in terms of a standard optimizing exercise with respect to codifying tacit knowledge, possibly incorporating the effects of adjustment, transaction and learning costs. Capabilities dependent on higher levels of tacit knowledge might diffuse more slowly because the full costs of diffusing them are relatively severe and the incentives to diffuse undermined as a result. To show what Zander and Kogut claim – that the diffusion rate is sometimes, perhaps often, too fast to be optimal – requires the presentation of a model which generates an unambiguous benchmark for the optimal transfer rate. This is not done – but even if it were, it seems quite likely that plausible parameterizations could predict a variety of transfer rates qualifying as 'optimal'. In other words, the *non*-optimality of coordination in Zander and Kogut's observations remains to be shown.

Third, the notion of capability in the Zander and Kogut analysis seems somewhat limited. It is confined to the nature of firms' manufacturing of the innovation (p. 81). Since this comes down to investment in production process, this is one reason why it is hard to see whether they are in fact observing evolutionary behaviour or something more akin to optimization. The idea of dynamic capability implies sense-making and perhaps opportunistic behaviour pitched at a higher strategic level in the firm and much harder to capture in terms of *ex ante* optimizing models. This may be implied by Zander and Kogut's analysis but it is not directly tested for.

Turning to a fourth point, there is firm evidence in this analysis that points to the value of non-imitable capabilities. Asked about the effects of continuing to build on an innovation, the sample firms saw continuous development of their current capabilities as an effective deterrent to imitation. But is the process supporting such development best described as 'evolutionary' – or might it equally well be framed in terms of a deliberate rational response to anticipated threats? We would argue that many innovators would be aware of the strategic danger of 'one-shot' innovation so that continuing development could be viewed, in general terms, as a deliberate and calculated attempt to invest in their future survival and profitability. Their behaviour could thus be modelled as optimizing under uncertainty. For our purposes the question is: could statistical analysis enable us to tell the difference? The statistical analysis performed by

Zander and Kogut does not enable us to discriminate: it could support either approach.

While Zander and Kogut focus on knowledge transferred, an evolutionary argument would, in addition to differences in knowledge, emphasize differences in coordination mechanisms (intra-firm diffusion routines) which, in turn, would have been shaped by past experience of success *and* failure. (Evidence seems to suggest that firms' routines reflect the painful memory of failure at least as much as they embody the lessons of past success.) If we recognize differences in coordination mechanism, Zander and Kogut's results are open to a quite different interpretation. Innovations may transfer at the same (say, sample mean) rate because of the same level of tacitness, *or* because high levels of tacit knowledge in one firm are balanced by highly effective coordination *or* because of poor coordination despite low levels of tacitness. If rate of transfer in response to competitive pressure is the key to understanding evolutionary advantage, then the characteristics and sources of variation in knowledge-processing require at least as much attention as the characteristics of the knowledge processed.

In summary, an analysis that sets out with every intention to describe the evolutionary firm finishes up with instructive and worthwhile findings – but, we would argue, not results that a model based on deliberate goal-seeking might be incapable of generating.

In an interesting development, building in part on Zander and Kogut, Subramaniam and Venkatraman (2001) look at the product development capabilities of 90 transnational companies with a view to analysing the relationship between their competitive advantage and the way they mobilize in-house tacit knowledge. Their key conceptual contribution is to argue that the competitive advantage of a firm in developing new products lies in the *combination* of tacitness of information about diverse overseas markets and the richness of the mechanisms they use to process that information. Their important finding is that firms with richer processing mechanisms relative to given levels of tacitness perform better than firms with poorer processing.

Subramaniam and Venkatraman's hypotheses (three in all) take the same general form:

> A 'fit' between the extent of tacitness in overseas information acquired and the richness of a (specified) information-processing mechanism will enhance transnational new product capability.

Subramaniam and Venkatraman find significant support for this hypothesis. This suggests tacit knowledge is relevant to building more generic capabilities (here, the ability to generate new transnational products) than were analysed in Zander and Kogut. The information-processing mechanisms identified (the use of cross-national teams, the use of teams with domestic members with prior overseas experience and the frequency of communication between team members and overseas managers) suggest HRD (human resource development) investments of various kinds by the companies involved. The crucial (and unanswered) question is how were such investments determined and, in particular, might not the processes involved be reasonably interpreted as optimizing behaviour?

IMPORTING AND ABSORBING TACIT KNOWLEDGE: EMPIRICS

A seminal paper linking in-house knowledge-building to external knowledge-sourcing is Cohen and Levinthal's 'Innovation and learning: the two faces of R&D' (1989). Their claim, supported by empirical analysis, is that firms invest in R&D – to some extent at least – in order to absorb technological knowledge developed beyond their boundaries. In essence, they discover that sectors in which much tacit knowledge would be required to convert new ideas into marketable products are those in which R&D expenditure for absorbing new knowledge appears to be greatest. It is a very short step to interpret the Cohen and Levinthal work as a representation of how firms deploy dynamic capabilities.[6] But their paper is in no way 'evolutionary'. In their analysis, firms are represented as profit maximizers within a game-theoretic framework.

The absorption of knowledge from beyond firms' boundaries rounds out the complete range of activities in which firms engage to build their knowledge. In the Nonaka–Takeuchi framework, 'combination' and 'internalization' both involve drawing on external sources. The institutional arrangements for engaging with other knowledge-generating agents can be anything from the most formal (acquisitions and mergers, joint ventures) to the most informal (conversations at conferences, workshops and social gatherings; factory visits; implicit trade in ideas). Most arrangements (perhaps 90 per cent) are informal (Hagedoorn et al. 2000) and some have hypothesized that the degree of informality in linkage arrangements is likely to be correlated with the degree of tacitness in knowledge exchanged (Faulkner and Senker 1996, p. 88).

Since tacit knowledge-building and its relationship to investments in more explicit knowledge is a key element in the evolutionary analysis of firms (see Nelson and Winter above), it would seem that any analysis that makes a claim to the evolutionary inheritance should incorporate or reflect the operation of such processes. In this connection, we shall look at the interesting, pioneering work of Orsenigo et al. (2001) which analyses multi-firm knowledge acquisition in what would appear to be the evolutionary tradition – but in which the role of tacit knowledge seems at most to be implicit. We shall ask whether this leads (unwittingly) to bias in the explanations offered, and whether the observations presented could be explained in terms of other traditions. Given the extent to which tacit knowledge is also both a component of and driver in developing dynamic capabilities, an evolutionary account of real firms (which, by our definition, would focus on dynamic capabilities) should show how tacit knowledge relates to dynamic capabilities. In this connection, we reflect on an analysis that seems to do this (Leonard-Barton 1995) but does not, *per se*, make a claim to the evolutionary frame of reference. We shall want to see if the behaviour could be described in terms of an evolutionary approach, whether other approaches might do an equally good job and whether the way questions have been asked in this case prevent us from seeing that elements of optimization could be at work but have been obscured.

Orsenigo et al. aim to establish a connection 'between the structure and evolution of scientific/technological knowledge and the structure and evolution of organizational forms in innovative activities' (p. 486). They examine 5000 collaborative agreements (16 types of contract relating to licensing, research, development, equity, supply, distribution and so on) among about 2000 firms and institutions in pharmaceuticals, 1978–97. Their main claim is that the specific properties of processes of scientific discovery in molecular biology have influenced patterns of evolution in the network of collaborative relationships in the industry. The way innovative activity is *organized*, they say, has to be understood (in part) as an *adaptive response* to the structural cognitive features of the *learning processes* involved (p. 488).[7] This sort of claim appears to fall fully within the evolutionary tradition, but Orsenigo et al. choose not to specify a model of how cognitive structures influence organizational forms. While this omission points to future work on the evolutionary research agenda, it is perhaps worth commenting that the Cohen and Levinthal model might, within its own tradition, be regarded as having already moved in that direction.

The empirical work undertaken in Orsenigo et al. involves mapping the cumulated number of agreements between pairs of firms, classified according to the year of entry into the network. As a very brief summary, they find that major new technological breakthroughs initially bring about the arrival of specialized technology 'originators' (new firms and institutions). Later, 'developers' build internal capabilities in the new fields. Together, new entry and the intensity of relationships among originators and developers generate shifts to new technology. Analysing the detail of these movements, Orsenigo et al. find evidence to support their more detailed hypotheses (see note 6). More generally, however, they say their findings may have implications for theories which aim to explain how innovation activities are organized – 'particularly those which emphasize the relevance of the notions of competencies, and dynamic capabilities of firms' (p. 500). In the case of pharmaceuticals, they argue that the evidence shows two sorts of trajectory in extending scientific knowledge have generated two associated trends in organizational structures: first, increasingly specific biological hypotheses have induced older firms working at higher levels of generality to form relationships with successive generations of new entrants to work with them on more specific ideas and techniques; and second, the development of transversal (field-spanning) techniques to generate and screen compounds and molecules has tended to disrupt this intergenerational structure. Importantly for the purposes of this chapter, Orsenigo et al. say, 'In both cases, established R&D-intensive pharmaceutical firms have been able to *absorb* new knowledge by interacting with new entrants' (p. 501, added emphasis). This evidence, they argue, supports the hypothesis that established, multi-technology firms build significant R&D capabilities to absorb new knowledge and techniques generated outside their boundaries.

We would make the following comments.

First, the Orsenigo et al. analysis does not attempt to distinguish tacit from explicit knowledge. Thus there is little to be learned *directly* about whether or to what extent firms' collaboration decisions are motivated by their desire to access the tacit knowledge of others or build their own. Given that acquiring tacit knowledge has strategic potential, this means that we are simply not in a position to judge whether the patterns Orsenigo, et al. observe are driven by the pursuit of competitive advantage rather than the cognitive structure of knowledge. Orsenigo et al. are in fact silent on firms' motivations. This could be taken as reflecting a belief that firms are not optimizers – but we would argue that from this work it is not possible to tell.

An associated implication relates to firms' in-house R&D. A persuasive interpretation of the Cohen and Levinthal absorption hypothesis is that when firms undertake in-house R&D, it is partly to surmount barriers to understanding about external developments in science and technology – barriers largely related to tacit knowledge. Undertaking R&D in this context lies at the core of exercising dynamic capabilities. Since, however, firms also undertake R&D for *other* reasons (associated with internal knowledge-building), the observation that R&D-intensive firms collaborate with other organizations is not sufficient to establish that the R&D is always being undertaken in order to absorb external knowledge or make sense of the external environment. Collaborations of the kind Orsenigo et al. observe are undertaken for a wide range of reasons and, even where they directly concern R&D, they may be for defensive rather than absorptive or acquisitive reasons. Furthermore, a large body of theory provides optimizing explanations for alliances and joint ventures without relying directly on issues around tacit knowledge. If one wanted to make the case that Orsenigo et al.'s firms are acting in a non-optimizing adaptive way, it would be necessary to show that elements of the knowledge transferred across boundaries were capable of giving rise to surprise. Separating out and identifying tacit elements would be a sufficient condition for implying that firms *needed* to undertake in-house R&D to absorb external knowledge.

Second, the data for analysis are *contractual* agreements and the meaning of 'network' within the analysis is the set of *formal* relationships defined by those agreements. Even if tacit knowledge were identified within the transfers and exchanges facilitated by the network Orsenigo et al. observe, much of potential importance in shaping the structure of innovation would be missed. This is because of the prevalence of *informal* networking, especially where tacit knowledge is concerned. We would argue that certain characteristics of collaboration might be determined by the degree of tacitness in knowledge involved – and that evolutionary accounts in particular should have regard to the way organizational arrangements respond to the presence of tacitness. (Luigi Orsenigo has commented to the author that abstracting from informal networks was deliberate. The Orsenigo et al. research is already heavily data-intensive.)

While it is even more difficult and time-intensive than observing networks of contractual arrangements, we would argue that analysis of interorganizational knowledge relationships should now focus on *collecting data on tacit knowledge* elements and their implications for the macro structures of innovation. An important question, we believe, is how variations in tacitness shape these structures – an issue analogous to that investigated at the level of the individual organization by Zander and Kogut, and by Subramaniam and Venkatraman, and one implicit in the work of Cohen and Levinthal. Until now such work has seemed beyond empirical reach, but tools are gradually emerging. In addition to using Likert scales to measure dimensions of tacitness (Zander and Kogut 1995 and Subramaniam and Venkatraman 2001), causal mapping techniques are now being proposed (Ambrosini and Bowman 2001). We would tentatively suggest that the degree and/or value of tacit knowledge might also be reflected in the strength of legal steps taken in employment contracts to constrain the mobility of employees – and their ability to transfer tacit knowledge. (Cowan et al. 2000 draw attention to the growing importance of such arrangements where tacit knowledge has strategic value.)

A further issue demanding attention is the effective *measurement* of absorption. It makes no sense to talk of in-house R&D to absorb external knowledge if absorption is consistently poor – and without such measures, it is impossible to test for the value of such investments. A prima facie case in favour of an optimizing model would consist in showing the expected benefits of absorption rising with R&D expenditure allocated for the purpose, with R&D-for-absorption reaching a maximum determined by a narrowing to zero of marginal net expected benefit. By contrast, evolutionary models might show either a zero correlation between R&D-for-absorption and absorption itself, or a tendency for firms with a higher absorption-to-expenditure ratio to grow at the expense of those with lower such ratios. Bozeman (2000) has suggested a variety of measures around technology transfer and it would seem worthwhile to pursue these in connection with tacit knowledge.

The force of this point is noted in Leonard-Barton:

> Even if . . . technological knowledge can be accessed from outside, tremendous management effort is required to nurture that initial outlay into an enabling or core capability . . . Companies vary as much in their ability to absorb new technology as they do in their skills at building technological capabilities from scratch. (1995, p. 155)

Leonard-Barton has useful advice for managing knowledge-absorption: create porous boundaries, close the 'readiness gap' (between technology as licensed or acquired and its use) and develop the ability to evaluate technology (which, among other things, calls for in-house R&D). Her work is not specifically located in the evolutionary paradigm but her study of the 'learning organization' Chaparral Steel has many of the characteristics we might seek in an evolutionary model. In particular, the culture (values) of the firm put it in continuous learning mode, seeking to build knowledge from internal and external sources which will underpin capabilities in the dimensions of skill, physical capital and management systems. While Leonard-Barton talks of *core* capability (contrasted with enabling and supplemental capabilities), it is clear that the learning processes she analyses at Chaparral constitute the exercise of what we have called dynamic capabilities.

Linking tacit knowledge to external acquisition, she points to the importance of *technological gatekeepers* and *boundary-spanners* – the former determining the relevance to their organization of external information, the latter 'people who understand the world of the source and the world of the receiver and translate as well as disseminate knowledge' (p. 158). While her case study draws together the elements we would expect to see in an evolutionary firm, answers to questions other than those she asks would be required to make a final judgement on the extent to which optimization is (or is not) considered. For example, if technological gatekeepers and boundary-spanners are important, how much does Chaparral spend on recruiting and/or training them, and how are these magnitudes determined? An optimizing approach would seek evidence of the value placed on what such people achieve – or would argue that limits on recruiting and training budgets in this area are an indication of value expected.

More generally, Leonard-Barton partitions knowledge-building activities into four types – of which accessing external sources is only one. Each of these activities has a cost, in terms of time, production sacrificed or financial outlays. The activities are presented as a dynamic, holistic process but surely there must be trade-offs among them. There must be limits to the time in-house employees will spend together sharing their knowledge attempting to solve the problem, for example, rather than calling in an external consultant. But what determines that limit, and what is the criterion for calling in outsiders? It may be that no accountant reckons out the net benefits, but careful observation of repeated decisions and choices may yield a consistent pattern relating implicit, perceived potential benefits to expected costs.

CONCLUSION

It can be argued that tacit knowledge has a key role in shaping the innovation process through underpinning the competitive advantage which makes it worthwhile for firms to innovate. Tacit knowledge also helps explain the importance of dynamic capabilities – which at their heart have much to do with making sense of a dynamically uncertain environment, adapting to it and contributing to the reshaping of it. This seems to be essence of the evolutionary firm at work. While tacit knowledge has established a key position in current debates about firms' strategy and competitive activity, empirical research taking account of the influence of tacit knowledge remains scarce and somewhat inconclusive. We need to know whether tacit knowledge varies in predictable ways from one firm to another and one sector to another and, if so, what relationship these variations bear to differences in competitive performance.

In conducting such analysis, a fundamental question is whether it makes sense to construct research questions within an optimizing framework or whether the evolutionary approach is, instead, more appropriate. As noted above, Johnson et al. (2002) are among those who have questioned whether the application of standard cost–benefit analysis at the margin makes sense in guiding decisions about the codification of tacit knowledge. While accepting their position might seem to place analysis of tacit knowledge and its impact beyond the bounds of an optimizing framework, it is nonetheless Nelson and Winter who pointed to the power of economic incentives in making tacit knowledge more widely accessible. The issue would seem to be how to incorporate the operation of such incentives in this case – and a missing element in all of the models noted above appears to be recognition of this point.

The selection of empirical work discussed in this chapter illustrates some of the difficulties and challenges confronting research into the relationships between knowledge in its various forms, capabilities, inter-firm knowledge transfers and competitive advantage. It also raises questions about whether findings that seem to support evolutionary interpretations might, in fact, be the outcome of behaviours which could equally well be cast as optimizing – albeit under uncertainty.

NOTES

1. The author gratefully acknowledges the comments of participants at the second Brisbane Club meeting in Manchester, 2002, and, in particular, inputs from Luigi Orsenigo, Esben Sloth Andersen, John Foster, Stan Metcalfe, Kurt Dopfer, Jason Potts, Paolo Saviotti, Andreas Pyka and Paolo Ramazzotti. Any shortcomings remain the responsibility of the author.
2. In simple selection models, firms differ but do not change: their production functions or 'routines' are given and fixed, and they neither adapt nor innovate. While there is scope under such conditions to model evolutionary selection, there is none for a theory of the evolutionary firm.
3. Richard Nelson shares the position taken by David Teece, Gary Pisano and Amy Shuen Nelson that the theory of dynamic firm capabilities emerged in the 1980s and underpinned various accounts of the firm following lines established by Chandler, and Nelson and Winter (see Nelson (1991) on the position that dynamic capabilities are the common element among all evolutionary theories). As a general idea, capabilities characterize resource-based theories of the firm and these, in turn, have been authoritatively viewed as nested within the evolutionary paradigm (Foss 1993).
4. As Teece et al. have emphasized, capabilities are ways of organizing and getting things done 'which cannot be accomplished by using the price system to coordinate activities . . . Firm capabilities need to be understood . . . mainly in terms of the organizational structures and managerial processes which support productive activity' (cited in Foss 1993, p. 269).
5. 'Codifiability' is meant to capture the degree to which knowledge can be encoded, even if the individual worker does not have the facility to understand it. 'Teachability' reflects the extent to which workers can be trained – in schools or on the job. 'Complexity' brings in inherent variations in combining different types of competency. 'System dependence' captures the degree to which a capability is dependent on many different experienced people for its production. 'Product observability' reflects the degree to which capable competitors can copy a production capability (Zander and Kogut 1995, p. 79).
6. Orsenigo et al. (2001) discussed below, for example, cite Cohen and Levinthal as a source for the hypothesis that 'significant capabilities' are put in place by established R&D-intensive corporations 'to absorb new knowledge and techniques generated outside their boundaries' (p. 501).

7. In particular, Orsenigo et al. make the following 'predictions': (1) the fast expansion or proliferation of relevant biological knowledge leads to an expectation of rapid network growth; (2) the hierarchical structure of knowledge growth (a general hypothesis spawning sub-hypotheses at successively lower levels of generality) should lead to a hierarchical network with a core and periphery; (3) the cumulative nature of knowledge growth should yield a relatively stable core of firms built on general and stable ideas alongside a more turbulent periphery shaped by specific and changing ideas; (4) the emergence of new general ideas or field-spanning 'transversal' techniques will, through the arrival of new firms, reduce hierarchization in the network (p. 489).

REFERENCES

Ambrosini, V. and C. Bowman (2001), 'Tacit knowledge: some suggestions for operationalization', *Journal of Management Studies*, **38** (6), 811–29.

Bozeman, B. (2000), 'Technology transfer and public policy: a review of research and theory', *Research Policy*, **29**, 627–55.

Cohen, W. and D. Levinthal (1989), 'Innovation and learning: the two faces of R&D', *Economic Journal*, **99**, 569–96.

Cowan, R., P. David and D. Foray (2000), 'The explicit economics of knowledge codification and tacitness', *Industrial and Corporate Change*, **9** (2), 211–53.

Faulkner, W. and J. Senker (1996), 'Networks, tacit knowledge and innovation', in R. Coombs, A. Richards, P.P. Saviotti and V. Walsh (eds), *Technological Collaboration: The Dynamics of Cooperation and Industrial Innovation*, Cheltenham, UK and Brookfield, USA: Edward Elgar.

Foss, N.J. (1993), 'Theories of the firm: contractual and competence perspectives', *Journal of Evolutionary Economics*, **3**, 127–44.

Hagedoorn, J., A. Link and N. Vonortas (2000), 'Research partnerships', *Research Policy*, **29**, 567–86.

Howells, J. (1996), 'Tacit knowledge, innovation and technology transfer', *Technology Analysis and Strategic Management*, **8** (2), 91–106.

Iansiti, M. and K.B. Clark (1994), 'Integration and dynamic capability: evidence from product development in automobiles and mainframe computers', *Industrial and Corporate Change*, **3** (3), 557–605.

Johnson, B., E. Lorenz and B.A. Lundvall (2002), 'Why all this fuss about codified and tacit knowledge?', *Industrial and Corporate Change*, **11** (2), 245–62.

Leonard-Barton, D. (1995), *Wellsprings of Knowledge: Building and Sustaining the Sources of Innovation*, Boston, MA: Harvard Business School Press.

Nelson, R.R. (1991), 'Why do firms differ, and how does it matter?', *Strategic Management Journal*, **14**, 61–74.

Nelson, R.R. and S. Winter (1982), *An Evolutionary Theory of Economic Change*, Cambridge, MA: Harvard University Press.

Nonaka, I. and H. Takeuchi (1995), *The Knowledge-Creating Company: How Japanese Companies Create the Dynamics of Innovation*, New York: Oxford University Press.

Nonaka, I., R. Toyama and N. Konno (2001), 'SECI, *Ba* and leadership: a unified model of dynamic knowledge creation', in I. Nonaka and D. Teece (eds), *Managing Industrial Knowledge: Creation, Transfer and Utilization*, London: Sage, pp. 13–43.

Orsenigo, L., F. Pammolli and M. Riccaboni (2001), 'Technological change and network dynamics: lessons from the pharmaceutical industry', *Research Policy*, **30**, 485–508.

Polanyi, M. (1967), *The Tacit Dimension*, New York: Doubleday.

Richardson, G.B. (1972), 'The organization of industry', *Economic Journal*, **82**, 883–96.

Rogers, E. (1980), *Diffusion of Innovations*, New York: Free Press.

Spender, J.-C. (1996), 'Making knowledge the basis of a dynamic theory of the firm', *Strategic Management Journal*, **17** (Winter), 45–62.

Subramaniam, M. and N. Venkatraman (2001), 'Determinants of transnational new product development capability: testing the influence of transferring and deploying tacit overseas knowledge', *Strategic Management Journal*, **22**, 359–78.

Teece, D. (1998), 'Capturing value from knowledge assets: the new economy markets for know how and intangible assets', *California Management Review*, **40** (3), 55–79.

Teece, D., G. Pisano and A. Schuen (1997), 'Dynamic capabilities and strategic management', *Strategic Management Journal*, **18** (7), 509–33; reprinted as ch. 19 in N. Foss (ed.), (1997), *Resources, Firms and Strategy: A Reader in the Resource-Based Perspective*, Oxford: Oxford University Press.

Von Hippel, E. (1988), *The Sources of Innovation*, New York: Oxford University Press.

Von Krogh, G., K. Ichijo and I. Nonaka (2000), *Enabling Knowledge Creation: How to Unlock the Mystery of Tacit Knowledge and Release the Power of Innovation*, Oxford: Oxford University Press.

Weick, K.E. (1995), *Sensemaking in Organizations*, Thousand Oaks, CA: Sage.

Winter, S. (1987), 'Knowledge and competence as strategic assets', in D. Teece (ed.), *The Competitive Challenge – Strategies for Industrial Innovation and Renewal*, Cambridge, MA: Ballinger, pp. 159–84.

Zander, U. and B. Kogut (1995), 'Knowledge and the speed of the transfer and imitation of organizational capabilities: an empirical test', *Organization Science*, **6** (1), 76–91.

PART II

Modelling Complexity

5. The complexity of structure, strategy and decision making

Peter M. Allen

INTRODUCTION

In several previous papers (Allen 1998, 2001a, 2001b), it was shown how the creative interaction of multiple agents is naturally described by co-evolutionary, complex systems models in which the agents, the structure of their interactions and the products and services that they exchange evolve *qualitatively*. In reality, complex systems thinking offers us a new, integrative paradigm, in which we retain the fact of multiple subjectivities, and of differing perceptions and views, and indeed see this as part of the complexity, and a source of creative interaction and of innovation and change (Foster 2000). The underlying paradox is that knowledge of any particular discipline will necessarily imply 'a lack of knowledge' of other aspects. But all the different disciplines and domains of 'knowledge' will interact through reality – and so actions based on any particular domain of knowledge, although seemingly rational and consistent, will necessarily be inadequate (Lyotard 1984; Cilliers 1998). Management or policy exploration require an integrated view. These new ideas encompass evolutionary processes in general, and apply to the social, cultural, economic, technological, psychological and philosophical aspects of our realities. Often, we restrict our studies to only the 'economic' aspects of a situation, with accompanying numbers, but we should not forget that we may be looking at very 'lagged' indicators of other phenomena involving people, emotions, relationships and intuitions – to mention but a few. We may need to be careful in thinking that our views will be useful if they are based on observations and theories that refer only to a small subspace of reality – the economic zone. The underlying causes and explanations may involve other factors entirely, and the economic 'effects' of these may be only delayed, ripples or possibly tidal waves. What matters over time is the expansion of any system into new dimensions and conceptual spaces, as a result of successive instabilities involving dimensions additional to those the current 'system' appears to occupy.

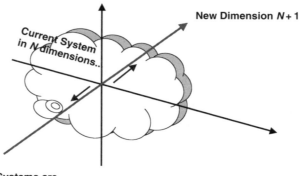

New Dimension *N* + 1

Current System in *N* dimensions...

Complex Systems are
emergent 'synergies'...

Figure 5.1   *The evolution of complex systems, at different possible levels within structures, is a 'dialogue' with the aspects and factors that are not playing an active part within it, at present*

In previous papers, a model of competing firms has been described showing how their strategies interact, and why an ability to adapt, learn, respond and 'make sense' of what is happening is a necessary strategy for survival. In this chapter it is proposed to continue further with these ideas and to show how the nested co-evolution of a complex system is about it 'dialoguing' with the dimensions that it does *not* occupy at present (see Figure 5.1).

This idea of evolution as a question of its 'invadability' with respect to 'invading' elements not yet in the system, was the subject of an early paper by the author (Allen 1976). Essentially then, systems are seen as temporary, emergent structures that result from the self-reinforcing non-linear interactions that result from successive 'invasions'. History is written not only by some process of 'rational improvement' in its internal structure but more fundamentally by its dialogue with elements that are *not yet* in the system – successive experimental linkages that either are rejected by the system, or 'take off' and modify the system irreversibly. Rational improvement of internal structure, the traditional domain of 'systems' thinking', supposes that the system has a purpose, and known measures of 'performance' which can indicate the direction of improvements. But, this more fundamental structural evolution of complex systems that results from successive invasions of the system by new elements and entities, is characterized by emergent properties and effects that lead to new attributes, purposes and performance measures. In the next sections therefore we attempt to show that this structural evolution is not in fact 'random' in its outcome, as successful invasions of a system are always characterized by the revelation of positive feedback and synergy, creating particular new, internally coherent, structures from a growing, explosively rich set of diverse possibilities (Allen and McGlade 1987; Allen 1990; 1993; 1994a; 1994b).

A CO-EVOLUTIONARY MODEL

In order to examine how the activities of different agents may evolve over time, let us consider 20 possible agent types or behaviours. In the space of 'possibilities', numbered 1 to 20, closely similar behaviours are considered to be most in competition with one another, since they occupy a similar niche in the system. Any two particular types of agent i and j may have an effect on each other. This could be positive, in that side-effects of the activity of j might in fact provide conditions or effects that help i. Of course, the effect might equally well be antagonistic, or of course neutral. Similarly, i may have a positive, negative or neutral effect on j. For our simple model therefore we shall choose values randomly for all the possible interactions between all i and j. fr describes the average strength of these, and $2*(rnd - 0.5)$ is a random number between -1 and $+1$.

This interaction is only 'potential' since the real effect of behaviour i on j will be proportional to the amount of activity of agent i – the population of type i. If agents of type i are absent then there will be no effect. Similarly, if j is absent, then there is no one to feel the effect of j. For each of 20 possible types we choose the possible effect i on j and j on i randomly:

$$Interaction(i, j) = fr * 2 * (rnd - 0.5) \qquad (5.1)$$

where random (j,i) is a random number between 0 and 1, and fr is the average strength of the interaction. Clearly on average we shall have an equal number of positive and negative interactions. (See Figure 5.2.)

Competition

Other effects positive or negative

Figure 5.2   Each pair of possible behaviours i *and* j *may interact in several ways; they may be synergetic, neutral or antagonistic*

Each agent type that is present will experience the net effect of all the other active agents present. Similarly, it will affect those agents by its presence:

$$\text{Net effect on } i = \sum_j x(j) \cdot \text{Interaction}(j, i). \qquad (5.2)$$

The sum is over j including i, and so we are looking at behaviours that in addition to interacting with each other also feed back on themselves. There will also always be a competition for underlying resources, which we shall represent by:

$$\text{Competition}(i) = \sum_j \frac{x(j)}{[1 + \rho \text{Distance}(i, j)]}, \qquad (5.3)$$

where ρ is an inverse distance in character space, scaling the distance (i, j) in character space. In other words, if distance is $\ll \rho$ then the competition is very strong, but if distance is $\ll \rho$ the competition is weak and activities can easily coexist. At any time, then, we can draw the landscape of synergy and antagonism that is generated and experienced by the populations present in the system. We can therefore write down the equation for the change in the volume of the activity i, the population x_i. It will contain the positive and negative effects of the influence of the other populations present, as well as the competition for resources that will always be a factor, and also the error-making diffusion through which populations from i create small numbers of offspring in $i + 1$ and $i - 1$:

$$\frac{dx(i)}{dt} = b * [fx(i) + 0.5 * (1 - f) * x(i - 1) + 0.5 * (1 - f) * x(i + 1)] *$$
$$[1 + 0.04 * \text{Neteff}(i)] * [1 - \text{Competition}(i)/N] - \qquad (5.4)$$
$$m * x(i) + \text{stochasticterm}$$

where f (which varies from 0 to 1) is the fidelity of reproduction that is the accuracy with which the behaviour is exactly passed on to new x, and $1 - f$ is a measure of the degree of 'exploration' of neighbouring behaviours. The term b reflects the value added or pay-off of the activity $x(i)$. The terms with 0.5 in equation (5.4) take into account that the exploration of behaviours is made equally to right or left, $i + 1$ and $i - 1$ since only the operation of the dynamics will reveal whether one of these offers a higher return than the other. The growth rate reflects the 'net effects' (synergy and antagonism) on $x(i)$ of the simultaneous presence of activities other than $x(i)$. There are limited resources (N) available for any given behaviour, so it cannot grow infinitely. The term $m * x(i)$ reflects the costs of the activity $x(i)$. The stochastic term concerns random jumps to explore new behaviours.

Let us consider an initial simulation. If we start initially with a single activity present, for example $x(10) = 5$, all other $x(i)$ are 0. If we plot the net effect of this activity on the pay-off of the 19 other possible behaviours it will provide a simple one-dimensional 'landscape' showing the potential synergy/antagonism that would affect the other activities *if they were present*. But they are not present and so the whole system may be unaware of this landscape of potential mutual interaction.

Consider that we launch activity $i = 10$, so that $x(i) = 10$. What happens? If the pay-off is greater than the costs then it grows, and if there is no exploration of other behaviours, the system rapidly reaches equilibrium. It grows until the activity is such a size that the pay-off is balanced by the costs. This is shown in Figure 5.3. There is no knowledge that other activities were possible, or that an advantageous division of labour might have been arrived at leading to a growth in the possible pay-offs, and hence an equilibrium with much higher activity.

If the same simulation is repeated with the same hidden pair interactions and the same initial conditions but this time there is a 1 per cent permitted diffusion (lack of fidelity) between neighbouring activities, then the result is shown in Figure 5.4. We see that the performance of the system increases to support a population of 72, the competition experienced per individual falls to 19 and the symbiosis per individual rises to 26.

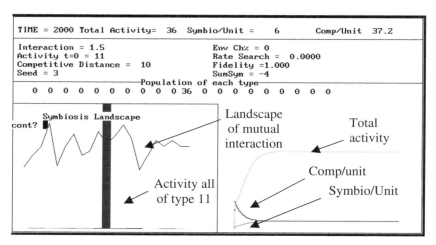

Figure 5.3   With no exploration in character space, fidelity f *= 1, the system remains homogeneous, but its performance will only support a total activity of 36*

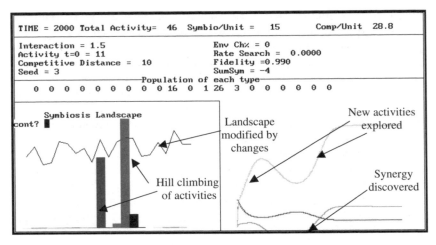

TIME = 2000 Total Activity= 46 Symbio/Unit =   15   Comp/Unit 28.8

Interaction = 1.5   Env Ch% = 0
Activity t=0 = 11   Rate Search =   0.0000
Competitive Distance = 10   Fidelity =0.990
Seed = 3   SumSym = -4
                    ─Population of each type─
    0   0   0   0   0   0   0   0   0 16   0   1 26   3   0   0   0   0   0   0

Figure 5.4   *Here the exploration of neighbouring possibilities leads activity*
              11 to hill climb into activities 10 and 13; these lead to an
              improved pay-off

In these figures, the lower left-hand graph is a moving histogram of populations $x(i)$ along the ordinate, 1 to 20 for the possible populations. Total activity is the sum of all populations. Symbio/unit is the amount of symbiosis (positive net effect) per individual. This is $[\Sigma_{ij}\, x(i) * x(j) * Neteff(i,j)]/$ *Total Population*2. Comp/unit is the amount of competition per individual.

In this simulation the activity 11 grows initially and begins to 'diffuse' into the types 10 and 12. Then 12 diffuses into 13 and the activities 10 and 13 discover a strong synergy. This leads to a higher level of activity 46, and much higher synergy per unit. However, in both simulations 1 and 2, the system has come to equilibrium and nothing more will occur. The system is 'trapped' in its routines.

Let us consider next the effect of adding in a 'stochastic term' that allows the random exploration of new activities. Instead of being trapped on the 'hill' the initial activity happens to be on, we can see whether these explorations allow a more successful ability to create new organizational forms of activity, leading to higher pay-offs and greater levels of activity (Figure 5.5).

What happens if we allow very frequent explorations? (Figure 5.6.)

An intermediate value of 0.01 leads to different possible *structural attractors* for the time 5000, as shown in Figure 5.7, where one started with activity 11 and the other with 18. This demonstrates the fact that the structural attractors discovered are 'history dependent', instead of

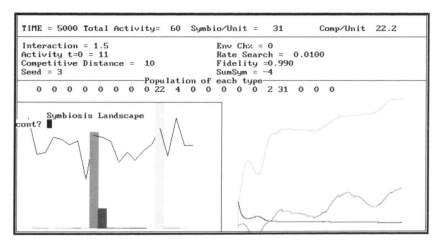

Figure 5.5   Here the occasional random explorations have allowed the system to find new hills to climb, and to climb them; total activity is 60, and synergy per unit is 31

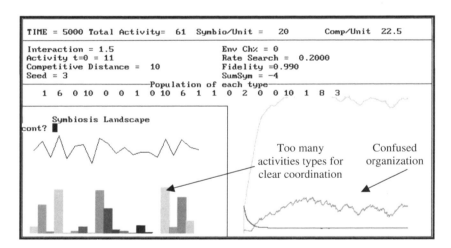

Figure 5.6   Here the frequent trials lead to some confusion, as the precise synergies and antagonisms are not clearly marked; total activity is high though

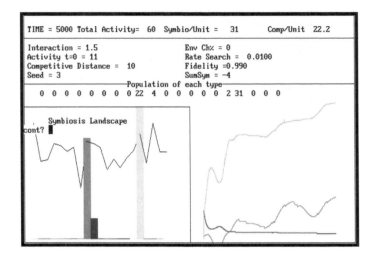

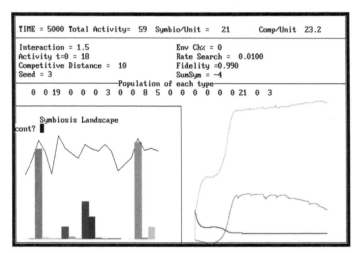

*Figure 5.7   For the same parameters, different initial conditions lead to
             different structural attractors*

running deterministically to a predictable result, the future is changed by
the action of chance in the present.

   Clearly, although the history that the simulation leads to is entirely
dependent on initial conditions and the parameters chosen, the
inclusion of exploratory mechanisms for learning does improve the performance. It allows our network to discover better organizational struc-

Different seed
for random
sequence
choosing pair
interactions

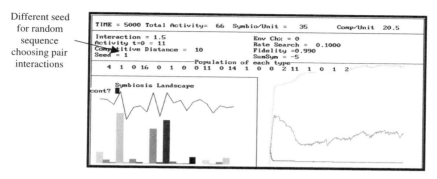

Figure 5.8　*Here a different set of pair interactions is successfully explored
by the system, leading to a high level of total activity*

tures. We can test these results by using other random seeds for choosing
the mutual pair interactions, and we can explore other initial conditions
(Figure 5.8).

This shows us that the key element that allows learning is the internal heterogeneity of a system, and its capacity to explore the potential complementarities that may be found within it, which shows us that the capacity
to try *only* neighbouring activities leads to hill climbing for the system,
improving its performance, but still staying trapped on the hill it happens
to be on. By adding an additional random exploration term the system can
considerably improve its behaviour and, through structural reorganization,
find new, more successful organizational forms. This shows us how a system
can learn what its internal possibilities are and how to make good use of
them in a particular environment.

STRUCTURAL ATTRACTORS

There are several important points about these results. The first is that the
model above is very simple and the results very generic. It shows us that for
a system in which we do not make the reductionist assumptions of average
types and average process rates (Allen 2001a) that take out the natural micro
diversity and idiosyncrasy of real-life agents, actors and objects, then
we automatically obtain the emergence of structural attractors such as
Figures 5.7 and 5.8. These are complex systems of interdependent behaviours whose attributes are on the whole synergetic. They have better performance than their homogeneous ancestors (initial states), but are less diverse
than if all 'possible' behaviours were present. In other words, they show how

an evolved entity will not have 'all possible characteristics' but will have some that fit together synergetically and allow it to succeed in the context that it inhabits. They correspond to the emergence of hypercycles in the work of Eigen and Schuster (1979) but recognize the importance of emergent collective attributes and dimensions. The structural attractor (or complex system) that emerges results from the particular history of search undertaken and from the patterns of potential synergy of the components that comprise it. In other words, a structural attractor is the emergence of a set of interacting factors that have mutually supportive, complementary attributes.

There are a number of implications of these structural attractors:

- Search carried out by the 'error-making' diffusion in character space leads to vastly increased performance of the final object. Instead of a homogeneous system, characterized by intense internal competition and low symbiosis, the development of the system leads to a much higher performance, and one that decreases internal competition and increases synergy.
- The whole process leads to the evolution of a complex, a 'community' of agents whose activities, whatever they are, have effects that feed back positively on themselves and the others present. It is an emergent 'team' or 'community' in which positive interactions are greater than the negative ones.
- The diversity, dimensionality and attribute space occupied by the final complex is much greater than the initial homogeneous starting structure of a single population. However, it is much less than the diversity, dimensionality and attribute spaces that all possible populations would have brought to the system. The structural attractor therefore represents a reduced set of activities from all those possible in principle. It reflects the 'discovery' of a subset of agents whose attributes and dimensions have properties that provide positive feedback. This is different from a classical dynamic attractor that refers to the long-term trajectory traced by the given set of variables. Here, our structural attractor concerns the *emergence* of variables, dimensions and attribute sets that not only coexist but actually are synergetic.
- A successful and sustainable evolutionary system will clearly be one in which there is freedom and encouragement for the exploratory search process in behaviour space. In other words, sustainability results from the existence of a capacity to explore and change. This process leads to a highly cooperative system, where the competition per individual is low, but where loops of positive feedback and synergy are high. In other words, the free evolution of the different populations, each seeking its own growth, leads to a system that is more cooperative than

competitive. The vision of a modern, free market economy leading to, and requiring a cut-throat society where selfish competitivity dominates, is shown to be false, at least in this simple case.

The most important point really is the generality of the model presented above. Clearly, this situation characterizes almost any group of humans: families, companies, communities and so on, but only if the exploratory learning is permitted will the evolutionary emergence of structural attractors be possible. If we think of an artefact, some product resulting from a design process, then there is also a parallel with the emergent structural attractor. A successful product is created by bringing together different components that together generate an overall performance that 'fits' the environment. But there are several dimensions to this performance, concerning different attributes, and these are correlated so that a change that is made in the design of one component will have complex consequences for the overall performance in its different attribute spaces. Some aspects of performance may be made better and some worse. We see that a successful product or service design corresponds to an emergent structural attractor. Clearly, a successful product is one in which the components interact synergetically leading to high average performance. From all the possible designs and modifications we seek a structural attractor that has components that generate performance attributes that work well in the multidimensional environment. Such structural attractors can only be revealed by research and development that must imitate the exploratory search of possible modifications and concepts which is 'schematically represented' by our simple model above.

An important point is that although our model shows us how exploration in character space will lead to emergent objects and systems with improved performance, it is still true that we cannot predict what they will be. The abstract model above used random numbers to choose pairwise interactions in an unbiased way, but in fact in a real problem these are not 'random' but reflect the underlying physical, psychological and behavioural reality of the processes and components in question, as illustrated if we think about an example such as a wine glass. The structural evolution of complex systems is about how explorations and perturbations lead to attempts to suggest modifications, and these lead sometimes to new 'concepts' and structural attractors that have emergent properties. The history of any particular product sector can then be seen as an evolutionary tree, with new types emerging and old types disappearing. But in fact, the evolution of 'products' is merely an aspect of the larger system of organizations and of consumer lifestyles that also follow a similar, linked pattern of multiple co-evolution. Let us look next at organizational evolution.

MANUFACTURING EVOLUTION

The previous sections demonstrate theoretically how micro diversity in character space, tentative trials of novel concepts and activities, will lead to emergent objects and systems. However, it is still true that we cannot predict what they will be. Mathematically we can always solve a given set of equations to find the values of the variables for an optimal performance. But we do not know *which* variables will be present, as we do not know what new 'concept' may lead to a new structural attractor, and therefore we do not know *which* equations to solve or optimize. The changing patterns of practices and routines that are observed in the evolution of firms and organizations can be looked at in exactly the same way as that of 'product' evolution above. We would see a 'cladistic diagram' (a diagram showing evolutionary history) showing the history of successive new practices and innovative ideas in an economic sector. It would generate an evolutionary history of both artefacts and the organizational forms that underlie their production (McKelvey 1982, 1994; McCarthy 1995; McCarthy et al. 1997). Let us consider manufacturing organizations in the automobile sector.

The organizational forms that have been identified are shown in Table 5.1 and Figure 5.9. If we consider the co-occurrences of particular features then we can begin to understand the probable synergy or conflict that different pairs of attributes actually have.

Figure 5.10 suggests the 'reasons' behind the emergent organizational forms, as being the hidden pair interactions between attributes. In our network simulations, successful evolution is about the discovery and

Table 5.1   Fifty-three characteristics of manufacturing organizations

Characteristic	Number
Standardization of parts	1
Assembly time standards	2
Assembly line layout	3
Reduction of craft skills	4
Automation (machine paced shops)	5
Pull production system	6
Reduction of lot size	7
Pull procurement planning	8
Operator-based machine maintenance	9
Quality circles	10
Employee innovation prizes	11
Job rotation	12

Table 5.1   (continued)

Characteristic	Number
Large-volume production	13
Mass subcontracting by sub-bidding	14
Exchange of workers with suppliers	15
Training through socialization	16
Proactive training programmes	17
Product range reduction	18
Automation (machine paced shops)	19
Multiple subcontracting	20
Quality systems	21
Quality philosophy	22
Open book policy with suppliers	23
Flexible multifunctional workforce	24
Set-up time reduction	25
Kaizen change management	26
TQM sourcing	27
100% inspection sampling	28
U-shape layout	29
Preventive maintenance	30
Individual error correction	31
Sequential dependency of workers	32
Line balancing	33
Team policy	34
Toyota verification of assembly line	35
Groups vs. teams	36
Job enrichment	37
Manufacturing cells	38
Concurrent engineering	39
ABC costing	40
Excess capacity	41
Flexible automation of product versions	42
Agile automation for different products	43
In-sourcing	44
Immigrant workforce	45
Dedicated automation	46
Division of labour	47
Employees are system tools	48
Employees are system developers	49
Product focus	50
Parallel processing	51
Dependence on written rules	52
Further intensification of labour	53

Modelling complexity

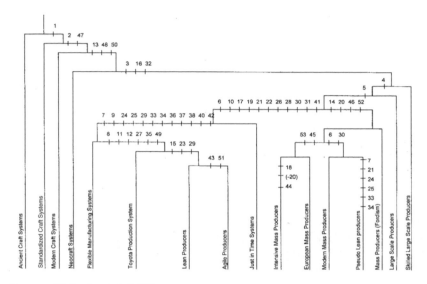

Source: McCarthy et al. (1997).

Figure 5.9 The cladistic diagram for automobile manufacturing organizational forms

Relative Specificity of the characteristics mutual occurrences

Characteristics	1	2	3	4	5	6	7	8	9	10	11	12
1	1	1	1	1	1	1	1	1	1	1	1	1
2	0.866667	1	1	1	1	1	1	1	1	1	1	1
3	0.6	0.714286	1	1	1	1	1	1	1	1	1	1
4	0.6	0.714286	1	1	1	1	1	1	1	1	1	1
5	0.333333	0.428571	0.666667	0.666667	1	1	1	1	1	1	1	1
6	-0.06667	0	0.166667	0.166667	0.4	1	1	1	1	1	1	1
7	-0.33333	-0.28571	-0.16667	-0.16667	0	0.428571	1	1	1	0.6	1	1
8	-0.6	-0.57143	-0.5	-0.5	-0.4	-0.14286	0.2	1	0.5	0.2	1	1
9	-0.46667	-0.42857	-0.33333	-0.33333	-0.2	0.142857	0.6	1	1	0.6	1	1
10	-0.33333	-0.28571	-0.16667	-0.16667	0	0.428571	0.6	1	1	1	1	1
11	-0.6	-0.57143	-0.5	-0.5	-0.4	-0.14286	0.2	1	0.5	0.2	1	1
12	-0.6	-0.57143	-0.5	-0.5	-0.4	-0.14286	0.2	1	0.5	0.2	1	1
13	0.733333	0.857143	1	1	1	1	1	1	1	1	1	1
14	-0.33333	-0.28571	-0.16667	-0.16667	0	-0.42857	-0.6	-1	-1	-1	-1	-1
15	-0.73333	-0.71429	-0.66667	-0.66667	-0.6	-0.42857	-0.2	0.333333	0	-0.2	0.333333	0.333333
16	0.6	0.714286	1	1	1	1	1	1	1	1	1	1
17	-0.33333	-0.28571	-0.16667	-0.16667	0	0.428571	0.6	1	1	1	1	1
18	-0.86667	-0.85714	-0.83333	-0.83333	-0.8	-1	-1	-1	-1	-1	-1	-1
19	-0.33333	-0.28571	-0.16667	-0.16667	0	0.428571	0.6	1	1	1	1	1
20	-0.46667	-0.42857	-0.33333	-0.33333	-0.2	-0.42857	-0.6	-1	-1	-1	-1	-1
21	-0.2	-0.14286	0	0	0.2	0.714286	1	1	1	1	1	1
22	-0.33333	-0.28571	-0.16667	-0.16667	0	0.428571	0.6	1	1	1	1	1
23	-0.73333	-0.71429	-0.66667	-0.66667	-0.6	-0.42857	-0.2	0.333333	0	-0.2	0.333333	0.333333
24	-0.33333	-0.28571	-0.16667	-0.16667	0	0.428571	1	1	1	0.6	1	1
25	-0.33333	-0.28571	-0.16667	-0.16667	0	0.428571	1	1	1	0.6	1	1
26	-0.33333	-0.28571	-0.16667	-0.16667	0	0.428571	0.6	1	1	1	1	1
27	-0.6	-0.57143	-0.5	-0.5	-0.4	-0.14286	0.2	1	0.5	0.2	1	1

Figure 5.10 The co-occurrences of 53 possible attributes in the 16 different organizational forms

exploitation of emergent synergies, and the rejection of conflictual attributes. As an illustration of the ideas behind the models we can use the co-occurrence matrix of Figure 5.10 to parametrize our 'pair interactions' instead of equation (5.1). If we do this and consider 53 possible characteristic behaviours instead of 20 as above, we can run an enlarged version of our model and see which organizational forms emerge.

The model starts off from a craft structure and is given characteristics 1, 2, 3 and 4. After that, the model tries to 'launch' new characteristics every 500 time units. These are chosen randomly and are launched as a small 'experimental' value of 1. Sometimes the behaviour declines and disappears, and sometimes it grows and becomes part of the 'formal' structure that then conditions which innovative behaviour can invade next. In the sequence shown below, our model depicts a particular evolutionary story. The history presented in Figure 5.11 is summarized in Table 5.2. It shows how from the initial situation where characteristics 1, 2, 3 and 4 are present, other innovations are tried out at intervals to see whether they will 'take off'. The condition for 'take-off' is not that the practice should necessarily improve overall performance in the long term, but merely that for the activities with which it is in interaction, those it affects, there should be a perception that it has made things go better, faster, cheaper and so on. So, it is based on a local perception of advantage since it is impossible in the short

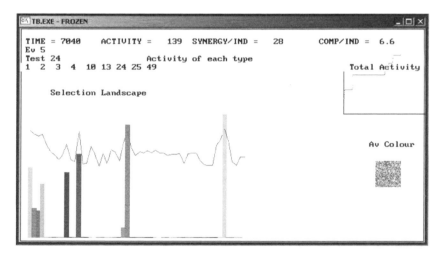

Figure 5.11   An evolutionary model tries to 'launch' possible innovative practices in a random order; if they invade, they change the 'invadability' of the new system

Table 5.2   A particular sequence of evolutionary events describing the
organizational changes that occurred over time

Characteristic	Time	Result	Structure
1,2,3,4	0	Succeeds	1,2,3,4
43	T = 500	Succeeds	1,2,3,4,43
42	T = 1000	Succeeds	1,2,3,4,43,42
9	T = 1500	Succeeds	1,2,3,4,43,42,9
48	T = 2000	Succeeds	1,2,3,4,43,42,9,48
17	T = 2500	Succeeds	1,2,3,4,42,9,49,17
20	T = 3000	Fails	1,2,3,4,42,9,49,17
28	T = 3500	Succeeds	1,2,3,4,42,9,49,17,28
14	T = 4000	Fails	1,2,3,4,42,9,49,17,28
15	T = 4500	Fails	1,2,3,4,42,9,49,17,28
34	T = 5000	Fails	1,2,3,4,42,9,49,17,28
45	T = 5500	Fails	1,2,3,4,42,9,49,17,28
45	T = 6000	Fails	1,2,3,4,42,9,49,17,28
19	T = 6500	Succeeds	1,2,3,4,42,9,49,17,28,19
13	T = 7000	Succeeds	1,2,3,4,42,9,49,17,28,19,13
15	T = 7500	Fails	1,2,3,4,42,9,49,17,28,19,13
38	T = 8000	Fails	1,2,3,4,42,9,49,17,28,19,13
5	T = 8500	Succeeds	1,2,3,4,42,9,49,17,28,19,13,5
16	T = 9000	Fails	1,2,3,4,42,9,49,17,28,19,13,5
10	T = 9500	Succeeds	1,2,3,4,42,9,49,17,28,19,13,5,10
20	T = 10000	Fails	1,2,3,4,42,9,49,17,28,19,13,5,10

term to know whether there will be a long-term overall gain or not when all the loops and interactions have worked themselves through. This is important since in reality, the full consequences will take a very long time to work through and it will be impossible to know exactly which consequences have arisen from which action very much earlier, or from other intervening decisions.

So, local judgement is used to amplify an experimental activity if it appears to work to those involved and this, once it has been integrated into the organization, changes the selection rules of compatibility or conflict for any new experiments that may follow. The model is able to describe how particular characteristics are tried out in a random fashion, and either can or cannot invade the system. Those that can invade change the structure of the organization qualitatively and produce a particular pathway through possibility space.

Different simulations lead to different structures, and there are *53!* (a very large number) possible 'histories'. This demonstrates a key idea in complex systems thinking. The explorations/innovations that are tried out next at a given time cannot be logically or rationally deduced because their overall effects cannot be known ahead of time. Therefore, the system has 'choices' about which new practice to try, and we mimic this by using a random number generator to actually choose in our simulation. In real life there would no doubt be debate and discussion by different people in favour of one or another choice, and each would cite their own projections about the trade-offs and the overall effect of their choice. However, the actual success that a new practice meets with is pre-determined by the 'fitness landscape' resulting from the practices already present.

But this landscape will be changed if a new practice does successfully invade the system. The new practice will bring with it its own set of pair interactions, modifying the selection criteria for further change. So, the pattern of what *could* then invade the system (if it were tried) has been changed by what *has already* invaded successfully. This is technically referred to as a 'path-dependent' process, since the future evolutionary pathways that are possible are affected by the path the system has taken previously.

At present the research described above is being extended by the author and by J. Baldwin and K. Ridgeway at Sheffield University. A survey of manufacturers is being conducted that will establish the 'real' pair interaction matrix of the 53 characteristics. This will allow us to calculate the evolving fitness landscape of simulations and demonstrate whether the observed organizational forms are 'structural attractors' of the interacting practices, or not. It will also make clear where irrevocable branching occurred in the evolutionary histories of organizations, and how many possible organizational forms there might really be.

It also highlights a 'problem' with the acceptance of complex systems thinking for operational use. The theory of complex systems tells us that the future is not completely predictable because the system has some internal autonomy and will undergo path-dependent learning. However, this also means that the 'present' (existing data) cannot be proven to be a *necessary* outcome of the past – but only, hopefully, a *possible* outcome. So, there are perhaps so many possible structures for organizations to discover and render functional, that the 16 actual organizational structures observed may be only a few of the several hundred that are possible. In traditional economics the assumption was that 'only the optimal survive', and therefore that what we observe is an optimal structure with only a few temporary deviations from average. But, in the new view derived from complex systems thinking, selection results from the competitive interactions of the other players, and if they have some qualitatively different emergent attributes, catering to a somewhat different market, and also sub-optimal at any particular moment, then there is no selection force capable

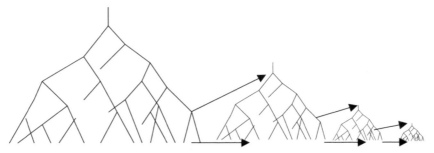

*Figure 5.12   The evolutionary process of exploration and selection is
nested in successive levels of the system; the 'innovation'
arises within an individual system, and is 'judged' by its
environment*

of pruning the burgeoning possibilities to a single, optimal outcome.
Complexity tells us that we are freer than we thought, and that there are
many possible pathways into the future, and the ability and willingness to
explore them are the basic mechanism that allows sustainability, adapt-
ability and learning to occur.

This picture shows us that evolution is about the successive discovery and
emergence of structural attractors that express the natural synergies and
conflicts (the non-linearities) of their particular underlying components.
Their properties and consequences are difficult to anticipate and therefore
require real explorations and experiments to be going on, based in turn on
a diversity of beliefs, views and experiences of freely acting individuals
(see Figure 5.12).

AN INTEGRATED VIEW OF AN ECONOMY

The ideas explored above show how organizations such as firms explore
possible functional innovations, and evolve capabilities that lead either to
survival or to failure. They describe a divergent evolutionary diffusion into
'possibility space'. Each of these is then either amplified or diminished
depending on the 'performance' of the products or services provided, which
depends on the internal trade-offs within them, on the synergies and conflicts that it encounters or discovers in its supply networks, retail structures
and in the lifestyles of final consumers.

Similarly, exploratory changes made in the supply network, in the retail
structures, or in the different elements of the lifestyles of different types of
individual all lead to a divergent exploration of possibilities. These are

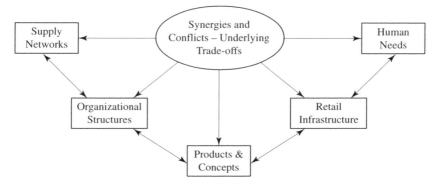

Figure 5.13   Throughout the economy, exploratory behaviour is amplified or suppressed as a result of both internal and external trade-offs

amplified or diminished as a result of the dual selection processes operating on the one hand 'inside them' in terms of the synergies and conflicts of their internal structures, and on the other hand 'outside them', in their revealing of synergy or conflict with their surrounding features (see Figure 5.13). So, a new practice can 'invade' a system if it is synergetic with the existing structure, and this will then either lead to the reinforcement or the decline of that system in its environment if the modified system is synergetic or in conflict with its environment. Because of the difficulty of predicting both the emergent internal and external behaviours of a new action, the pay-off that will result from any given new action can therefore generally not be anticipated. It is this very ignorance that is a key factor in allowing exploration at all. Either the fear of the unknown will stop innovation, or divergent innovations will occur even though the actors concerned do not necessarily intend this. Attempting to imitate another player can lead to quite different outcomes either because the internal structure or the external context is found to be different.

Throughout the economy, and indeed the social, cultural system of interacting elements and structures we see a generic picture at multiple temporal and spatial scales in which uncertainty about the future allows actions that are exploratory and divergent, which are then either amplified or suppressed by the way that this modifies the interaction with their environment. Essentially, this fulfils the early vision of dissipative structures, in that their existence and amplification depend on 'learning' how to access energy and matter in their environment. Can they form a self-reinforcing loop of mutual advantage in which entities and actors in the environment wish to supply the resources required for the growth and maintenance of the system in question? In this way, structures emerge as multi-scalar entities of cooperative, self-reinforcing processes.

What we see is a theoretical framework that encompasses both the evolutionary and the resource-based theory of the firm – and not only of the firm, but of the social and economic system as a whole. It is the complex systems dialogue between explorations of possible futures at one level, and the unpredictable effects of this both at the level below and the level above. There is a dialogue between the 'trade-offs' or 'non-linearities' affected inside and outside the particular level of exploration. But it is also true that all levels are exploring. Unless there is an imposition of rigid homogeneity up and down the levels of the system, there will necessarily be behavioural explorations due to internal diversity. And internal diversity can only be suppressed by an active selection strategy that *immediately* knows which entity will be effective, and which will not. But this is impossible, since the process is dynamic and takes time to register the relative performances. Because of this, diverse behaviours will invade the system and will coexist for a considerable time, with selection operating only gradually. In this way, the multi-level systems are precisely the structures that can 'shield' the lower levels from instantaneous selection, and allow an exploratory drift to occur, which can generate enough diversity to eventually *discover* a new behaviour that will grow. Without the multiple levels, selection would act instantly, and there would be no chance to build up significant deviations from the previous behaviour.

CONCLUSIONS

This chapter sketches out an integrated theory of economic and social evolution. It suggests how the different types of people channel their needs into particular patterns of need for different products and services. These are delivered according to the non-linear interactions of synergy and conflict that lead to particular retailing structures, both expressing natural 'markets' and within that complementarities between product categories and lines.

Products themselves exist as embodiments of attributes that cluster synergetically, and different product markets emerge naturally as a result of inherent conflicts between attributes. For example, a palmtop computer cannot have a really easy-to-use keyboard (under existing design concepts) and so notebooks and laptops exist in a different market from palmtops. Similarly, toasters and telephones also occupy separate markets because answering a call on a toaster/telephone can set your hair on fire. So, again it is the 'complementarities and conflicts' of possible attributes that structures the space of possible product or service markets.

On the supply side, the capabilities of organizations, and the products and services that they create, are the result of a creative evolutionary process in which clusters of compatible practices and structures are built up, in the context of the others, and discover and occupy different niches. At each moment, it is difficult to know the consequences of adopting some new practice – such as 'best' practice, since the actual effect will depend on both the internal nature of the organization and its actual context and relationships it has developed. For this reason it is bound to be an exploratory, risky process to try new practices, and new products. In the short term it will always be better to simply optimize what already exists and not to risk engaging on some innovation. But over time, without engaging in evolution extinction becomes not simply possible, but actually certain.

The synergies and conflicts of the supply network exhibit similar properties as new technologies provide possible opportunities and threats, and it may be necessary for new technologies and new knowledge to be adopted if extinction is to be avoided later. It is necessary to couple the driving potentials of 'human needs' to the products and services that are consumed to satisfy them, and the technologies, the structures and the organizations that form and evolve to create new responses to their changing embodiments. The whole system is an (imperfect) evolutionary, learning system in which people learn of different ways that they could spend their time and income, and what this may mean to them. Companies attempt to understand what customers are seeking, and how they can adapt their products and services to capture these needs. They attempt to find new capabilities and practices to achieve this, and create new products and services as a result. These call on new technologies and materials, and cause evolution in the supply networks. Technological innovation, cultural evolution and social pressures all change the opportunities and possibilities that can exist, and also the desires and dreams of consumers and their patterns of choice and of consumption.

This seemingly utopic view of 'restless capitalism' (Metcalfe 1998, 1999) is of course not the whole picture. This imperfect learning process means that decisions will tend to reflect the short-term positive performance of something with respect to the dimensions of which we are aware, but obviously, in a complex system, there will be other, less obvious dimensions that will perhaps be adversely affected, perhaps over the longer term, but even quite immediately. In other words, what we choose to do is dependent on 'what we are measuring', and so the system changes that we implement reflect our limited understanding of what will actually affect us. This is because our actions are based on our limited understanding and knowledge of the complex systems we inhabit, and their evolution therefore bears the imprints of our particular patterns of ignorance. So, we may grab economic gain, by pushing 'costs' into the 'externalities', or we may seek rapid satis-faction from consuming some product that actually harms us, or our com-munity, or our region, or the ozone and so on, over the longer term.

Complex systems thinking is not simply telling us that we are for ever doomed to evolve into an unknown future, with sometimes interesting, sometimes painful consequences. It is also telling us that the alternative to innovation and change is decline and impoverishment. There are two basic messages that are slightly contradictory. One is that some models of par-ticular situations can help you understand what it is you believe is going on, and therefore how you might behave in ways that are most advantageous to you. The second is that since this knowledge is extremely dubious, it is always better to have multiple options, hidden diversities and multiple interpretations available to deal with what you cannot understand and could not anticipate. The old adage is that it is better to travel than to arrive and we would suggest that the message from complex systems thinking is that nobody ever arrives. Life is not about arrival but about travelling, and although our knowledge can make some sense of the present, the future will not emerge from this, but from the whole system of sense, nonsense and that which has not yet been given words.

REFERENCES

Allen, P.M. (1976), 'Evolution, population dynamics and stability', *Proceedings of the National Academy of Sciences*, **73** (3), 665–8.

Allen, P.M. (1990), 'Why the future is not what it was', *Futures*, July/August, 555–70.

Allen, P.M. (1993), 'Evolution: persistent ignorance from continual learning', ch. 3 in *Nonlinear Dynamics and Evolutionary Economics*, vol. 8, Oxford: Oxford University Press, pp. 101–12.

Allen, P.M. (1994a), 'Evolutionary complex systems: models of technology change', in L. Leydesdorff and P. van den Besselaar (eds), *Chaos and Economic Theory*, London: Pinter, pp. 1–19.

Allen, P.M. (1994b), 'Coherence, chaos and evolution in the social context', *Futures*, **26** (6), 583–97.

Allen, P.M. (1998), 'Evolving complexity in social science', in G. Altman and W.A. Koch (eds), *Systems – New Paradigms for the Human Sciences*, Berlin and New York: Walter de Gruyter.

Allen, P.M. (2001a), 'Knowledge, learning and ignorance', *Emergence*, **4** (2), 149–80.

Allen, P.M. (2001b), 'A complex systems approach to learning, adaptive networks', *International Journal of Innovation Management*, **5** (2), June, 149–80.

Allen, P.M. and J.M. McGlade (1987), 'Evolutionary drive: the effect of microscopic diversity, error making and noise', *Foundations of Physics*, **17** (7), July, 723–8.

Cilliers, P. (1998), *Complexity and Post-Modernism*, London and New York: Routledge.

Eigen, M. and P. Schuster (1979), *The Hypercycle*, Berlin: Springer.
Foster, J. (2000), 'Competitive selection, self-organization and Joseph A. Schumpeter', *Journal of Evolutionary Economics*, **10** (3), 311–28.
Lyotard, J.-F. (1984), *The Post-Modern Condition: A Report on Knowledge*, Manchester: Manchester University Press.
McCarthy, I. (1995), 'Manufacturing classifications: lessons from organizational systematics and biological taxonomy', *Journal of Manufacturing and Technology Management – Integrated Manufacturing Systems*, **6** (6), 37–49.
McCarthy, I., M. Leseure, K. Ridgeway and N. Fieller (1997), 'Building a manufacturing cladogram', *International Journal of Technology Management*, **13** (3), 2269–96.
McKelvey, B. (1982), *Organizational Systematics*, Berkeley, CA: University of California Press.
McKelvey, B. (1994), 'Evolution and organizational science', in J. Baumand and J. Singh (eds), *Evolutionary Dynamics of Organizations*, Oxford: Oxford University Press, pp. 314–26.
Metcalfe, J.S. (1998), *Evolutionary Economics and Creative Destruction*, London: Routledge.
Metcalfe, J.S. (1999), 'Restless capitalism, returns and growth in enterprise economics', mimeo, ESRC Centre for Research on Innovation and Competition, University of Manchester.

6. Knowledges, specialization and economic evolution: modelling the evolving division of human time

Esben Sloth Andersen[1]

INTRODUCTION

To study economic evolution we need a clear answer to the question: 'What evolves?'. If we want to cover only limited aspects of the overall process of economic evolution, adequate answers are 'technologies', 'strategies' or 'routines'. But for researchers who want to cover larger parts of the history of economic evolution, it is helpful to try out the more general answer that what evolves is 'knowledge'. Unfortunately, this is very imprecise and it also leaves open serious ontological and methodological problems (Potts 2000, pp. 58–60). So Boulding's (1978, p. 33) more cautious 'glimmering' of an answer seems more appropriate: 'what evolves is something very much like knowledge'. This gives some direction for research, but it also emphasizes the urgent need for a further specification.

Not all types of knowledge show the same degree of evolution. In this respect there is a radical difference between the basic knowledge about how to behave economically and the concrete knowledge about how to produce and exchange particular economic goods. The former type seems to be pretty universal for *Homo sapiens*, so it is not the basic economizing knowledge that shows permanent evolution. A more likely candidate for evolvable knowledge is found in close relation to the concrete economic activities of production and exchange. Here we do not, however, find knowledge at the Platonic level of abstraction, where it is clearly separated from the workers and their activities. To emphasize this fact we shall introduce the concept of 'knowledges', that is, bodies of knowledge that are created and learned for performing the different activities in the system of economic activities. Thus we take the 'fundamentalist' view of Metcalfe (2001a, p. 568) and many others: it is only individuals that know and their knowing is directly or indirectly motivated by their economic activities. According to this view the core area of study comprises special purpose knowledges that are applicable for particular economic activities. In this and several other respects the concept of knowledges clearly relates to Adam Smith's (1976) analysis of the division of labour.

The next question is: 'How do knowledges evolve?'. Here Smith's answer seems to be that knowledges evolve as an automatic consequence of the changing division of labour and that this evolution is a major cause of productivity growth. An alternative and probably better answer implies some degree of decoupling between the change in division of labour and the change in knowledges. The simplest specification of this decoupling would be that the labour time spent in a particular economic activity will increase the activity-specific knowledge in a stochastic manner. This means that firms that are equally engaged in two activities will not have exactly the same knowledges about these activities. Thus they will for random reasons have clues about how to specialize. A further decoupling may be obtained by allowing for the different allocations of knowledge-improving labour towards the different knowledge areas. Although the improvement of an area of knowledge will ultimately have to be related to the corresponding productive activity, this more radical decoupling will potentially speed up the diversification of knowledges in the economic system.

In the long run, knowledges evolve both by deepening and widening. In each knowledge area there is a deepening that is reflected in the improved productivity of workers engaged in the related economic activity. The speed of this deepening depends on the number of productive workers and/or research workers in the area. This deepening takes place over the whole set of economic activities and the related knowledges. But this set may also widen to include new elements (and shrink due to the deletion of old elements). Here the gradual differentiation of final demand due to increased incomes plays a crucial role, but this topic will not be covered in this chapter. Instead we shall consider only the widening that is related to intra-industrial division of labour – both within and between firms. In the simplest case the final good is produced by an open-ended series of intermediate goods. In this setting a firm may improve its competitive position both by deepening its knowledge on an existing intermediate good and by creating a new intermediate good, which is then offered to other firms. However, as soon as the new good is created, other firms may also engage in the related knowledge deepening and production.

The study of the evolution of knowledges raises fundamental problems for both theorizing and measurement. These problems may to some extent be confronted by theoretical studies on evolutionary epistemology and by basic reflections on measurement issues. But there is little hope of resolving the problems in a purely bottom-up manner by starting from the theory of cognition and moving towards macroscopic economic evolution. There is also a need for playing the 'phenotypic gambit' (Grafen 1984). This strategy is less secure in evolutionary economics than in evolutionary biology, where there it is well supported by heritability studies. However, in economics it is important to avoid the hopeless search for a full specification of the underlying knowledges. Instead, we study the consequences of economic behaviours – not least productivities – that are assumed to be based on differential knowledges. This strategy has the advantage of specifying the kind of knowledges that we are looking for. Furthermore, it allows an abstract confrontation with some of the problems of the measurement of knowledges – including the knowledge-input problem, the knowledge-investment problem, the quality-improvement problem and the obsolescence problem (Aghion and Howitt 1998, pp. 437–41).

In order to attack directly the problem of the evolution of knowledges it is useful to start from a model of a pure labour economy. In such an economy, final output is ultimately produced by labour alone. But labour is not necessarily used only for the direct production of final output. It is also to be used for the improvement of knowledges and it may be used in the production of intermediate goods that are used in the production of final output. Thus a model of a pure labour economy analyses the division of human time across a set of activities that are directly or indirectly related to the production of final output. In an evolving labour economy this division of human time is not due to any grand design in the style of Plato's *Republic*. Instead we have to study the emerging divisions of labour and knowledges by means of 'population thinking' (Mayr 1976; Metcalfe 2001b).

Although such a form of thinking is embodied in any realistic notion of economic competition, it has been surprisingly difficult to apply it in a systematic manner. The easiest task has been to handle what may be called intra-population thinking, where we appreciate the heterogeneity of knowledges within a well-defined population and study the resulting competitive process. But to handle the evolving division of labour we also have to master the emergence of new specialities – that is, we have to apply intra-to-inter-population thinking. Furthermore, we have to deal systematically with the co-evolution of specialities by means of inter-population thinking. More generally, the study of the evolving division of human time requires a multi-level analysis of overall economic evolution. The pure labour economy is the simplest possible context in which we may try out different kinds of population thinking.

Any society may be viewed as a pure labour economy. Thus we may analyse the division of labour and knowledge in an ant colony or in a group of stone-age humans. But in this chapter we shall not try to operate at such a level of generality. Instead we shall assume that we have already reached a monetary economy, where firms operate in at least a market for final output and a market for labour. This simple economy may be viewed in two ways. First, it may be modelled as an unstructured production economy. In such uni-activity models each firm has a given level of knowledges that is normally shared by all its employees. Second, we may add the production of knowledges. Since knowledge production may be performed in different ways, we have to develop oligo-activity models for the study of this situation. However, in both uni-activity and oligo-activity models we basically operate with a single population of firms. But this analytical situation changes drastically when we move to multi-activity models in which firms are engaged in the production of a number of intermediate goods as well as in the production of the final good. If firms in such a multi-activity setting engage in knowledge production, then they will in some way or another generate productivity differentials that can be exploited by specializing in and exchange of intermediate goods. At the same time firms face difficult questions about their specialization profile – both with respect to production of goods and production of knowledges.

The suggested family of multi-activity models of economic evolution has several similarities with models developed within the mainstream of endogenous growth theory that treat the emergence of novelty as the driver of the growth process. For example, in Romer (1990) and Aghion and Howitt (1998) novelty is largely modelled as new sectors in which monopolists produce intermediate goods. Thus an increasing number of specialized inputs are supplied to the final good sector and thereby the whole economy obtains an increase in productivity. In this way an increasingly heterogeneous set of firms create growth, but these firms do not constitute a population. Instead there is one population in the final good sector, where all firms are identical, and an increasing number of intermediate good-producing 'populations', each consisting of one firm. So we are facing inter-population diversity but no intra-population variance. Furthermore, these firms have rational expectations in the sense that they know the probability of obtaining an innovation and are able to calculate the optimal research and development (R&D) effort (given that they are risk neutral).

Both the lack of population thinking in new growth theory and its assumption of substantive rationality exclude any analysis of the evolutionary process that in real economic life generates much of the observed economic growth. Against this background it seems premature when Romer (1993, p. 559) suggests 'a natural division of labour in future research' between 'mainstream theorists and appreciative theorists' (p. 556). The former provide 'simple abstract models', while the latter provide 'aggregative statistical analysis and in-depth case studies' (p. 559). While Romer's diagnosis about the deficiencies of the formal tools of appreciative theorists of economic evolution might be correct, his prescription has a big problem. It ignores the fact that the supposed suppliers of evidence – Romer (1993) mentions David, Fagerberg, Mokyr, Nelson and Rosenberg – are dealing with heterogeneous populations of boundedly rational agents that are not adequately formalized by the new growth theorists (compare Andersen 1999, pp. 34–7).

This chapter is squarely based in population thinking. The formalization of this kind of thinking is by no means easy – as pointed out, for example, by Metcalfe (2001b) and Saviotti (2001). So the chapter suggests a double strategy. On the one hand, it deals with formal tools and basic model specifications that implement the different aspects of population thinking in the context of economic evolution. On the other, it draws on simulation exercises that explore different aspects of the evolution of knowledges and specializations in a pure labour economy. Both strategies are necessary, but to relate to Romer's challenge, it might be remarked that formal tools have an underestimated descriptive function. We really need tools that help us to become population thinkers. Here the chapter emphasizes a formula for the decomposition of short-term evolutionary change that is surprisingly powerful. This is the formula of George R. Price (1970, 1972) that has recently started to spread into evolutionary economics from its stronghold in the analysis of social evolution in evolutionary biology. The application of Price's formula helps us to think clearly about the selection processes that form the backbone of economic evolution, but it also elucidates innovation processes and their consequences. Furthermore, it eases the move from single-level population thinking to multi-level thinking. So Price's formula is a major tool for the analysis of many aspects of the evolving division of human time.

UNI-ACTIVITY MODELS

Background and Specification

The task of all the models of this chapter is to depict the macro phenomenon of economic evolution. In the basic models only one homogeneous good is produced, so economic growth is easily measured as growth in the per capita production of the good. In the simplified uni-activity setting output is produced by only two factors of production: labour and knowledge (that determines labour productivity). In the simplest case, growth is obtained because firms with above-average productivity increase their share of total employment. Thus the favoured firms over time supply a larger and larger proportion of the output of the economy. Through this simple selection process, both average productivity and total output is increased.

The basic assumption of the whole model family is that because firms have limited information and are boundedly rational, they have to apply the limited knowledges that often take the form of routines for productive activities and market-related decision-making. The starting point is to specify the routines that are related to the transformation of labour input to final output. In other words, we consider production-related knowledges as defining routines of production. To each particular production routine there corresponds a particular productivity level. Thus we may represent a given production routine by a real-valued productivity that for a given firm is defined by $A = Q/L$.

In contrast to most models that deal with economic evolution, the present model family is designed to cover whole economies. The reason for this is not primarily that the results can immediately be interpreted in relation to theories of economic growth. The main purpose of the whole-economy approach is to define a robust test bed for different evolutionary mechanisms. If we choose a partial-economy test bed, then we will have to specify the relationship to the rest of the economy by means of more or less arbitrary parameters – as is the case with the Nelson–Winter models of Schumpeterian competition (Nelson and Winter 1982, chs 12–14). This problem is removed by the whole-economy approach. Here, of course, we have to define explicitly the available factors of production as well as the price system that regulates the allocation of factors and goods, but we will have fewer and more fundamental parameters than in the case of partial-economy models.

The elements of the economic system of the uni-activity model are households and firms that are held together by two markets: an output market and a labour market. The final good is sold and bought in a simple output market that takes place at the end of each period. In the market-place, households spend all the income that they have obtained during the period. Firms supply their maximum output – given their employment and their productivity. The output price is determined so that it clears the market. Labour provides a homogeneous service, so there is no difference between newly hired employees and long-term employees. The labour services are sold and bought in a market that takes place at the end of each period. Households earn their income for the next period by supplying a fixed amount of labour at a fixed wage rate that is set to unity. Thus each employee receives an income of one monetary unit in each period. Firms employ labour on one-period contracts, which imply that wages are paid after one period of employment. In practice the labour market concerns only workers who are moving between firms. A worker who is fired from a shrinking firm is immediately available for employment in an expanding firm.

These descriptions of the uni-activity model may be summarized more formally:

1. The model describes an economy in which output is produced by the production function $Q_i = A_i L_i$, where A_i is the fixed productivity and L_i is the changing employment of firm i. The wage rate $w = 1$, so the firm has fixed unit costs, $c_i = 1/A_i$.
2. The aggregate employment of the economy is $L = \Sigma L_i$, aggregate output is $Q = \Sigma Q_i$, the employment shares of the firms are $s_i = L_i/L$ and the mean productivity is $\overline{A} = \Sigma s_i A_i$.
3. Households spend all their income on the output. So since wage is equal to unity, monetary demand $D = L$. This means that the market-clearing price $P = D/Q$. Since $Q = \overline{A}L$, we have that $P = 1/\overline{A}$.
4. For firm i profit $\pi_i = PQ_i - L_i$. Positive and negative profits lead to corresponding hiring and firing, so $\Delta L_i = \pi_i$.

From the viewpoint of the individual firm, things are pretty simple in this uni-activity model. If the market price is larger than the firm's unit cost (that is, if $P > 1/A_i$), then it obtains a positive profit and expands its employment correspondingly; if the price is smaller, it contracts. Furthermore, the output price is inversely related to the mean productivity of the economy. This market price allows us to study the logic of the change of the firm's employment. Here we see that for firm i, the change $\Delta L_i = \pi_i = (A_i/\overline{A} - 1)L_i$. Thus the change of employment depends on the relation between the firm's productivity and the mean productivity. This behaviour of the individual firms implies that there is no aggregate change of the economy's employment ($\Delta L = 0$).

Given this result, it is easy to find the rate of change of the firm's employment share. It is determined by the difference between a firm's employment change and the zero change of aggregate employment. Thus:

$$\Delta s_i = s_i \left(\frac{A_i - \overline{A}}{\overline{A}} \right).$$

This is the well-known replicator dynamic equation. Since the dynamics of the uni-activity model is governed by a system of such equations, the population shows a distance-from-mean dynamics (Hofbauer and Sigmund 1998, Part 2; Metcalfe 1998, ch. 2). If for a particular firm productivity is equal to the mean, then this firm has an unchanged employment share. If its productivity is higher than the mean, it increases its employment share. If the productivity is less than the mean, the employment share decreases. Over time the expanding high-productivity firms will influence the mean in an upward direction. In the long run, mean productivity will become equal to that of the firm with the highest productivity. The rest of the firms will have shrunk to zero employment.

This expansion of the study of uni-activity models into the long run is, however, dependent on the assumption of fixed productivities. But such an assumption was not made in the above description, where it was made clear that we have not yet included an endogenous source of productivity change. But such change may come from exogenous sources. So it is not wise to introduce too readily the assumption that for all firms $\Delta A_i = 0$.

Price's General Formula for Evolutionary Change

Since the uni-activity models of this chapter are just the starting point for further and more complex studies, it is useful to study them by means of general tools for evolutionary economic analysis. Here, replicator dynamics is just one of several more or less equivalent ways of formalizing evolutionary change (Hofbauer and Sigmund 1998; Page and Nowak 2002). Each of these formalisms serves to highlight aspects of the evolutionary process. But formalisms that emphasize the statistical aspects of the process are especially important to promote population thinking. So we shall apply one such formalism in our analysis of the uni-activity models.

The basic result on the selection process in a model that shows replicator dynamics was obtained by Fisher (1999, p. 46), who summarizes it by the statement: '[t]he rate of increase of fitness of any species is equal to the genetic variance in fitness'. This theorem concerns only the selection process, so it is actually a special version of a much broader population thinking that also includes innovation processes. Even though this innovation process was excluded from the above specification of a uni-activity model, we shall include it in the following general analysis. Here we apply a formalization of the Fisher principle that was made by Price (1970, 1972).

Price's contribution is mainly based on a deep and novel analysis of generalized processes of selection (compare Price 1995). On this background he made a general decomposition of the evolutionary change that included not only the effect of selection but also the effect of causes that increase variation. Frank (1995, 1997, 1998) has been a major contributor to the development and diffusion of Price's equation. His contributions demonstrate that a large number of evolutionary problems can be clarified by means of Price's equation. Frank also makes clear that many researchers have been moving in the same direction as Price without noticing the full generality of their results and their relationship to Price. This aspect of Frank's contribution is emphasized by Metcalfe (2002): 'For some years now evolutionary economists have been using the Price equation without realizing it'. This statement holds for Metcalfe's (1998, ch. 2; 2001b) contributions to theoretical evolutionary economics, but it has also some truth for Nelson and Winter's (1982) pioneering contributions to evolutionary economics.

While, by means of replicator dynamics, we study the change of employment shares, Price's equation focuses directly on the change of mean productivity $\overline{A} = \Sigma s_i A_i$. The task is to decompose change in this mean productivity into two effects. The first of these is the selection effect. Here selection is understood as the differential change in employment that is caused by differences in productivities. The second effect is often somewhat more difficult to handle, but in the present case we may consider it as an innovation effect. Price's decomposition states that:

$$\text{Total change} = \text{Selection effect} + \text{Innovation effect.}$$

Such a decomposition of evolutionary change has obvious advantages, but it cannot be understood without a little formal analysis. To decompose evolutionary change we study the firms in two periods, where we denote variable values for the first period with their ordinary names and variable values for the second period by adding primes. Thus our basic task is to decompose $\Delta\overline{A} = \overline{A}' - \overline{A}$.

To perform this decomposition we need to define a new firm-level variable that corresponds to a clear concept of selection. This is the firm's reproduction coefficient of labour ρ_i. If we multiply the first-period employment of a firm by its reproduction coefficient, we obtain the size in the next period. Thus we have the new employment $L_i' = \rho_i L_i$. Given this variable, we define selection as differential reproduction coefficients. Since there is no change in aggregate employment in the uni-activity models, we have that $\overline{\rho} = 1$, so that $s_i' = s_i \rho_i$.

To study the selection effect we need basic population-level statistics. Here it is useful to start from the regression coefficient of reproduction on productivity, which is denoted $\beta_{\rho,A}$. This regression coefficient shows the degree to which selection exploits differential productivities. Normally we deal with partial regression coefficients, but in the present discussion we shall operate as if productivity is the only determinant of the reproduction coefficient. Thus its meaning can be caught by considering the linear relationship:

$$\rho_i = \beta_{\rho,A} A_i + \text{error.}$$

The next population variable is the variance of the productivities $\text{Var}(A) = \Sigma (A_i - \overline{A})^2$. The variance describes the differences that selection operates on. If $\text{Var}(A) = 0$, selection cannot produce any change of mean productivity. Given non-zero values of both the regression coefficient and the variance, we have a contribution to observed change of mean productivity.

The information on the regression coefficient and the variance may be replaced by the covariance between reproduction coefficients and productivities:

$$\text{Cov}(\rho, A) = \sum s_i(\rho_i - \bar{\rho})(A_i - \bar{A}) = \beta_{\rho, A}\text{Var}(A).$$

This study of the innovation effect starts from firm-level change in productivity $\Delta A_i = A_i' - A_i$. The effect of this change on mean productivity is dependent on the firms' employment shares in the second period, so we need to introduce the reproduction coefficients (since $s_i' = s_i\rho_i$). The total size of the effect is the mean or the expected value of all the firm-level contributions to the innovation effect $\overline{\rho\Delta A} = \text{E}(\rho\Delta A) = \Sigma s_i\rho_i\Delta A_i$.

Given the specifications of the selection and innovation effects, we can readily understand two different versions of Price's decomposition of evolutionary change in the uni-activity model. Price's equation states that mean productivity change,

$$\Delta\bar{A} = \frac{\text{Cov}(\rho, A)}{\bar{\rho}} + \frac{\text{E}(\rho\Delta A)}{\bar{\rho}} = \frac{\beta_{\rho, A}\text{Var}(A)}{\bar{\rho}} + \frac{\text{E}(\rho\Delta A)}{\bar{\rho}}. \tag{6.1}$$

This is the general version of Price's equation that may be used for the decomposition of any kind of evolutionary change. In the uni-activity models, equation (6.1) may be significantly simplified. First we note that since there is no change in aggregate employment in the uni-activity models, we have that $\bar{\rho} = 1$. Furthermore, we have that the individual reproduction coefficients,

$$\rho_i = L_i'/L_i = 1 + \pi_i = A_i/\bar{A}.$$

Thus Price's equation for the uni-activity models becomes:

$$\Delta\bar{A} = \frac{\text{Cov}(A, A)}{\bar{A}} + \frac{\text{E}(A\Delta A)}{\bar{A}} = \frac{\text{Var}(A)}{\bar{A}} + \frac{\text{E}(A\Delta A)}{\bar{A}}. \tag{6.2}$$

The uni-activity model version of Price's equation demonstrates that the selection effect is simply the variance of the productivities divided by mean productivity. This demonstrates that a very simple selection mechanism is ingrained in the uni-activity models. Similarly, the innovation effect is simply the employment-share weighted mean of the productivity times productivity change, divided by mean productivity. If we assume that there is no firm-level productivity change, we have found a version of Fisher's theorem for the uni-activity models. This is close to the result obtained by Nelson and Winter (1982, p. 243). However, the application of Price's equation for such a narrow purpose is just the beginning of a much larger research agenda. For those who want to follow this agenda, it is useful to know that Price's equation is an identity that can be derived fairly easily (see, for example, Frank 1995; Gintis 2000, pp. 267–8).

Developing the Uni-activity Models

The application of Price's formula to the basic uni-activity model demonstrates that the assumption of no productivity change is just one of several possibilities. In this case it is crucial to introduce variance from the very beginning. In Figure 6.1(A) we see a simulation that starts from productivities that are drawn randomly from a normal distribution with a mean productivity of 0.16. Given four firms that initially have even employment shares, two of them start to increase their employment shares since they have above-average productivities. At the same time mean productivity is also growing, so after some time the second-best firm becomes a below-mean performer and its employment share begins to fall. In the end, all employment is concentrated in the best-performing firm.

This story is dependent on a constant number of firms, but in the pure labour economy it is easy to introduce entry and exit. The exit process is not very important for the dynamics of the model (and the assumptions of the model ensure that low-performing firms are always able to pay the employees who are left). So the real issue is entry. Within the logic of uni-activity models the best way of introducing entry is through spin-offs from or fissions of existing firms. Thus the new firms may inherit the productivity level of the mother firms. If fissions take place in the productivity, then we are able to avoid monopoly. But there is no change in the dynamics of mean productivity. Actually, the logic of Price's decomposition requires us to treat spin-offs as parts of their mother firm.

Another version of uni-activity models is used in Figure 6.1(B), where we turn to the case of a truncated random walk in the productivities. This means that each firm will in each period have a small but random upward move in its productivity, no matter whether the firm has a large or a very small market share. This means that all productivities move upward such that the distance between the firms would show a random walk. In Figure 6.1(B) we see the turbulence of market share, but also that one firm appears to take over in the

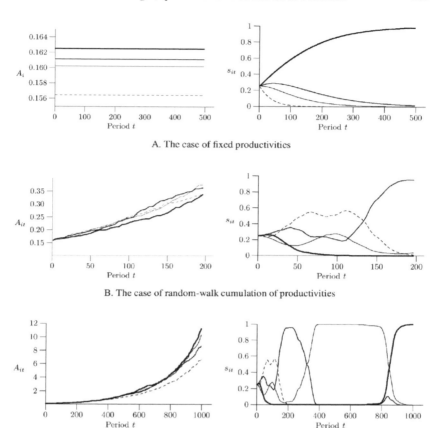

A. The case of fixed productivities

B. The case of random-walk cumulation of productivities

C. Longer run of the case of random-walk cumulation of productivities

Note: Left subfigures show productivities and right subfigures show employment shares. (A) Fixed productivities are drawn randomly from a distribution with a mean of 0.16. (B) In each period productivity increases by draws from a random distribution with a mean equal to the present productivity level of the firm. (C) A continuation of the simulation of panel B that demonstrates that no lock-in situation has yet emerged.

Figure 6.1   Simple dynamic patterns from simulations of uni-activity models with four firms

end. But as the random walk was defined there will sooner or later come a sequence of random numbers for another firm that will bring it up in front. In Figure 6.1(C) we actually see a succession of near-monopoly positions in the industry. This warns us against telling 'just-so stories' about phenomena that are fully of a stochastic nature and where firms probabilistically are exactly alike. Thus the results are like those in Arthur's (1994) random walk case. However, the basic selection dynamics is still working forcefully and, in the long run, the probability of a revival of very small firms moves towards zero. The next issue is whether we can find an equivalent to Arthur's case of lock-in because of increasing returns. The production function shows constant returns to scale, but large firms make more efficient use of productivity changes than small ones. No matter whether a given increase in productivity is applied in a large or a small firm, its effect covers all employees in the next period. Thus the most effective use of a productivity change is to apply it in a firm with a market share of 1.

This dynamic can be analysed by means of the model-specific version of Price's equation (6.2). One aspect of the random-walk process is to introduce new variety and thus allow for a renewed selection effect. However, most of the time variance is close to zero, so mean productivity change is largely due to the innovation effect, that is, $\Sigma s_i A_i \Delta A_i$. Even before the model shows a full lock-in to a monopoly situation, we see most of the time that only one firm has a significant employment share. So it is practically only productivity change in that firm that accounts for the innovation effect.

Since we have a pure labour model, the dynamics may be followed at the level of the main employment of each individual worker. In Figure 6.2 this is done by considering the economic system from the viewpoint of the households of the economy. We assume that there are five firms and 100 households in the economy. Each household supplies one worker that has a primary attachment to one firm (a few households have a secondary employment in another firm). Initially all firms have 20 employees. When one expanding firm has a net demand of a full employee, an employee changes primary employment to this firm from the firm that is closest to firing a full employee. The selection among its employees takes place on a first-in-first-out basis. The whole simulation is based on the assumption that firms have fixed productivities, which are drawn from a normal distribution.

In Figure 6.2, households are placed on a two-dimensional lattice and their primary employment is depicted by the colour of the primary employer. The first 20 households are initially employed by the black firm, the next 20 by the dark-grey firm and so on for the medium-grey firm, the light-grey firm and the near-white firm. The intensity of colouring reflects the productivity of firms, so the black firm has the highest productivity and the near-white firm has the lowest productivity. After two periods the first employee moves employment from the near-white to the black firm (panel A). After 10 periods (panel B) both the light-grey and the near-white firm have dismissed employees. The receivers are the black firm (four new employees) and the dark-grey firm (two new employees). After 30 periods

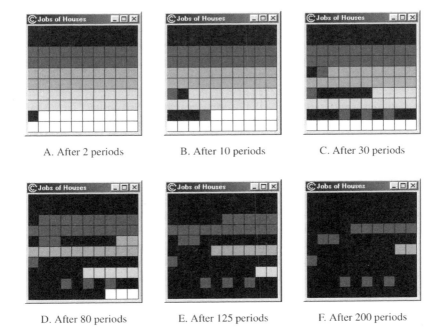

A. After 2 periods   B. After 10 periods   C. After 30 periods

D. After 80 periods   E. After 125 periods   F. After 200 periods

Note: The lattice consists of a 10 × 10 grid in which 100 single-person households are distributed with locations corresponding to their initial employment. The relationship of households to firms is indicated by the shades of grey. The black firm has the highest productivity, while the near-white firm is the worst performer.

Figure 6.2   Replicator dynamics in the uni-activity model depicted by a lattice of households

(panel C) the medium-grey firm has also dismissed two employees. Thus the working of the replicator dynamics is pretty obvious.

Panels D, E and F of Figure 6.2 follow the further development of the selection process. In panel D the dark-grey firm has just begun to dismiss employees. During the previous development it has received six new employees, but now the black firm receives one of its employees according to the first-hired-first-fired principle. It is clear that this principle makes it easy to follow both gross and net movements of employees. Let us call the rows of the lattice R1, . . . , R10 and the columns of the lattice C1, . . . , C10. Thus the households of the initial employees of the dark-grey firm were R3C1 to R4C10. The fired employee comes from household R3C1, but still we can see the households of the employees that were previously hired by the firm, for example, R5C2 and R9C4. This possibility of following both net and gross movements will in the end disappear, but the simulation – even after 200 periods – has not moved far enough to demonstrate the effect for the dark-grey firm. Instead we see how the shrinking firms gradually become unable to employ a full employee. After 125 periods (panel E) the near-white firm has no full employees and after 200 periods (panel F) the light-grey firm has also disappeared from the scene of primary employments.

The use of a lattice for depicting the dynamic process immediately suggests a whole series of possible uni-activity models. Such models are based on the fact that the computer keeps track of the movements of individual employees and it is not difficult to add further information on these employees. One characteristic of employees is their personal productivity. As we shall see in the next section, Price's equation allows a two-level decomposition of productivity change, so it may be used for exploring selection at both the economy and the firm levels. Presently, we may just note that an individual worker's productivity may increase from the level of the firing firm to the level of the hiring firm during a learning period and this learning may influence the design of the model. Even at the lattice level such learning effects would be obvious. The reason is that they suggest that firms that follow the first-hired-first-fired principle will perform worse than firms that follow the last-hired-first-fired principle. The learning mechanism would also function as a brake on the expansion of high-productivity firms. The reason is that the newly hired employees will not only have a productivity that is lower than the average productivity of the firm but also a productivity that is below the economy average.

OLIGO-ACTIVITY MODELS

Basic Specification

The uni-activity models did not include any endogenous mechanism of productivity change. In the more interesting case, firms improve their individual productivities – and thus the average productivity – by means of imitative and innovative activities. In this case it also becomes more interesting that the firms may merge and split up. To be more specific, we shall assume that firms improve their productivity by means of R&D work. Thus each of the firms needs a research intensity decision routine (or rule of thumb), which relates research efforts to its level of employment. It also needs related rules of how to divide research into subactivities (for example, innovative research and imitative research).

The structure of oligo-activity models is summarized in Figure 6.3, where

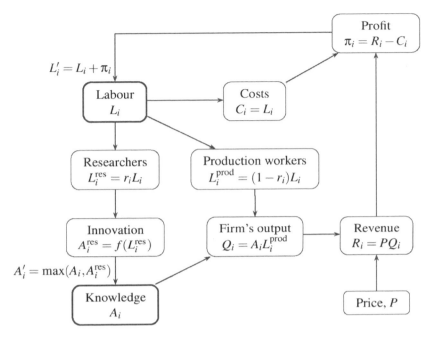

Figure 6.3   *The structure of oligo-activity models from the viewpoint of a particular firm* i *(price is determined at the population level)*

we see the model from the viewpoint of a particular firm. Much of the model structure is the same as in the uni-activity models. The firm produces the good by means of labour and knowledge, which is equally available to all employees. We have already seen that selection process uses up its own fuel, that is, the employment-share weighted productivity differentials. So if we observe a case of continuing evolutionary change, we infer that the system includes a mechanism that generates new variety in pace with the variety reduction due to the selection mechanism. In evolutionary economic models it is customary to identify this variety creating mechanism with R&D, but this is mainly for convenience since formal R&D is just one of several contributors to variety creation. Therefore, it is important to note that oligo-activity models are designed to function as test beds for different 'regimes' of variety creation.

Let us, however, assume that the firm divides its stock of employees L_i into two activities, production and research, according to a fixed decision parameter r_i. Labour for production is $L_i^{\text{prod}} = (1 - r_i)L_i$ and labour for research is $L_i^{\text{res}} = r_i L_i$.

The firm's production workers, L_i^{prod}, produce output according to the firm's labour productivity and a full-capacity utilization rule, that is,

$$Q_i = A_i L_i^{\text{prod}} = A_i(1 - r_i)L_i.$$

Thus it obtains the profit:

$$\pi_i = PQ_i - L_i = PA_i L_i^{\text{prod}} - L_i = [P(1 - r_i)A_i - 1]L_i.$$

The activity of the firm's research workers, L_i^{res}, is to produce knowledge and this production is modelled as a two-stage stochastic process. The success or failure aspect of R&D is modelled as a stochastic variable $Z_i \in \{0,1\}$, where $Z_i = 1$ means success and $Z_i = 0$ means failure. The firm's research workers have a fixed productivity that is measured as the average number of successes per period per researcher, $1/\lambda$. The result of the firm's total research activities is modelled as a Poisson process with average waiting time for a success equal to λ times the number of researchers. Thus $\text{Prob}(Z_i = 1) = \lambda L_i^{\text{res}}$.

The research workers apply different R&D methods according to fixed parameters that determine the degree to which the researchers focus on different ways of improving knowledge: (a) cumulation of the firm's own knowledge, (b) imitation of the leading firm in the industry, (c) application of the industry's average knowledge and (d) application of general knowledge. Firm i's fixed degree of emphasis on method x determines directly the probability that an R&D success is obtained by method x. The core method in this chapter is cumulative knowledge. In this case the outcome of a success is basically drawn from a normal distribution with mean determined by the firm's present productivity A_i and standard deviation as a constant σ. To ensure scale-independent research outcomes, in the normal distribution we set the mean to $\ln(A_i)$ and then use the inverse exponential function to find the result.

Innovation-based Dynamics

The consequences of introducing R&D in the family of oligo-activity models may be discussed in relation to Price's equation. The introduction of research workers implies that the model-specific simplification in equation (6.2) is not fully correct. The problem can readily be seen if we set the research intensity of one of the firms close to 1. This firm may for a while make significant progress with respect to productivity. However, as long as we do not assume huge research productivity, selection works strongly against this firm because there are far too few production workers to exploit its productivity gains. Thus the individual reproduction coefficients are more complex than before. As a consequence we have to apply the general version of Price's equation (6.1). However, our assumptions for the oligo-activity models imply that the mean reproduction coefficient is still zero.

Let us first consider how the research intensity influences the selection effect. This is simply the mean productivity change that is obtained between two points of time based on the given productivities. So if the productivity leaders spend more on research than the other firms, then the selection process is slowed down. The reason is that they earn less money than they could otherwise have done, so they expand less and consequently con-tribute less to productivity growth than they could otherwise have done. This effect of their research activity may, however, be counterbalanced by their contribution to the innovation effect. Furthermore, the productivity gains are potential sources for their long-run success.

Instead of formally analysing the effects of R&D work, we shall presently explore them by means of simple simulations. These simulations are made in continuation of those that were recorded in Figure 6.2. Thus we study the dynamics of the productivities and employment shares of four firms under different R&D conditions. So let us consider the results recorded in Figure 6.4.

In Figure 6.4(D) we see the result of a simulation of the usual four firms where there is a gradual removal of firms from the progress of productivi-ties to the fixed-productivity state that we saw in the treatment of replica-tor dynamics. There are two interrelated reasons for this result. First, firms use a fixed share of their labour force for research, so a large firm will spend more than a small firm and this has a larger probability of success (contrary to the random-walk case). Second, as mentioned above the large firm applies its research results more efficiently than a smaller firm. As time pro-gresses weak firms become smaller and smaller and their probabilities of innovative success move towards zero. The movement of the employment shares demonstrate that in the beginning of this process it is impossible to predict who is going to become the monopolist. Thus we see that the firm marked with the dashed line has a period of market share leadership before the firm with the thick line takes over.

The two last simulations represent attempts to avoid the march towards monopoly. In the case of Figure 6.4(E) we have made a distinction between two firms that have no R&D expenses while the two others perform research. Initially the firms without R&D produce more, obtain a higher profit and grow at the expense of the firms with research. One of the R&D firms is lucky to obtain an innovation while the other disappears more quickly than those without research. It is not difficult to make simulation setups where all R&D firms disappear, but then the empirical fact of evo-lution also disappears from the simulation.

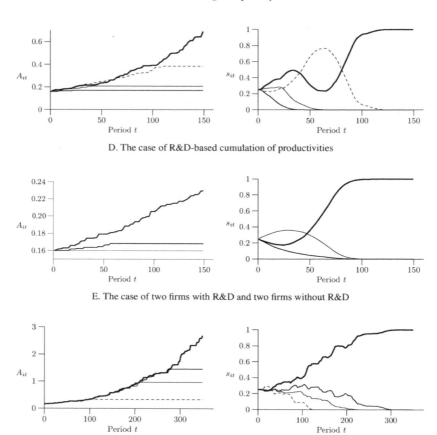

D. The case of R&D-based cumulation of productivities

E. The case of two firms with R&D and two firms without R&D

F. The case of firms that are both innovators and imitators

Note: (D) All firms have the same positive R&D intensity and the innovative results have their mean value in the present productivity of the firm. (E) Two firms perform R&D as in panels D, while the two other firms have no R&D and thus obtain an initially higher profitability. (F) All firms have the same intensity of innovative R&D and the same intensity of imitative R&D.

Figure 6.4   Dynamic patterns from simulations of oligo-activity models with four firms (in continuation of Figure 6.1)

The last simulation (Figure 6.4(F)) represents yet another way of weakening the dominant firm, namely by making it very easy to imitate the position of the leading firm. This means that all firms follow a narrow band of productivity growth, until they drop out – one after the other. The reason is that both innovation and imitation require resources to perform imitations, so in the end we still see that one firm takes over. So even if imitating firms obtain the productivity of the leading firm, they do not become better by imitation alone. Instead they succumb after periods of 'bad luck'.

The study of the simulation results brings out clearly a simple message. Even when we do our best to protect against the movement towards monopoly, we cannot avoid it. This unrealistic result may be called the monopoly paradox of evolutionary modelling. There are two reasons for the result. First, we are operating in a simplistic selection environment, where there are no niches that may serve as a (temporary) refuge. Second, the movement towards monopoly is heavily based on the characteristics of R&D.

Two-level Evolution in Oligo-activity Models

Until now we have used Price's formula for studying situations where it was useful but not strictly necessary. However, Price's decomposition may also deal with more structured populations than an industry in which every firm competes directly against any other firm. Actually, Price's formula has found a primary area of use for the study of more structured populations – both in evolutionary biology and, more recently, in economics among evolutionary game theorists (Gintis 2000, ch. 11). In both areas it has allowed the introduction of group-level selection to explain such issues as the evolution of 'altruistic' behaviour. One example may be an economy that is structured into districts (indexed by j) that consist of firms (indexed by ji). Another example is an economy consisting of firms (indexed by j) that consist of employees (indexed by ji). To explore the functioning of such groups we shall start by expressing Price's equation for the group level of the population – like industrial districts. To emphasize that we are operating at this level, we add group subscripts to the variables at the right-hand side of the equation. Furthermore, we multiply both sides of equation (6.1) by $\bar{\rho}$. Thus we have Price's equation for the group (district) level, where:

$$\bar{\rho}\Delta\bar{A} = \text{Cov}(\rho_j, A_j) + \text{E}(\rho_j\Delta A_j). \tag{6.3}$$

This format of Price's equation might appear more mysterious than that of equation (6.1), but it has an advantage that is revealed by studying equation (6.3) under the new interpretation in terms of groups.

The left-hand side is still dealing with means of the whole economy, but on the right-hand side we are also dealing with mean values. They are taken over the firms (indexed by ji) of each district. Thus:

$$\rho_j = \bar{\rho}_j = \sum s_{ji}\rho_{ji},$$

$$A_j = \overline{A}_j = \sum s_{ji} A_{ji},$$

and

$$\Delta A_j = \Delta \overline{A}_j = \sum s_{ji} \Delta A_{ji}.$$

Given this interpretation, we may return to equation (6.3) and observe that the left-hand side $(\overline{\rho \Delta A})$ says the same as the right-hand side's product in the expectation term $(\overline{\rho_j \Delta \overline{A}_j})$ – except for the group subscript. Since Price's formula is general, it can also be used to decompose this product. Thus we have that:

$$\rho_j \Delta A_j = \overline{\rho}_j \Delta \overline{A}_j = \text{Cov}(\rho_{ji}, A_{ji}) + \text{E}(\rho_{ji} \Delta A_{ji}).$$

Here we see how productivity change within a district (or any other group) can be decomposed into a selection effect and an innovation effect. By inserting this result into equation (6.3), we obtain the two-level Price equation:

$$\overline{\rho \Delta A} = \text{Cov}(\rho_j, A_j) + \text{E}[\text{Cov}(\rho_{ji}, A_{ji}) + \text{E}(\rho_{ji} \Delta A_{ji})]. \qquad (6.4)$$

According to this equation we study change of mean productivity at the economy level in terms of three effects. First, there is selection between the districts of the economy. Here we can either directly use the covariance between district reproduction coefficients and district productivities or use the formulation with the regression coefficient and the variance of district productivities. Second, there is the expected value of the intra-district selection effects. If the mean of these effects is important, it is due to the fact that there are differences in the selection process in different districts. Third, there is the expected value of the innovation effects – first over firms and then over districts. By means of district-level selection systems and externalities from firm-level innovative activities we may try to give meaning to the last two effects. However, to explore more fully the multi-level process of evolution it is necessary to move beyond the limits of the oligo-activity models.

TOWARDS MULTI-ACTIVITY MODELS

Motivation and Structure

In the preceding sections we have explored formal intra-population thinking and stretched it to its limits. But the analysis of evolutionary processes also requires that we are able to handle the emergence of new specialities and the interaction between different industries. Thus we have to add intra-to-inter-population thinking and inter-population thinking. Unfortunately, these forms of thinking are more complex and less supported by formal tools than intra-population thinking. But this caveat should not lead to an abandonment of the study of crucial forms of economic evolution. Instead we should confront these forms of evolution and thereby we might even find that some of the more narrow tools are of great help. This has been demonstrated by, for example, Saviotti (1996, 2001) within the tradition of replicator dynamic analysis. In relation to this chapter, it should be remarked that the complementary tradition based on Price's formula has also been able to exploit its generality to handle aspects of surprisingly difficult issues.

There seem to be two major strategies for moving beyond intra-population thinking. The first strategy is to turn directly to the diversity of the market environment (Andersen 2002). The second is to start from the inner diversity of the firms or households (Andersen 2001). We shall apply the second strategy by starting from multi-activity firms, so the task is to explain why and how individual activities become outsourced and coordinated by more-or-less clear-cut market mechanisms. Here we relate to the traditions in industrial economics and growth theory that can be traced back to the Smith-inspired ideas of Young (1928) and Marshall (1949). In this tradition there is an intense interest in the close relationship between the internal economies of firms and the external economies which arises from inter-firm specialization with respect to production and knowledge creation. To obtain a quick and concrete picture of these relationships, it is helpful to quote Young's (1928, pp. 537–8) description of his favourite example: the disintegration of the printing trade:

> The successors of the early printers, it has often been observed, are not only the printers of today, with their own specialized establishments, but also the producers of wood pulp, of various kinds of paper, of inks and their different ingredients, of typemetal and of type, the group of industries concerned with the technical parts of the producing of illustrations and the manufacturers of specialized tools and machines for use in printing and in these various auxiliary industries. The list could be extended, both by enumerating other industries which are directly ancillary to the present printing trades and by going back to industries which, while supplying the industries which supply the printing trades, also supply other industries, concerned with preliminary stages in the making of final products other than printed books and newspapers.

This story is Young's answer to the monopoly paradox that arose from Marshall's (1949) allowance into his system of economies of scale. There is no real paradox as long as we allow into our models the indefinite divisibility of production activities. This divisibility often makes a small well-focused firm more productive than a large firm with a broad scope of activities. Although concentration is a real process, the trend is broken by the evolution of markets for more and more intermediate goods that slowly undermine many of the industrial giants. Even in relation to such models one might, however, ask whether the limits of divisibility will be met 'at the end of the road'. In a Smithian context, Richardson's (1975, p. 357) answer is 'that the end of the road may never be reached. . . . For just as one set of activities was separable into a number of components, so each of these in turn become the field for a further division of labour'. The opening up of these possibilities is part of the evolutionary process itself: 'the very process of adaptation, by increasing productivity and therefore market size, ensures that the adaptation is no longer appropriate to the opportunities it has itself created' (ibid., p. 358).

Although there are clear needs for multi-activity generalizations of the uni-activity and oligo-activity models, it is by no means simple to design such models. A major obstacle is the tendency of modelling to become too ambitious with respect to the handling of many interdependencies between the different production activities and knowledge areas. But in an evolutionary model even the simplest attempts of handling emerging production chains and emerging knowledge chains tend to become too complex for most analytical purposes (compare the suggestions by Andersen 1996a, 1996b). To move forward it seems necessary to start from a radical simplification of the input–output structure of production and knowledge creation, but we need to stick to the heterogeneity principle. Thus we cannot follow the otherwise very interesting approach of Arrow et al. (1998) and Yang (2001). Instead the present chapter follows a kind of disintegration approach, whose basic structure is shown in Figure 6.5 seen from the viewpoint of an individual firm.

The starting point is simple oligo-activity models. As we have already seen, each firm has only one production activity and one R&D activity (combining process innovation and process imitation). To obtain multiple activities we can simply think of these activities as being simple aggregates of m subactivities. Thus we have m production activities and m related R&D activities. The R&D activities function as in the oligo-activity models. The only difference is that an individual innovation concerns only one of the activities, so the size of the productivity increase has to be m times as large to give the same overall productivity effect as in the oligo-activity models.

The generalization to m production activities (indexed by j) is slightly more complex. The problem is how the different production activities should relate to the production of final output. The solution chosen in the multi-activity models is to have one production activity that combines

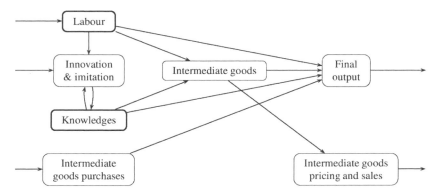

Figure 6.5   Structure diagram that only covers a single firm's activities in the multi-activity version of the pure labour economy (compare with Figure 6.3)

$m - 1$ intermediate goods into final output. This final good activity operates according to a Leontief production function. The Leontief function means that to produce one unit of final output, activity #1 in firm i needs one unit of each of the $m - 1$ intermediate goods as well as $1/A_{i1}$ units of direct labour. The production functions for the $m - 1$ activities that produce intermediate goods are much simpler, since these activities use only labour and knowledge, so that $Q_{ij} = A_{ij}L_{ij}$.

To obtain the same results as in oligo-activity models, this decomposition presupposes that all subactivities have the same productivity, $A_{ij} = mA_i$. This can be seen from the following: in oligo-activity models firm i needed $1/A_i$ units of labour to produce one unit of final output. In multi-activity models we need $\Sigma_{j=1}^{m} 1/A_{ij} = 1/A_i$ units of labour, that is, exactly the same. Concerning R&D things are equally simple. If the size of an innovation is m times that of oligo-activity models, the firm obtains the same aggregate productivity gain as before. So multi-activity models may seem to be an unnecessary complication of oligo-activity models. There is, however, one crucial difference: even though two multi-activity firms have exactly the same aggregate productivity, they need not and will not in practice be equal with respect to their productivity profile. The reason is, of course, that for stochastic reasons two firms will not have improved the same productivities to the same degree. So even two firms with the same overall productivities might gain from trade. Therefore, intermediate goods markets may emerge endogenously in multi-activity models – simply because of the stochastic process of activity-specific productivity change.

The make-or-buy decisions and the sell-or-use decisions of firms in multi-activity models are, in principle, quite simple. The potential seller of an intermediate good sets a supply price that covers its costs times a mark-up factor. The potential buyer compares the supply price with its reservation price (determined by its unit costs). If both parties gain from the exchange, a contract is made and the intermediate goods are supplied just in time for the finalization of the final output in the period under consideration. This looks pretty straightforward, but from a modelling point of view things are more complex since we have to specify precisely how the system of intermediate goods markets is functioning. It is, however, not difficult to specify an algorithm for the functioning of the intermediate markets. In multi-activity models it is assumed that the intermediate market with the largest differences between supply prices and reservation prices comes first. Within each market it is assumed that the supplier with the lowest price comes first and serves as many as possible of the customers (from the end with the highest reservation prices) before the next cheapest supplier enters. In this way a precise market process takes place.

To control the degree of trade in multi-activity models, there is added an extra feature that is not normally dealt with in evolutionary models: transaction costs. These costs are modelled in the simplest possible way (compare Yang 2001, pp. 131–2): if the supplier has costs that would give x_{ij} units for in-house use, the purchasing firm only receives $X_{ij} = (1 - \kappa)x_{ij}$ units of the good. If the transaction costs parameter κ is close to 1, it is practically impossible to obtain productivity differences large enough to motivate exchange. If κ is close to 0, even relatively modest productivity differences will lead to exchange.

The core issues of multi-activity models are connected to R&D. As long as all firms are self-sufficient with respect to intermediate goods, the firm's choice of R&D specialization is fairly easy. But as soon as exchange emerges, the problem of R&D specialization becomes pretty complex for the boundedly rational decision makers of multi-activity models. The reason is that the firm cannot be sure whether in the future it will uphold its position with respect to sales and purchases of intermediate goods. Therefore, the question is whether the firm should strengthen its given positions by a narrow R&D specialization or whether it is better to spread its researchers over a larger set of activities. In other words, multi-activity models are test beds for a large set of strategies of R&D specialization. Closely connected to these R&D strategies are the pricing strategies for the suppliers of intermediate goods. The dynamic problem concerns the sharing of the ever-changing gains from exchange of intermediate goods. If the supplier gets too large a part of the gains, its customers will do relatively badly in the dynamic process of labour accumulation and this will in turn influence the profits of suppliers with high mark-ups. Another dynamical trade-off concerns the fact that a successful supplier may outgrow its chosen intermediate goods market. In this case the successful firm has to take up other production activities, and this works best if R&D has prepared for the firm's path of expansion.

An additional difficulty for firms in multi-activity models is that there is a possibility for a type of R&D whose results increase the number of intermediate goods. This so-called structural R&D results at first in an increase in the decomposition of the firm's production activities. This increased decomposition is carried out in a productivity-neutral way, so that it makes little sense for autarkic firms to engage in structural research. However, in an economy with exchange of intermediate goods, it may be very profitable to perform structural innovations since the first innovator will have a productivity advantage in that area (although there is a spillover to other firms so that they can easily reorganize their production). It is especially firms that have relatively strong positions in many knowledge areas that can easily benefit from decomposition since the initial productivity in the new area is influenced by the firm's general level of productivity.

Exchange

A major issue of multi-activity models concerns the distribution of labour across the different activities. We may, for instance, ask how labour is distributed between final good production and the production of the intermediate goods that are used as inputs in the production of the final good. We may also ask for the relation between in-house production of intermediate goods and intermediate goods produced for the market. The possibility of asking such questions indicates that multi-activity models have not only introduced a simple input–output structure but have also endogenized the borderline between the 'sectors' of production. In this way multi-activity models differ from other sectoral models of the Nelson–Winter model family, like the two-sector model by Chiaromonte and Dosi (1993) and the multi-sectoral model of Verspagen (1993, ch. 7).

Within the framework of the present chapter it is impossible to give a full analysis of multi-activity models. Instead we shall explore some of the basic characteristics of the models, and here it is convenient to start from the distinction between the final good market and the intermediate goods market. The main thing to understand is that these markets are radically different. This difference will both be discussed in general and illustrated by a simple multi-activity computer simulation with 20 firms that are engaged in both a final good activity and one intermediate good activity. To simplify further, we let the evolution take place in a situation where transaction costs are so high that there is no trade. Then we stop the simulation and ask what will

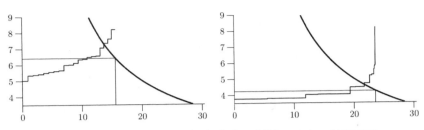

A. Price schedule and firms' costs for the final good #1 in an early and later stage

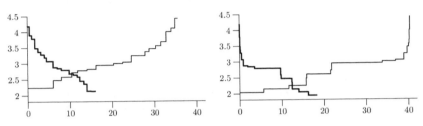

B. Potential demand and supply for intermediate good #2 in an early and later stage

Note: (A) the final good market #1 and (B) a potential intermediate good market #2.
The horizontal axis shows quantities and the vertical axis shows prices. Thick lines deal
with demand and the medium lines with supply. The thin lines of (A) shows the market
price under the conditions of no intermediate good trade, a capacity-determined supply,
and a market clearing through a price set by demand with unitary elasticity. Panels
(B) show the room that is available for mutually profitable trade for the intermediate good.

Figure 6.6   Two types of market at two stages of development

happen if transaction costs at that point of time are reduced to zero. The
results are presented in Figure 6.6.

The final good market is depicted in Figure 6.6(A). It is modelled just as
in uni-activity and oligo-activity models. This means that firms produce as
much as their capacities allow, while the consumers pay a given amount of
money (all their income) for this output. Thus the final good market shows
unitary elasticity of demand. This price function is the same in both subfigures – the thick curve. The simulation has been started with stochasti-
cally distributed productivities across the 20 firms that all have the same
employment of labour. For each firm we find the aggregate productivity,
that is, how much output is produced by one worker – given that this worker
also has to take care of the necessary intermediate input and the related
R&D. Then we find the aggregate unit costs, which is simply the inverse of
the productivity. These unit costs have to be compared with the market

price for the final good. For this purpose we construct a long-term supply schedule by taking the firms in ascending order according to their unit costs. The first horizontal part of the supply curves in Figure 6.6 represent the firm with the lowest unit costs and its length is the capacity of this firm. Then comes the second firm and so on, to the twentieth firm.

The supply curve that we have constructed does not influence output in the short run. This output is simply the sum of the capacities of all the firms. This means that in Figure 6.6(A) firms produce about 15.6 units of output at a price about 6.4 – as indicated by the thin lines. This price divides firms into two classes. Those that have unit costs below 6.4 will have positive profits and thus they will expand their labour force. Those that have unit costs above 6.4 will have negative profits and contract their labour force. Even if unit costs were fixed, we would thus over time see a movement of the supply schedule so that the profitable firms would expand their capacity and increase aggregate output, so that marginal firms would become unprofitable. This is one of the reasons for the shift of the supply schedule from the left to the right panel of Figure 6.6(A), where we see: (i) that the price is lowered, (ii) that the profitable firms have obtained large capacities and (iii) that many of the unprofitable firms have contracted to a negligible capacity. There is, however, another reason for the shift, which is obvious from the fact that the profitable firms have significantly lowered their unit costs. This is, of course, that the firms have been performing innovations. Since the larger firms have larger-scale R&D activities, they also show the largest productivity advances.

The potential intermediate good market of Figure 6.6(B) has a rather different interpretation. Here we are not yet dealing with a functioning market but rather with the possibilities for such a market. The thick lines represent the potential demand schedules. In the left panel we have firms with fairly equal capacities, so the size of their potential demanded quantities do not differ much. There are, however, substantial differences between the costs they can save by getting rid of the labour they use for the intermediate good activity. Thus their reservation prices range from about 4.4 to 2.2. The quantities that are potentially demanded are determined by the quantity of the final good produced in the last period. Since the market has not yet been opened up for intermediate trade, all firms are represented on the demand side. Similarly, all firms are potential suppliers of the intermediate good. If they become fully specialized in intermediate production, they use their whole labour force (except the researchers) for this purpose and they can supply their whole production. Therefore, the overall size of the potential supply is – in the two-activity case – about double the demand. However, it is obvious from the figure that only three firms can enter into mutually profitable exchanges with the potential buyers.

Because of labour accumulation and R&D, the demand and the supply schedules will change over time. This is the case even if no trade were introduced in the early stage. The right panel of Figure 6.6(B) depicts a later stage where the firms' behaviour has not yet been coordinated and disciplined by an intermediate good market. Thus it is production and innovation for the final good market that have created the new schedules. On the potential demand side we see that the highest reservation prices come from firms that, because of their low aggregate productivity, have been reduced to a very small size. There are, however, some profitable firms whose strength is in the final good activity rather than in the intermediate good activity, so that they represent a significant demand. On the supply side, there are three firms that can enter into mutually profitable exchanges.

R&D Specialization

The discussion of exchange in multi-activity models has demonstrated the crucial importance of productivity differentials. Like in the classical theory of international trade, there is simply no exchange of intermediate goods unless there are substantial differences in the demand and supply schedules. The problem is then how these differences arise. In the previous section the differences were produced somewhat artificially. It was simply assumed that the firms randomly chose whether to innovate in the final good activity or the intermediate good activity. There are, however, reasons to believe that this choice will not be made randomly. This is the issue dealt with in Figure 6.7.

The figure depicts the strange (but fairly realistic) conditions of autarkic production and the related productivity enhancement under Leontief technology. In the figure we assume that each firm has to produce one unit of each of three intermediate goods and to add a fixed amount of labour to produce one unit of the final good. In this setting we follow a succession of three major innovations that are performed according to two different strategies of R&D specialization. The first strategy is to emphasize the productivity strengths of the firm and thus to continue to innovate with respect to a (randomly obtained) stronghold. This specialist strategy is called the 'top strategy' in the first row of Figure 6.7. The second strategy is to obtain a more or less equilibrated enhancement of the productivities. This generalist strategy is called the 'bottom strategy' in the second row of the figure. In both cases the labour shares in the different activities are depicted by pie charts with different shades of grey for each of the four activities, while the area of each pie is the unit labour costs.

The effects of the two strategies become immediately clear from the figure. The top strategy serves to innovate in the activity where least labour

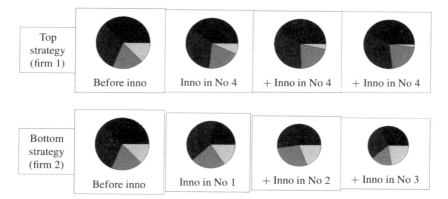

Note: The area of each pie is the labour costs of producing one unit of final output. The slices of the pie are the labour costs in individual activities. Activity number 1 is black, while activities number 2, 3 and 4 have decreasing intensities of grey.

Figure 6.7   Examples of the development in a four-activity model of employment shares and total labour costs for two types of strategy when there is no intermediate goods trade

is spared by each innovation, while the bottom strategy at any point of time focuses on the activity in which most labour can be spared for each innovation. Thus the rule of R&D allocation seems to be clear: focus on the costly areas of production and ignore any tendency to make a follow-up of past successes. A somewhat less efficient strategy, which is however much better than the top one and much easier than the bottom one, is to allocate researchers in exactly the same proportions as the production workers. These rules are, of course, dependent on the specifications of multi-activity models, but they provide good rules of thumb for process innovations.

Unfortunately, there is one problem with these nice rules. This problem is that if they were followed strictly and if innovations could take place in sufficiently small increments, the strategies would undermine the possibility of moving from autarky to trade in intermediate goods. Instead we recognize easily that the top strategy is the best and fastest way of promoting the emergence of trade. The shift from the bottom or production-oriented strategy to the top strategy is, however, not easy – neither at an early stage of development nor for large and complex firms. One problem is that rules of thumb become deeply ingrained in organizations and larger social structures. To see this it is useful (and realistic) to think of a large firm whose many different activities are taking place in organizationally separate departments and plants. Each of these departments have their specialized activity in the production of an intermediate good or intermediate services. The easiest way of upholding an organizational truce (compare Nelson and Winter 1982, pp. 107 ff.) between these departments is to have a more or less balanced productivity advance for all departments. This is the major background for what looks like a slowly improving 'circular flow' (p. 98) of large firms. But the result of the resultant all-round R&D strategy is that these firms become poorly suited for participating in intermediate goods exchange. Thus we seem to have found an endogenous reason for the limits of the march towards monopoly and decreasing diversity.

In developing countries there are further reasons for the discouraging results of the specializing top strategy. Here we not only find vested interests against major changes but also a well-founded scepticism against intermediate supplies that are not adapted to the circumstances and that might not be sufficiently sustainable. Furthermore, there are high and oscillating transaction costs. So under such conditions it is wise to uphold a broad (although not advanced) in-house competence in many production activities. Unfortunately, this wisdom often leads to vicious circles. In such a context, multi-activity models provide no easy suggestions. On the contrary, it demonstrates that the emergence of economically coordinated R&D strategies takes place through a difficult and turbulent process. As soon as we operate in terms of two-level population thinking, we recognize the source of the difficulties. The problem is that the intra-firm selection environment is not necessarily in correspondence with the inter-firm selection environment. This problem will, of course, be overcome if each firm specializes in a single activity: in this case there is no internal selection taking place within firms and thus no conflict. However, the set of economic activities is not fixed. As soon as a firm appears to be fully specialized, it starts to decompose its chosen activity into subactivities. Since this suggests the possibility of outsourcing, the difficulties of R&D specialization emerge in a new form. Thus we really need a three-level analysis of evolutionary change.

The Evolving Multi-sectoral Economy

Multi-activity models can be interpreted as multi-sectoral growth models with (i) a household sector that sells labour and buys final goods, (ii) a final good sector that buys labour and intermediate goods and sells final goods and (iii) a set of intermediate goods sectors that buy labour and sell intermediate goods. But because multi-activity models take their starting point in multi-activity firms and exclude any fixed sector boundaries, they represent a rather special kind of multi-sectoral growth models. However, even for such fuzzy models Price's formula allows us to single out any sector for further analysis. The most obvious help is provided for the handling of intermediate goods sectors. The untraditional problem is that each of these sectors is in principle represented by all the firms of the economy. The reason is that all of them are able to produce all intermediate goods – but often with ridiculously low productivity. The evolution of the social division of labour implies that firms move from self-sufficiency to specialization with respect to each intermediate good. Furthermore, at a given point of time there may be firms that produce an intermediate good for their own use, while other firms have entered a stage of full specialization. But this is really no problem for our analysis.

Let us first consider Price's equation (6.1). Now we are dealing with mean productivity change with respect to the jth intermediate goods sector. This is simply the change in the sector's employment-share weighted mean productivity $\overline{A}_j = \Sigma s_{ji} A_{ji}$. Before exchange has emerged in this sector, all producers of final output are engaged in this area of production. Thus the reproduction coefficients are only weakly related to the productivities in this sector. This situation changes drastically with the emergence of a market for the intermediate good. Now the reproduction coefficients of the specialized firms are much more narrowly connected to their productivities in their speciality. Therefore, they tend to focus their research and thus the innovation effect increases significantly. The consequence of their focus for the selection effect is more ambivalent. During a transition period an increased variance emerges, so the increased regression coefficient has fuel to work on. This transition period may, however, be fairly short. Low productivity firms quickly shift from make to buy and competition among specialized suppliers means yet another decrease of variance. However, it is obvious that Price's formula gives us the discipline to analyse clearly all the stages.

The two-level Price equation (6.4) may provide further help in structuring the problems. Thus we may distinguish between the group of firms that produces the intermediate good for its own use and the group of specialized suppliers. But this equation also forces us to define precisely the selection levels of the economic system. As long as there is only a well-developed market for final goods, each firm is selected according to the mean of its activity-specific productivities. Thus inter-firm selection concerns the firm as a whole, while intra-firm selection deals with individual activities. As soon as intermediate goods markets emerge, market selection works on (some of) the intra-firm activities, but this is also an area for intra-firm selection. So conflicts may emerge. The conflict we discussed in the previous section concerns the innovation effect of equation (6.4). When exchange has emerged, the generalist strategy implies relatively small

productivity changes with respect to intermediate good *j*, while the specialist strategy secures a larger innovation effect because research is focused.

Quite another issue concerns the handling of what may be called the
paradox of Leontief technology. It is obvious from the description that
multi-activity models build squarely on Leontief technology. We can also
construct simple and evolving input–output tables from simulation runs
with multi-activity models. But nevertheless multi-activity models do not
show the kind of 'knife-edge' problems that otherwise characterize this
realistic type of technology. The reason is, of course, that no firm is entirely
dependent on the intermediate supplies of other firms. For instance, if
supplies are vanishing because of a sudden increase in transaction costs,
production will carry on through a changed division of labour between and
within firms. The firm may even continue for some time (in a shrinking
manner) if it is pushed out on the intermediate goods markets and
performs badly with respect to the final good. These properties would be
even more prominent if we added some flexibility in the wage level for a
firm's labour force. But it must be underlined that the tractability of multi-
activity models is heavily dependent on simplifying assumptions and not
least those that relate to the labour market and the homogeneity of wages,
labour qualifications and so on.

When we study the long-term evolution of the multi-sectoral economy,
it becomes clear that it does not provide a full-blown solution to the
paradox of Leontief technology. The problems of multi-activity models
become most clear if we somehow (for example, by limiting the efficiency
of the R&D strategies of large firms, by introducing frequent fissions of
firms and so on) obtain a relatively stable selection environment. In such an
environment we will see many full specializations in particular activities
(so-called corner solutions), so that highly specialized R&D strategies will
become profitable. This means that each firm becomes highly inefficient in
producing outside its current activity portfolio. So if supplies of a particular input are discontinued for some reason, the firm will suffer a major
setback and disappear quickly (unless all the other firms have the same
problem).

Luckily there are several reasons why this scenario is rather unlikely. The
most important is that life as an intermediate goods supplier can be quite
harsh. Even a position in the lucky end of the supply schedule (compare
Figure 6.6(B)) is by no means a steady one. First, because of the potentially
substantial profits, the strongest firm can outperform the other suppliers
and in the end grow so large that it has to take up an additional activity. To
be prepared for this eventuality means applying an R&D strategy that goes
beyond the core competence. Second, the potentially quite profitable
ability to introduce new intermediate goods presupposes a broad range of

competencies. This gives a certain advantage to large firms with a wide range of activities. Third, there is always the risk that another firm makes a huge productivity increase that in a relatively short time pushes a firm out of its stronghold and into other activities. This gives yet another reason for a fairly broad R&D strategy.

Any systematic treatment of these and other issues of the evolving multi-sectoral economy presupposes both analytical work and simple and systematic computer simulation exercises. Both these tasks bring us beyond the limits of this chapter. Similarly, we cannot discuss the emergence of an institutional framework that structures and stabilizes economic life (Nelson 2001). But the suggested type of model might serve as a test bed for both evolutionary institutional analysis and for the deeper issues of the history specificity of economic evolution (Dopfer 2001). Actually, the present multi-activity models have not primarily been developed as solutions to a number of issues that seem to be intrinsic to the Nelson–Winter tradition of studying industrial dynamics. Their major advantage can probably be found when we turn to broader and more interdisciplinary issues.

DISCUSSION AND CONCLUSIONS

This chapter started with a sketchy account of knowledges and their evolution and against this background it emphasized the need of including these issues in an evolutionary framework that relates to the models of Schumpeterian competition in the tradition that was pioneered by Nelson and Winter. The modelling framework of the chapter emphasizes that knowledges and the related specializations of production do not emerge from scratch. Instead, knowledges evolve largely through a gradual process of deepening and widening of existing knowledges. To be more specific, the evolution of knowledges is depicted as going hand in hand with the changing allocation of labour and the increased specialization of the economy. Such an account is definitely in contrast to Schumpeter's vision of economic development, which did not see evolution as a gradual branching process. On the contrary, Schumpeter (1934, p. 216) asks: 'does this whole development, which we have been describing proceed in unbroken continuity, is it similar to the gradual organic growth of a tree? Experience answers in the negative'. Instead the account may be seen as a return to the ideas of the division of labour and the related evolution of knowledges that can be traced from Adam Smith via Marshall to Young and modern theorists. Take, for instance, the famous discussions of the long-term evolution from more or less autarkic family farming to the modern industrial farming supported by manufacturing industries and services. During this evolution ever more subtasks of the original farms have branched out to separate activities. Thus the scope of knowledges of individual firms has become radically narrowed down while the depth of their knowledges has increased enormously. It is this and similar stories that are supported by the chapter's concepts and models.

Although there is thus an obvious contrast to the Schumpeterian vision, Schumpeter has nevertheless directly and indirectly inspired the modelling framework. To understand this inspiration it is helpful to consider the Schumpeterian pattern of evolution through disruptive entrepreneurs as a complement rather than an alternative to the Marshallian pattern of the knowledge-based branching of economic activities – both in industrial districts and in the economy as a whole (Andersen 1996a). This complementarity becomes clear when we recognize that Schumpeter often placed the Marshallian pattern in the so-called circular flow of economic life. Thus his circular flow is far more than a Walrasian system that has been transformed into routine behaviour. It is rather a way of removing all more-or-less automatically functioning economic processes from attention in order to focus on a kind of innovative economic behaviour that is not at all automatic. To the extent that economic evolution is such an automatic process, it is thus not a part of the core of Schumpeterian analysis. But here two comments are important. First, such automatic evolution is still – even according to Schumpeter – a part of economic life. Second, there are important parts of the division-of-labour-like economic evolution that are not at all automatic and which include difficult innovative interventions.

Schumpeterian ideas have largely entered the chapter's modelling framework through the Nelson–Winter tradition. According to this tradition, R&D is a separate activity that may be taken as a first approximation to the difficult topic of entrepreneurship. In the present chapter further approximations were included – like fissions of firms, the problems related to the creation of new markets and the quite difficult problems of a research specialization strategy in a very unstable system of intermediate goods production. But it must be admitted that these aspects of the modelling framework were somewhat de-emphasized in order to allow for a quick description of core aspects of the presented models. In the future it will be important to return to the more disruptive parts of especially the multi-activity model of a pure labour economy. In this connection it will also be important to analyse the interaction between radical and incremental innovators in this model.

The stepwise development of the chapter's modelling framework started with a pure labour economy in which only a single final good is produced and gradually included more complex issues. Although the chapter's family of models has close connections with the Nelson–Winter models, there are also several novelties. First, the chapter focuses on growth models – which may later be specialized to cover partial processes of industrial dynamics. Second, the concentration on labour and knowledge led to an explicit treatment of research as one of the firm's activities in line with the production activity/activities. Third, the concentration of labour led to a certain emphasis on organizational issues, for example, in the question of how new firms emerge. In the Nelson–Winter models this emergence has a parametric character while pure labour models suggest quite another solution: new firms emerge by fissions of old firms. Fourth, the models got rid of some of the other parameters of the Nelson–Winter models – thus obtaining a higher degree of endogenization of the elements of the evolutionary process. The design of the pure labour models as general rather than partial coordination models plays an important role in this result. Fifth, the relative simplicity of the models suggested that Nelson and Winter's split between specialized formal models and complex simulation models is not always necessary. It was especially emphasized that Price's equation for the decomposition of evolutionary change helps us both to handle descriptive issues and to recognize the possibility of deriving mathematical theorems for our models. Sixth, the models make it relatively easy to perform computer simulations and related analytical work in order to explore the conditions for the creation of knowledge as well as imitative behaviour.

The basic function of the chapter's uni-activity and oligo-activity models was to provide stepping stones in the construction of multi-activity models of the evolution of a pure labour economy. Given these models, the core analytical step in the construction of multi-activity models was really quite simple: instead of considering all the activities of a firm as an aggregate for which innovations and imitations are performed in a single step, multi-activity models split up this aggregate activity into a number of subactivities that have their own productivities and their related R&D activities. This decomposition was the starting point for a number of extensions. First, the fact that the productivities for the production activities can be improved individually, in practice makes each firm unique because of stochastic events. Second, the existence of multiple activities led the chapter into a discussion of how these activities are related. The multi-activity solution is to have a production function for the final good activity that includes labour, knowledges and intermediate goods. Third, the multi-activity approach not only suggested the existence of specialized R&D activities in relation to each production activity but also the existence of structural R&D that serves to decompose the existing activities of the firm. This allows an endogenous evolution of an economic system that starts with the single-activity firms and gradually creates a more and more complex system. Fourth, the multi-activity models include the endogenous emergence of intermediate goods markets based on spontaneously emerging productivity differentials. These differences function like dynamic comparative advantages in international trade theory. Fifth, the issue of trade in intermediate goods suggested a renewed discussion of the problem of R&D specialization. It was shown that for autarkic firms it is rational to use a variant of the generalist R&D strategy. However, this strategy functions as a brake on the emergence of productivity differentials sufficiently large to allow for widespread exchange in intermediate goods. Therefore, alternative, more or less specialized R&D strategies become important parts of the long-term evolution of knowledges and specialization.

The multiform set of issues included in the chapter has not allowed any systematic coverage of the underlying forms of population thinking. In the introduction it was suggested that this kind of thinking is not only crucial for evolutionary analysis but that it is also more multi-form than normally recognized. Thus evolutionary economists not only need the fairly well-established intra-population thinking. In addition we need intra-to-inter-population thinking as well as co-evolutionary inter-population thinking. All these types of thinking have to some extent been included in the chapter, but it is obvious that both the discussion and the formal tools have largely supported intra-population thinking. However, an important theme of the chapter was that Price's formula for the decomposition of evolutionary change is surprisingly powerful in supporting manifold tasks of evolutionary analysis. So although it is apparently a natural extension of the statistically oriented intra-population thinking in the tradition of R.A. Fisher, it may also help to transcend this tradition. The reason is partly that Price's formula avoids making strong assumptions about the kind of evolutionary processes that can be covered. This means that the formula is not sufficient to define a long-term path of evolutionary change. But this limitation should be seen as its strength rather than its weakness. For instance, it is far too easy to forget about the web of inter-population links when a system of replicator equations is projected into the long run. Price's formula helps us to be more modest by pointing to the many assumptions underlying such long-run dynamics. Presently, the major task for our understanding of the evolution of the division of human time is, probably, to deepen our analysis of its shorter-term aspects.

NOTE

1. The research underlying the chapter was supported by the Danish Research Unit for Industrial Dynamics (DRUID), initially for computer simulation exercises. Previous versions of the chapter were presented at DRUID's Nelson and Winter Conference, Aalborg University, 12–15 June 2001 and the Brisbane Club Workshop, University of Manchester,

5–7 July 2002. Discussions here and with my Aalborg colleagues have helped to develop the chapter. Stan Metcalfe made the crucial suggestion to study Steven Frank's work. The usual caveat applies with extra force to the present version of this chapter.

REFERENCES

Aghion, P. and P. Howitt (1998), *Endogenous Growth Theory*, Cambridge, MA and London: MIT Press.

Andersen, E.S. (1996a), 'The evolution of economic complexity: a division-and-coordination-of-labour approach', in E. Helmstädter and M. Perlman (eds), *Behavioral Norms, Technological Progress, and Economic Dynamics: Studies in Schumpeterian Economics*, Ann Arbor, MI: University of Michigan Press, pp. 97–119.

Andersen, E.S. (1996b), 'From static structures to dynamics: specialisation and innovative linkages', in C. DeBresson (ed.), *Economic Interdependence and Innovative Activity: An Input–Output Analysis*, Aldershot, UK and Brookfield, US: Edward Elgar, pp. 331–53.

Andersen, E.S. (1999), 'Multisectoral growth and national innovation systems', *Nordic Journal of Political Economy*, **25**, 33–52.

Andersen, E.S. (2001), 'Satiation in an evolutionary model of structural economic dynamics', *Journal of Evolutionary Economics*, **11**, 143–64.

Andersen, E.S. (2002), 'Railroadization as Schumpeter's standard example of capitalist evolution: an evolutionary–ecological interpretation', *Industry and Innovation*, **9**, 41–78.

Arrow, K.J., Y.-K. Ng and X. Yang (eds) (1998), *Increasing Returns and Economic Analysis*, London: Palgrave Macmillan.

Arthur, W.B. (1994), *Increasing Returns and Path Dependence in the Economy*, Ann Arbor, MI: University of Michigan Press.

Boulding, K.E. (1978), *Ecodynamics: A New Theory of Societal Evolution*, Beverly Hills, CA and London: Sage.

Chiaromonte, F. and G. Dosi (1993), 'The micro foundations of competitiveness and their macroeconomic implications', in D. Foray and C. Freeman (eds), *Technology and the Wealth of Nations: The Dynamics of Constructed Advantage*, London: Pinter, pp. 107–34.

Dopfer, K. (2001), 'History-friendly theories in economics: reconciling universality and context in evolutionary analysis', in Foster and Metcalfe (eds) (2001), pp. 160–87.

Fisher, R.A. (1999), *The Genetical Theory of Natural Selection: A Complete Variorum Edition*, Oxford: Oxford University Press.

Foster, J. and J.S. Metcalfe (eds) (2001), *Frontiers of Evolutionary Economics: Competition, Self-Organization and Innovation Policy*, Cheltenham, UK and Northampton, MA, USA: Edward Elgar.

Frank, S.A. (1995), 'George Price's contributions to evolutionary genetics', *Journal of Theoretical Biology*, **175**, 373–88.

Frank, S.A. (1997), 'The Price equation, Fisher's fundamental theorem, kin selection, and causal analysis', *Evolution*, **51**, 1712–29.

Frank, S.A. (1998), *Foundations of Social Evolution*, Princeton, NJ: Princeton University Press.

Gintis, H. (2000), *Game Theory Evolving: A Problem-Centered Introduction to Modelling Strategic Behavior*, Princeton, NJ: Princeton University Press.

Grafen, A. (1984), 'Natural selection, kin selection, and group selection', in J.R. Krebs and N.B. Davies (eds), *Behavioural Ecology: An Evolutionary Approach*, 2nd edn, Sunderland, MA: Sinaur, pp. 62–84.

Hofbauer, J. and K. Sigmund (1998), *Evolutionary Games and Population Dynamics*, Cambridge: Cambridge University Press.

Marshall, A. (1949), *Principles of Economics: An Introductory Volume*, reprint of the 8th edn, Basingstoke and London: Macmillan.

Mayr, E. (1976), *Evolution and the Diversity of Life: Selected Essays*, Cambridge, MA and London: Belknap/Harvard University Press.

Metcalfe, J.S. (1998), *Evolutionary Economics and Creative Destruction*, London and New York: Routledge.

Metcalfe, J.S. (2001a), 'Institutions and progress', *Industrial and Corporate Change*, **10**, 561–85.

Metcalfe, J.S. (2001b), 'Evolutionary approaches to population thinking and the problem of growth and development', in K. Dopfer (ed.), *Evolutionary Economics: Program and Scope*, Boston, MA: Kluwer, pp. 141–64.

Metcalfe, J.S. (2002), 'Book Review: Steven A. Frank. 1998. *Foundations of Social Evolution*', *Journal of Bioeconomics*, **4**, 89–91.

Nelson, R.R. (2001), 'The co-evolution of technology and institutions as the driver of economic growth', in Foster and Metcalfe (eds) (2001), pp. 19–30.

Nelson, R.R. and S.G. Winter (1982), *An Evolutionary Theory of Economic Change*, Cambridge, MA and London: Belknap/Harvard University Press.

Page, K.M. and M.A. Nowak (2002), 'Unifying evolutionary dynamics', *Journal of Theoretical Biology*, **219**, 93–8.

Potts, J. (2000), *The New Evolutionary Microeconomics: Complexity, Competence and Adaptive Behaviour*, Cheltenham, UK and Northanpton, MA, USA: Edward Elgar.

Price, G.R. (1970), 'Selection and covariance', *Nature*, **227**, 520–21.

Price, G.R. (1972), 'Fisher's "fundamental theorem" made clear', *Annals of Human Genetics*, **36**, 129–40.

Price, G.R. (1995), 'The nature of selection', *Journal of Theoretical Biology*, **175**, 389–96.

Richardson, G.B. (1975), 'Adam Smith on competition and increasing returns', in A.S. Skinner and T. Wilson (eds), *Essays on Adam Smith*, Oxford: Clarendon, pp. 350–60.

Romer, P.M. (1990), 'Endogenous technological change', *Journal of Political Economy*, **98**, S71–S102.

Romer, P.M. (1993), 'Idea gaps and object gaps in economic development', *Journal of Monetary Economics*, **32**, 543–73.

Saviotti, P.P. (1996), *Technological Evolution, Variety and the Economy*, Cheltenham, UK and Brookfield, USA: Edward Elgar.

Saviotti, P.P. (2001), 'Considerations about a production system with qualitative change', in Foster and Metcalfe (eds) (2001), pp. 197–227.

Schumpeter, J.A. (1934), *The Theory of Economic Development: An Inquiry into Profits, Capital, Credit, Interest and the Business Cycle*, London: Oxford University Press.

Smith, A. (1976), *An Inquiry into the Nature and Causes of the Wealth of Nations*, Oxford: Clarendon.

Verspagen, B. (1993), *Uneven Growth Between Interdependent Economies: An Evolutionary View on Technology Gaps, Trade and Growth*, Aldershot: Avebury.

Yang, X. (2001), *Economics: New Classical Versus Neoclassical Frameworks*, Malden, MA and Oxford: Blackwell.

Young, A.A. (1928), 'Increasing returns and economic progress', *Economic Journal*, **38**, 527–42.

PART III

Empirical Perspectives

7. Erring to be right: the paradox of error in the foundation of probability in economics

Francisco Louçã[1]

INTRODUCTION

This chapter is a first instalment of my research on the nature of the concept of errors in economic theories, models and equations, and proceeds to an investigation of some of the evolving discussions among economists on the nature of randomness and determinism, probability and certainty. The next section describes some of the antecedents, followed by a section summarizing the intellectual context of the probabilistic revolution in economics. Finally, the conclusion recapitulates the argument and presents some sceptical considerations in relation to the foundational dichotomy of law and 'chaos', or order and chance. The conceptualization of the 'error' in evolutionary biology is suggested as an alternative theoretical framework to be considered in economics.

This research emerges from a puzzle that can be expressed by a simple question. Why are so few economists seemingly unconcerned with the obvious discrepancy between concepts such as: 'error'; 'shock'; 'residual'; 'perturbation'; 'disturbance'; 'innovation'; 'stimuli'; 'noise'; 'aberration'; and so many others used to describe one of the core operational terms in our models?

Reading this list of nine different names for the statistical error brings to mind Joan Robinson's remark on the teaching of the concept of 'capital'. She once wrote that this concept was so abstruse or ill-defined that, as a teacher presenting it to students, she secretly hoped that no one would ask the difficult question, namely: 'what exactly do you mean by, "capital"?' in order that the course could proceed on an albeit shaky, but unshaken, basis. Likewise for the case of the concept of 'error', or whatever synonym is currently in use, since so many of its translations encapsulate a distinct if not diverse meaning. It suffices to open any handbook of statistics, in particular those designed for undergraduates beginning their course, and evidence emerges of the pervading epistemic ambiguity of the distinctive concepts, which creates a constellation of colliding meanings and semantic instability.

Johnston (1987) uses both the concept of 'disturbance' and that of 'error' in the sense of discrepancies between the expected values from the working of a model and the actually observed values. These discrepancies are explained by the heterogeneity among agents, given all possible small influences on their behaviour, aggravated by the unpredictable randomness in human diversity (ibid., pp. 14–15). In other words, 'error' is a feature of the model and the price of its limited power of explanation. Judge et al. (1988, pp. 160–61) also explain the error term as being simply the unexplained part of reality, given the model: $y_t - \beta = e_t$. The random vector represents the unpredictable or uncontrolled errors associated with the outcome of the experiment and, consequently, 'the random vector is often referred to as the noise' (ibid., pp. 179–80).

Maddala (1992, pp. 64–5) equates the concepts of 'error' and 'disturbance', and defines three possible origins for that error: the unpredictable randomness in human behaviour, the large number of omitted variables and the measurement error in the endogenous variable. Griffiths et al. (1993, pp. 175–6) use the same explanation, adding the possible approximation error provoked by the assumption of linearity. Greene (1993, pp. 142–3) defines the error as the aggregation of omitted variables and errors of measurement.

This list is obviously heterogeneous, since at least seven different explanations are proposed for the error term, namely:

1. measurement errors;
2. influence of omitted variables;
3. intrinsic randomness in society;
4. theoretical misspecification of the model;
5. functional misspecification;
6. general inadequacy of the model; and, in general,
7. irregularities, or what Frisch called 'aberrations'.

This heterogeneity of reasons highlights the problems with the use and misuse of the listed concepts: although some of these names for 'error' are clearly synonyms, the fact is that others are contradictory or diverse. In addition, the proposed explanations are also partly contradictory. While some of the arguments place the 'error' in the universe of the model (residual), and it is observable, others emphasize that it is in the nature of reality (disturbance), but it is unobservable. Some are intrinsic (error of measurement), others are extrinsic to the model (unpredictable random behaviour of humans). Some are eventually corrigible (neglected influence of omitted variables, approximation error imposed by the assumption of linearity), others are not (heterogeneity among agents). Some refer to variables defined in the universe of the model itself (stimuli), whereas others refer to attributed features of reality (perturbation). Some refer to exogenous causes (shocks), while others argue that they are irrelevant (noise), although it is this very irrelevance that is the basis for its useful statistical properties. The concept of error hides a forest of deviant meanings.

But these discrepancies did not pass unnoticed. Goldberger (1991) argued that there is a substantial difference between the interpretation of the model of the residual and that of the model of the disturbance. The two models are contrasted: Judge et al.'s ε is simply the disturbance vector, the deviation of the random vector $\mathbf{y}$ from its expectation $\mu = \mathbf{X}\beta$. Thus, for a scalar random vector y with $E(y) = \mu$ and $V(y) = \sigma^2$, one might write $y = \mu + \varepsilon$, $E(\varepsilon) = 0$, $E(\varepsilon^2) = \sigma^2$. There is no serious objection in doing so, except that it tends to give disturbance a life of its own, rather than treating it as merely the deviation of a random variable from its expected value. Doing so may make μ the 'true value' of y and ε an 'error' or 'mistake'.

For example, Judge et al. (ibid., p. 179) say that the disturbance ε 'is a random vector representing the unpredictable or uncontrollable errors associated with the outcome of the experiment', and Johnston (1987, p. 169) says that 'if the theorist has done a good job in specifying all the significant explanatory variables to be included in $\mathbf{X}$, it is reasonable to assume that both positive and negative discrepancies from the expected value will occur and that, on balance, they will average out at zero'. Such language may overdramatize the primitive concept of the difference between the observed and the expected values of a random variable. In any event, we will want to distinguish between the *disturbance* vector $\varepsilon = y - \mu$, which is unobserved, and the *residual* vector $e = y - \hat{y}$, which is observed (Goldberger, 1991, pp. 170–71).

Between the mere statistical tool, and the disturbance with a life of its own, there is a world of difference. Furthermore, there are strong implicit ontological statements in this story, since a limited concept of order requires the 'true' value to be $E(y)$, not y, which allows for the attribution to ε of the denomination of a real 'error'. Indeed, these questions are deeply rooted in the history of economic statistics.

The next section briefly presents some of the main contributions for the introduction of the concepts of probability and error in economics, arguing that this epistemic instability was in fact better detected and discussed in the first period of the installation of econometrics than it is today. So, let us look back.

HIC SUNT LEONES, OR THE DANGER OF THE UNKNOWN

According to the Bible, one of the matrices of western culture, 'Chaos' prevailed at the beginning of time, but then came God and the Creation. Other mythical accounts share that view of disorder turned into order. Yet, as the tale goes, even when order was imposed – an exogenous order, in any possible way – something essential continued in the management of human affairs: order frequently occurred by chance. Matthias was chosen by lot to become the twelfth Apostle (Acts 1: 26), and the Almighty did not hesitate to indicate guilt by lot: such was the case in the trials of Jonathan (1 Sm. 14: 37–43), of Jonah (Jon. 1: 1–10) and of Achan (Josh. 7: 10–23).

The drawing of lots occurs repeatedly: the Roman soldiers drew lots for Jesus' tunic (John 19: 23–4 and Ps. 22: 18). Julius Caesar uses chance to decide on his destiny and that of the Empire: the dice decide, *alea jacta est*. Again, one of the founding fathers of the Catholic Church presents the argument for chance as an expression of order: according to Augustine (Ps. 30: 16, enarr 2, serm 2) '*Sors non est aliquid mali, sed res, in humana dubitatione, divinam indicans voluntatem*, lots are not bad in and for themselves, for they indicate the Divine will when man is in doubt' (Ekeland 1993, pp. 8–9; 75–9). Some of the later reference literature gives new examples: in *Gargantua and Pantagruel*, by Rabelais, the honourable Judge Bridlegoose passes sentences by rolling dice.

Of course, the use of chance is as old as history itself. Games of chance are known in all ancient civilizations, with lots, cards and dice pervading all narratives of antiquity. Institutions used it as well as laymen, and they were certainly required to do so: according to Stigler, at least since 1100 there is evidence of 'institutionalized numerical allowance for uncertainty', with the *Trial of the Pyx*. The London Mint, in order to check the quality of its procedures, used the *pyx*, a box containing a sample of coins, whose weight was compared to the standard control values. Certainly there was long-lasting resistance against combining measures taken under different circumstances, for fear that an error would contaminate rather than counterbalance all the measurements (Stigler 1986, p. 3). Sampling was not easily understood and accepted, although it was recognizably the only accessible method for control in large production. Order is the taming of chaos, and that was the work of probability methods and concepts.

The history of statistics and of the definition of probability exceeds the limits of this chapter. It is a long history, from the puzzles established by the Chevalier de Méré (1654), going through Blaise Pascal, the correspondence between Gottfried Leibniz and Jacob Bernoulli on the law of large numbers (1703), the definition of the normal distribution by Abraham de Moivre (1730) and the principle of maximum likelihood by Daniel Bernoulli (1778). Yet it was only in the early nineteenth century that a theory for the distribution of errors in measurement was advanced by Karl Friedrich Gauss (1809) and the central limit theorem was first formulated the following year by Pierre Simon Laplace. Almost simultaneously, but independently, the concept of error was introduced in practical methods of statistics (Klein 1997).

The application of these concepts to social sciences was not trivial. But it was powerful enough to challenge the resistance: the characteristics of order in a population were more valuable than disorder and differences among individuals. Adolphe Jacques Quételet argued that the behaviour of individuals was fundamentally unpredictable, but added that the aggregation of evidence and measurements describing the behaviour of a large crowd would necessarily lead to a law of behaviour – certainly one of the first 'certainty equivalents' in modern social sciences. That equivalent is the law of the distribution of errors in the deviations from the average. This powerful result gained credibility in the scientific community: it could be empirically checked in a number of instances and it allowed for measurement, control and prediction. Karl Pearson assumed that the law of errors was conveniently represented by the normal distribution, and the profound consequence of such a choice was to affirm the primacy of order over chance: random variations were recognized to exist, but were domesticated, and consequently variation could no longer challenge the capacity of science to uncover causality.[2]

In parallel, in 1805 Adrien-Marie Legendre established his *Nouvelles Méthodes pour la détermination des orbites des comètes*, defining the first approximation to the ordinary least squares (OLS) method. Given:

$$a_i = -b_i x - c_i y - f_i z - \ldots + E_i,$$

E_i being the error that should be nullified (Stigler 1986, p. 56). Although the author recognized an element of arbitrariness in the 'distribution of errors among the equations' (ibid., p. 13), this method was supposed to approach truth: 'By this method, a kind of equilibrium is established among the errors which, since it prevents the extremes from dominating, is appropriate for revealing the state of the system which most nearly approaches the truth' (Legendre, quoted in Stigler ibid.).

Legendre's OLS method was immediately adopted[3] and in 10 years it was the standard. But the method implied no formal treatment of probability and was precisely defined in relation to a specified scientific field: errors of measurement in relation to an accepted *true* law of the universe.

Indeed, it depended on the verification of the Newtonian laws and was generalized as part of the Laplacean vision of determinism.

Within the context of post-Newtonian scientific thought, the only acceptable grounds for the choice of an error distribution were to show that the curve could be mathematically derived from an acceptable set of first principles. As the inverse square law was the touchstone of mathematical astronomy, so the principle of equally likely cases was that of mathematical probability. If a choice of a curve of errors was to be found acceptable, it must be reducible in some sense to a description in terms of cases supposed equally likely, or indifferently indistinguishable. Both Laplace derivations fall within this paradigm (ibid., p. 110).

In this framework, the notion of 'error' depended only on the limits of the apparatus of observation, since the theory would necessarily provide the correct coordinates of the astronomic object. As far as Newton's laws were accepted, the concept of error was therefore precisely defined; it could have no other origin than the measurement itself – it is indeed an error, in the full sense of the word. There are no mixture of causes, no new variables, no extrinsic influences, no undefined agents, no strange and surprising behaviour to generate the error. The model had only a few degrees of freedom and it was supposed to be able to describe exactly the state of nature and its evolution. The error is just an error.

The following semantic instability of the concept is consequently alien to its origin; it emerges later on from the extension to the social sciences. Of course, in social sciences there is no equivalent to the Newtonian laws, no single causality, no general authoritative equation representing the trajectory of a system, not even a single authoritative theory for the discrimination of the variables and their functional form. Consequently, the error became a 'residual', that is, it was accepted that it would depend on the theory and its model determining the measurement. This consequential conceptual shift dominated the introduction of the modern concept of statistical 'error' in social sciences, and in economics in particular.

In fact, there are profound differences between the concept of error in astronomy and this new social concept: the *error* only equates with the *residual* if one can assert as a dogma that the model is true. In the Newtonian world, error is an exact measure of the deviation to the correct orbit, established without a shred of a doubt by theory, since it defines invariant mass points on which exogenous forces act, giving the balance between forces that determines the position and momentum of the bodies. The causality of the registered deviation, consequently, can be unquestionably attributed either to the error of the apparatus of measurement itself, or to other and ignored forces at work, influencing gravitation. Alternatively, in the social sciences framework, the residual is a derivation of the model, interpreting a state of nature, irreducible variation impinging perturbations on the system.

It must be added that, for many economists, this simply could not be accepted, since economics should mimic astronomy and physics. The mechanics of the universe would be inconceivable without order, and the very concept of order excludes chance and surprise: 'Happily the universe in which we dwell is not the result of chance, and where chance seems to work it is our own deficient faculties which prevent us from recognizing the operation of Law and Design' (Jevons, quoted in Aldrich 1987, p. 236). The deeply rooted tradition of mechanical determinism in economics abhorred chance. General equilibrium and neoclassical economics, consequently, favoured order. But order was itself redefined as being so powerful as to emerge even out of disorder – and that was at the core of the probabilistic revolution.

Of course, this was not exactly what the theory was proposing at that time, since no assertion was being made on reality, but simply on a possible representation and on the measurement of the adequacy of the model. The notorious consequences of this conceptual deviance – as errors were treated as residuals – were not ignored, and were largely discussed. It is certain that many economists felt that, as the early explorers wrote as they approached *terra incognita*, there was the danger of the unknown: this part of the map is the territory of beasts, *hic sunt leones*.

FRISCH AND THE THREE MUSKETEERS OF THE PROBABILISTIC REVOLUTION: TINBERGEN, KOOPMANS AND HAAVELMO

When probability entered the province of economics, there were two main available approaches: that of astronomy and that of biology. For astronomy, things were apparently simpler: errors in measurement were possible but could easily be corrected, since the analytical universe was composed of independent observations, those could be multiplied for the sake of precision, and the true model was supposed to have just a few degrees of freedom (Hendry and Morgan 1995, p. 9). For biology, evolution and consequently time-dependent observations dominated, but several were available at each point, and therefore the crucial question became the relation between the population and the sample.

Ragnar Frisch, the founder of econometrics, argued strongly for the first alternative, and favoured the introduction of the concepts derived from astronomy, vigorously opposing the probabilistic approach championed by R.A. Fisher. Indeed, 'he felt that probability and the sampling approach to statistical analysis, developed for use with experimental data in the work of Fisher, was not appropriate for the non-experimental data of econometrics and so he developed his own method of statistical analysis' (ibid., pp. 40–41). Consequently, Frisch developed the confluence method for addressing multicollinearity and the identification problem, and the bunch maps method for variable selection and model choice, leading to instrumental variables (IV) estimation later introduced by his colleague Olav Reiersol.

At that time, three major models were available to explain discrepancies between data and theory. The differences were explained: (i) as measurement errors, that is, errors in variables; (ii) as omitted variables, that is, errors in equations; and (iii) through a probabilistic approach, which was more general, given the fact that both (i) and (ii) assumed a deterministic system (Morgan 1990, pp. 193, 241).

Frisch clearly favoured (i), arguing that sampling theory could only be applied in conditions of controlled experiments, whereas Koopmans argued for (ii), the omitted variables approach. For more than one decade (approx. 1930–44), probability theory was kept at bay: it was rejected by Warren Persons, on the grounds that in social sciences observations are time related, and by Morgenstern, under the argument of lack of homogeneity in data (ibid., pp. 235–36). Vilfredo Pareto, Wesley Mitchell and many others identified cases of statistical deviations from normality, and Persons and Lionel Robbins challenged the probabilistic methods under the argument of lack of homogeneity through time, anticipating John Maynard Keynes's critique of Tinbergen.

Nevertheless, it was Frisch, the econometrician, who was the champion of the resistance. For him,

> [A] regression was considered properly specified if it was 'complete', meaning that it contained all the relevant variables and so did not contain an error term. This was the standard framework that explained residual variance in terms of measurement errors in the variables. Frisch's innovation was to extend the framework to encompass what he termed the 'complete system', that is, the total of n equations that presumably were needed to determine the n variables appearing in the equation of interest. He took pains to avoid mentioning the market equilibrium problem in order to emphasize his notion of a system as a general feature of any econometric movement. (Epstein 1987, p. 38)

Completeness was the necessary and sufficient condition for a system of equations to explain an economic process. Consequently, Frisch favoured the notion that a determinate system was the best way to describe the functioning of the economy and, in his famous paper on cycles (Frisch 1933), the inclusion of an error term was not even theoretically justified, and was used just for the sake of a better fit to reality. Finally, Frisch introduced the error term as a representation of laboratory stimuli impinging on a deterministic system tending to equilibrium: this was as far as he went on the introduction of probability concepts.

Yet, he did not explain that error term: 'The concrete interpretation of the shock e_k does not interest us for the moment' (ibid., pp. 200–201), he argued. Further in the same paper, the erratic shocks are presented as a 'source of energy in maintaining oscillations', and a model for Joseph Schumpeter's forced pendulum is presented as a relevant example: in that case, innovations are that source of energy. Following on from the early pendulum models for explaining cycles, such as those of Fisher (1925) or Yule (1927), Frisch also used the insights from Slutsky (1927), which used purely random shocks – and the divergence went unexplained. Indeed, the two references used by Frisch in order to explain the nature of shocks, those of Slutsky and Schumpeter, were clearly orthogonal to each other. But it is plausible that Frisch did not fully understand Schumpeter's arguments on the nature of innovations under capitalism, in spite of much correspondence and discussion on the matter, or at least that he was unable to formally represent the model Schumpeter had in mind (Louçã 1999).

It was up to a disciple and colleague of Frisch, Haavelmo, to change the balance of forces in favour of a sampling approach, essentially with his 1944 paper on 'The probability approach in econometrics'. Until then, statistical analysis and OLS methods were used, but the probability framework was not generally accepted (Morgan 1990, p. 229). Haavelmo knew about, and for a while shared, Frisch's resistance to the introduction of probability concepts, but then was convinced by Jerzy Neyman and, although accepting that no experiments were made in economics and that only passive observations were possible, suggested that the probability approach could be used nevertheless. Haavelmo and Koopmans, in contrast with Frisch, adopted Fisher's view, which assumes a hypothetical infinite population, the actual data being regarded as a random sample of it. By the end of the 1940s, this was largely accepted: that was the second departure for econometrics, the period of 'mature econometrics' (ibid., p. 242).

Frisch proffered no strong arguments against the introduction of probability concepts – his resistance was focused on the denial of the core assumptions of the new approach, and consequently there was no common ground for cooperation or even debate. He never shared the new vision of his colleagues; however, rather than a prima facie rejection, there is evidence that he looked for, but did not find, ammunition for the battle. As Koopmans was researching in the small Oslo Institute of Economics in 1935, and the discussion had already been engaged, Frisch even tried to recruit some help. When Paul Hoel, whom he had met when lecturing in Yale in 1930, wrote to him about the possibility of coming to Oslo to study statistics, Frisch answered at length and invited him to come and to compare both approaches:

> At the present time Mr. Tjalling Koopmans, of Amsterdam, is here working on a doctor thesis in mathematical statistics. He is particularly interested in building a bridge between the approach in my book *Confluence Analysis* and the R.A. Fisher sampling approach. The difference between these two points of view is this. In sampling theory, in order to test the significance of a statistical observation, one puts up the fiction of a 'universe', that is some big collection from which the actual observations are 'drawn' in a more or less 'accidental' manner. Whatever assumptions one makes are made in the form of *assumptions about this universe*. This point of view is fruitful, it seems to me, in problems concerning experiments that *can be controlled*. For instance, agricultural or biological experiments. But this theory is very inadequate when it comes to applications in economics, or in social sciences in general, where we most of the time have to accept observations that are presented to us without our being able to influence the results to any considerable extent. In these cases all the problems of confluence analysis crop up, and these can, it seems to me, be better treated by another type of analysis, namely, an analysis where the assumptions being produced *are assumptions about the sampling itself*. For instance, one may assume that each observation is a sum of a systematic part and a 'disturbance', and then introduce assumptions concerning what has been the connection, or lack of connections, between the disturbances *in the sample*. In this way one arrives at identities, exact upper and lower limits, etc., not results which are formulated in probability terms. One does have a means of investigating how a particular constellation of assumptions entails a particular consequence for the result obtained. This analysis of the effects of *alternative assumptions* is very important for applications to economics.
>
> This is of course a very rough outline of the difference between the two approaches. If I should give a fuller statement, I would have to explain that, in some sense, the notion of probability comes in my approach and that, after all, there may be some points of contact between the two approaches. But it would lead too far to go into this in a short letter. I mention it in order to suggest to you a field of research, which, I think, is particularly important and very intriguing. (Frisch to Paul Hoel, 15 October 1935, Oslo University Library, original emphases)

The effort was inconsequential, no bridge was built – if any was intended – and the differences remained a dividing line in the first generation of econometricians. During that period, two strategies competed to overcome the limits Frisch imposed on statistics and probability: Tinbergen, on the one hand, and Haavelmo and Koopmans, on the other, were the main proponents of such strategies.

Tinbergen, a physicist by training and education, concentrated on the explanation of economic cycles. Like Frisch, his main concern in economics was the social implication of depressions. In order to assess and to control those processes, he used models of harmonic oscillators to mimic cycles, the implication being that 'supply and demand were exact relationships among the observables, with any lack of fit due to errors in variables or nonlinearities' (Epstein 1987, p. 34). In that framework, Tinbergen understood exogenous variables as shocks: 'Tinbergen was primarily interested in estimating the coefficients of the lagged endogenous variables that determined the oscillatory behaviour of the system. The exogenous variables represented specific outside economic shocks that excited the equations' (ibid., p. 171), and therefore the general class of exogenous variables could be divided into two categories: errors and other variables, all being treated on the same grounds. But this classification was unsatisfactory for everyone: it did not challenge Frisch's reservations, and it did not share the points of view that Koopmans and Haavelmo were spreading. It allowed for structural estimation – which became the programme for econometrics for two decades – accepting the intellectual framework of the laboratory experiment, but the empirical experience was disillusioning.

In 1939, Tinbergen published his famous study on the theories of business cycles based on an econometric model and estimation. This ignited two parallel lines of debate: Keynes criticized econometric methods, and the econometricians stood by Tinbergen; but, simultaneously, Frisch strongly expressed his own reservations on Tinbergen's research. Once again, the core of the problem was the assessment of shocks, or errors, or the nature of probability in economics.

In his critique of Tinbergen's conclusions, Frisch proposed to distinguish between two operational concepts: that of 'nature' or 'constitution', the structure of the system represented by the equations, and the 'disturbance', being 'a deviation from that situation which would have existed as a consequence of the structure'. The disturbances could be conceived of either as 'aberrations', not affecting the subsequent states of the system, or as 'stimuli', affecting the future of the system (Frisch 1938, p. 408). A stimulus is clearly a reference to the laboratory framework. Furthermore, Frisch doubted that highly autonomous equations could be established and estimated, meaning that the real explanations for the phenomena were frequently inaccessible, since only coflux equations were deductible from data (ibid., p. 416). Consequently, the programme for structural estimation was considered to be utopian.

Tinbergen, in his book published the following year, carefully addressed this discussion, and tried to establish a bridge between the concept of measurement error and that of error representing the influence of omitted variables and the problems of sampling:

> According to this method ['classical method', Laplace, Gauss, R.A. Fisher], it is assumed that the unexplained parts – the residuals – are due to the circumstance that the 'explained variate, though essentially a linear function of the

"explanatory" variates, contains an additional component representing the influence of neglected explanatory variates and may, moreover, be subject to errors of measurement. ... The probable average magnitudes of these differences [in relation to 'true' values] are derived from the assumption that the disturbances in subsequent time are to be considered as "random drawings" from the "universe" of all possible values of these disturbances. In ordinary speech, small disturbances will be numerous and large disturbances will be few, their frequency obeying a simple law'. (Tinbergen 1939, vol. I, p. 28).

Tinbergen recognized that this was in contradistinction to Frisch's views:

Professor Ragnar Frisch, in his treatment of these problems, does not use the concept of some unknown 'universe' from which a 'sample' is drawn. He considers *every* variate as being built of a systematic part and a disturbance. The relations assumed between the variates are supposed to hold good exactly between the systematic parts and the regression coefficients in these relations are called the true coefficients. (ibid., p. 29, Original emphasis)

In spite of this, in his applied work, Tinbergen restricted his assumptions to the concept of error representing the omitted variables, as in the investment equation (ibid., p. 38), imposing furthermore the restriction of no correlation between the 'erratic components' or 'disturbances' of the different variates, as well as no correlation between the disturbances and the systematic part, or between the disturbances and the systematic parts of the other variates (ibid., p. 30).

The difficulty emerged out of the effort to explain the rationale for these 'extra economic factors' or 'autonomous factors'; what could eventually be represented in this pot-pourri of variables? Inventions, political events, abnormal acts, surprises, what more? Tinbergen did not ignore the problem and tried to distinguish between two classes of events, according to their impact:

These influences are considered in this analysis as non-systematic disturbances which act largely accidentally, in an irregular way, like lottery drawings. In general, such influences will exist whenever many mutually independent and small forces are acting, which will be the case in normal times. This is the approach to business cycle problems which is known as the 'shock theory of cycles'. Some very exceptional events which do not obey these 'laws' will be generally known, so that they may easily be eliminated before the analysis. This has been done, e.g. with the English coalminers' strike in 1926. (ibid., p. 38).

The difficulty is obvious from the nature of the 'shocks' here considered, as they are distinguished by Tinbergen according to their dimension and distribution and by Frisch according to their durability, with no hypothesis attached to any distribution. In spite of this difference, Tinbergen did not generalize the implication of the random drawing he suggested. He even suggested, quoting Koopmans, that the 'classical method' and Frisch's were complementary and not contradictory (ibid., pp. 32–3). But almost 50 years later, after a life dedicated to statistical economics, to econometrics, to models and estimation, Tinbergen suspected that the error term was still ill defined:

> The error term is introduced as a catchall for less important independent variables and for measuring errors of both the dependent variable and the independent variables. ... Essentially the introduction of an error term is a second best setup and in a way a *testimonium paupertatis*. (Tinbergen 1990, p. 201)

Tinbergen interpreted this as reason enough to suspect probability and statistical estimation and, like Frisch, he retired from econometrics soon after the Second World War. Koopmans and especially Haavelmo instead built their contribution to econometrics on the assumption that Fisher's concept of sampling error was the key to generalized procedures of estimation, and consequently was much more important for economics than pure measurement errors in models with few degrees of freedom, such as those applied to astronomy. Consequently, the crux of the matter was to extend the concepts forged for laboratory experiments and sampling. For Koopmans, exogeneity was the core conceptual feature of the statistical universe:

> By viewing exogeneity as a statistical property it is possible to introduce many economic factors into a model that have the same interpretation as laboratory stimuli ... exogeneity was essential in the simultaneous equations methodology because it provided the conceptual basis for understanding economic data as the result of experiments. (Epstein 1987, p. 171)

Yet, it is surprising that Koopmans kept defining the 'disturbance' just as the cocktail of omitted variables:

> The investigator specifies a number of behavioural equations, the variables entering into each, a simple mathematical form for each equation, and a rather wide class of probability distributions for the disturbances of the various equations. The disturbance in any one equation is here looked upon as the aggregate effect of many individually unimportant or random variables not explicitly recognized in setting up the behaviour equation in question. (Koopmans 1957, p. 200)

Koopmans himself did not present a convincing explanation for these shocks, and even eventually challenged the concept of the economic time series as random drawings from a hypothetical universe:

> In a great deal of problems variables are developing in time in cyclical oscillations, apparently to a large extent governed by some internal causal mechanism,

and only besides that influenced, more or less, according to the nature of the variable, by erratic shocks due to technical innovations, variations in crop yields, etc. At any rate, they are far from being random drawings from any distribution whatever. (1937, p. 277)

Nevertheless, he argued that 'it may be better to have some point of support obtained by the use of a set of simplifying assumptions, than none at all' (ibid., p. 278) – an accepted *testimonium paupertatis*, in any case.

It was up to Haavelmo to stabilize the new research programme. In particular, Haavelmo strongly challenged the idea that 'small shocks' could be added without any reference to an explicit model defined in a probabilistic approach, an obvious critique of Frisch's approach:

> Without further specification of the model, this procedure [assuming small shocks] has no foundation, and that for two main reasons. First the notion that one can operate with some vague idea about 'small errors' without introducing the concepts of stochastical variables and probability distribution is, I think based on an illusion. For, since the errors are not just constants, one has to introduce some more complex notion of 'small' and 'large' than just the numerical values of the individual errors. Since it is usually agreed that the errors are 'on the whole small' when individual errors are large only in rare occasions, we are led to consider not only the size of each individual error but also the frequency with which the error of certain size occur. And so forth. If one really tries to dig down to a clear formulation of the notion of 'small irregular errors', or the like, one will discover, I think, that we have, at least for the time being, no other practical instrument for such a formulation than those of random variables and probability distributions, nor is there any loss of generality involved in the application of these analytical instruments, for any variable may be 'probabilized', provided we allow sufficiently complicated distribution functions. (1943, pp. 457–8)

Furthermore, for Haavelmo, the probabilistic framework was necessary for two main epistemological reasons: for the generalization of the useful statistical applications and for the correct representation of the 'nature of economic behaviour'. On one hand, 'We need stochastical formulations to make simplified relations elastic enough for applications' (ibid., p. 454), and on the other:

> [T]he necessity of introducing 'error terms' in economic relation is not merely a result of statistical errors of measurement. It is as much a result of the very nature of economic behaviour, its dependence upon an enormous number of factors, compared with those which we can account for explicitly in our theories. (ibid.)[4]

It is also important to note that Haavelmo argued that the assumed distribution of probabilities was merely a feature of the model, that is, of the imagination of the modeller:

The rigorous notion of probabilities and probability distribution 'exist' only in our rational mind, serving us only as a tool for deriving practical statements ... 'Since the assignment of a certain probability law to a system of observable variables is a trick of our own, invented for analytical purposes, and since the same observable results may be produced under a great variety of different probability schemes, the question arises as to which probability law should be chosen, in any given case to represent the true mechanism under which the data considered are being produced. (1944, pp. 48, 49)

Consequently, the introduction of the probabilistic approach derived from utilitarian arguments: the forerunners did not argue that it was the most appropriate concept to interpret reality, but instead that it was useful to represent it. Furthermore, as stochasticity was introduced through the concept of error, and statistical inference is only possible if the error has certain desired properties, the whole edifice was based on narrow foundations.

Later on, a new argumentative strategy was established, as the Cowles Commission became, in the 1940s and 1950s, the centre for the econometric research on structural estimation: a Walrasian model, based on the aggregation of agents, was adopted, and consequently the cycle was defined as a deviation from the equilibrium. Mechanical determinism was back. This combination of external shocks plus neoclassical deterministic equations, or uninformative white noise plus equilibrium, was the basis for the Cowles method.

Frisch provided the dichotomy between the stabilizing system and the exogenous shocks but did not accept the full consequences of this approach, since he did not share the representation of the economies as random drawings from the hypothetical universe of experiments. Then the three musketeers, Tinbergen, Koopmans and Haavelmo, came and introduced the generalized probabilistic approach. However, as in the old story of the musketeers, at least one of them, Tinbergen, did not continue along the road with his pals and retired to his empirical castle, looking defiantly at the work of econometrics.

DETERMINISM AND RANDOMNESS

If the adequate model of an evolving process can be represented by the summation of an equilibrium system and well-behaved random disturbances then control, prediction and inference would be trivial. Yet, they are not. How could this be so simple?

This modern interrogation echoes older ones. In particular, some distinguished physicists challenged the bucolic universe of certainty and mechanical determinism in different fields of science, including their own. For a long time, Poincaré and Maxwell had argued that this difficulty of matching equilibrium and change, or order and disorder, was to be expected, given complexity – the nature of the systems or the multiplicity of explanatory variables, generating perturbations from the working of the system itself. Maxwell, who suspected all causal explanations, argued in 1876 that '[i]t is a metaphysical doctrine that from the same antecedents follow the same consequents', namely, given the presence of instability related to the large number of variables acting on a system.

In his *Science et méthode* (1908), Poincaré detected cases for which 'a very small cause which escapes our notice determines a considerable effect that we cannot fail to see, and then we say that that effect is due to chance'. Moreover,

> Why have meteorologists such difficulty in predicting the weather with any certainty? Why is it that showers and even storms seem to come by chance, so that many people think it quite natural to pray for rain or fine weather, though they would consider it ridiculous to ask for an eclipse by prayer? We see that great disturbances are generally produced in regions where the atmosphere is in unstable equilibrium. The meteorologists see very well that the equilibrium is unstable, that a cyclone will be formed somewhere, but exactly where they are not in a position to say; a tenth of a degree more or less at any given point, and the cyclone will burst here and not there, and extend its ravages over districts it would otherwise have spared. If they had been aware of this tenth of a degree, they could have known of it beforehand, but the observations were neither sufficiently comprehensive nor sufficiently precise, and that is the reason why it all seems due to the intervention of chance. (ibid., 1908, pp. 67–8)

Previously, writing about the 3-bodies problem, Poincaré had already indicated that not all dynamic equations are integrable and, consequently, that there is no possible prediction of the trajectories of all systems. In these cases, new qualitative methods are needed to study differential equations: the world of astronomy was suddenly understood to be not so simple as Newton's laws and the measurement errors suggested. But the consequences for this story of the debate in economics are devastating, since the first interpretation of errors was derived from the solid foundations of astronomy, as errors of measurement. Yet, at that time, this simplification was already being challenged in physics. Furthermore, in economics the alternative was not easier: the generalized probabilistic approach was interpreted in the framework of the juxtaposition of strong equilibrating forces plus irrelevant shocks, and consequently randomness was artificially insulated. In any case, under the influence of Ludwig Boltzman and others, quantum physics and statistical mechanics defined the landscape of the long probabilistic revolution in the period up to 1920. Since chance is the 'intersection of independent causal consequences', and it can be understood only in relation to human experience in precise historical situations, Ekeland concludes that chance is always an answer to a question posed by humans (Ekeland 1993, pp. 121–22).[5] But in economics, the prevailing interpretation is that order and chance are strictly dichotomic, independent and simply additive. And, although Haavelmo and Koopmans initially argued that the probabilistic framework was just a desired feature of the models, this dichotomy became a dogma for the interpretation of time series.

Moreover, legitimate order was interpreted by neoclassical economics as a structure of relations representable in a Hamiltonian framework, in which everything is known, and all events are exogenous. Consequently, the errors – whatever they are – should necessarily be considered as external to the system and, since fixing causality in strict exogeneity is a weak epistemological strategy, their theoretical status should be diminished as a consequence. This permits the understanding of the dogmatic resistance against any alteration of the general equilibrium framework of conservation of energy: if instead the economic systems were conceptualized as dissipative, then the coherence of this scheme would explode, since intrinsic randomness may emerge from the interaction of variables, known and unknown. In that case, randomness is not a stream of 'errors' or 'perturbations', but part of the essential structure of events and relations, and that was the insight both from Maxwell and from Poincaré. And, one may add, in social sciences we deal with yet another level of complexity, the intersection of institutions, strategies and choices.

Evolutionary biology developed one of the possible conceptual frameworks for the consideration of such complexity. Natural selection is defined as a two-stage process, emerging out of sexual combination and random mutation, which produces variation that is independent of adaptive advantage and selective pressure. Then there is a second process, natural selection by external constraints – there are internal and external causes of evolution, and they are independent and parallel. Charles Darwin himself did not know enough about genetic evolution to be able to draw this conclusion, but he established the basis for this new science, and the later interpretation of Gregor Mendel's experiments provided the missing link in the theory.

It is relevant to notice that, eight years after the publication of *The Origin of the Species* in 1859, Darwin was challenged by statistical wisdom. Jenkins, a physicist from Glasgow, argued that it would be highly improbable that variation could overcome the conservative effects of inheritance, and that normally a regression to the mean would operate after mutation, imposing a conservative evolution of the transmission of traits.

Francis Galton, who shared this view of the role of the regression to the mean, argued nevertheless that discontinuous variation was still possible. Darwin, himself, held the same view: small changes could be positively selected, through a slow process of cumulative changes, *natura non facit saltum* – had he known genetics, he would be able to prove that no regression to the mean were possible.

It was in this framework that two mathematical biologists, R.A. Fisher and a Cambridge professor, Udny Yule (1927), investigated evolution and developed a number of techniques to assess change and mutation, such as the analysis of variance. Fisher did not appeal to indeterminacy or exogenous stochasticity; he simply considered a multiplicity of causes to determine mutation and the play of adaptation and selection. As a consequence, order, or necessity, and disorder, or chance, were conceptualized as parts of the same universe of determination. In particular, the understanding of dynamic processes of evolution with inherent stochasticity, the consideration of the characteristics of populations and not just of samples, and the description of these universes using non-parametric methods, are being developed by ecology and may provide insightful inspiration for social sciences, given the centrality of the same type of problems: evolution through time and complexity emerging out of interaction among agents.

My argument is that the very concept of *error* is pivotal for this appropriation and learning. In fact, in economics, the 'error' lived through three major epochs. It was first defined as a measurement error, as in astronomy, claiming for economics the Laplacean certainty that physics was supposed to exhibit. This was too much and too scarce to interpret social processes, so then the 'error' was reconceptualized as a residual from the estimation of a model. Consequently, the notion of 'error' in economics was never stabilized but the physics envy was still present as the legitimate model for models. This explains the dogmatic interpretation of the 'residual' equating the 'error', provided that an authoritative law describes the universe. But the law itself is the problem, since general equilibrium excludes change, and therefore the residual is necessarily treated as a 'perturbation', or 'shock' – an external impact on the equilibrating system, the third major interpretation of the 'error'.

Economists never agreed upon these three interpretations, but the last one tended to dominate. Frisch rejected the comparison of economics to other sciences able to deliver controlled experiments, and rejected as a consequence the assumptions about the sample, denying probability altogether. Koopmans assumed probability just as a simplifying assumption with no necessary ontological statement. Tinbergen used but suspected these analytical tools. Haavelmo was indeed the first to assume stochasticity as the nature of economic behaviour, but accepted, essentially for computational reasons, as other Cowles researchers did after him, the framework of general equilibrium as a convenient representation of this system of behaviour. This, of course, had a tragic implication, since in the context of Walrasian economics no change is possible except from outside the economic system.

In biological evolution, instead, errors arise from random mutations, and are selected in the interplay of social and natural forces. Exogenous and endogenous stochasticity are interdependent and, once a mutation is selected, the 'error' may generate a path-dependent trajectory of change. The *error* is therefore part of a construction of change: this implies a strong ontological claim on the nature of evolution. The population can be understood following the rules of the game: replication, variation, selection. One may wonder whether this identification of rules as a privileged tool for understanding dynamic processes is not an alternative for investigating social evolution, populations, agents and institutions.

NOTES

1. This chapter was presented at the Manchester conference of the Brisbane Club, 5–7 July 2002. I thank Stan Metcalfe, John Foster and other participants for their comments.
2. There was an important exchange of views between Francis Galton, the British promoter of positivism and a cousin of Darwin, and Alfred Wallace, the co-founder of modern biology. Galton argued that there is an immanent structure of order, that of the normal law: 'I know of scarcely anything so apt to impress the imagination as the wonderful form of cosmic order expressed by the "law of frequency of errors"(quoted in Peters, 1994, p. 14). The law . . . reigns with serenity and in complete self-effacement amidst the wildest confusion. The larger the mob, and the greater the apparent anarchy, the more perfect is its sway. It is the supreme law of Unreason. Whenever a large sample of chaotic elements are taken in hand and marshalled in the order of their magnitude, an unsuspected and most beautiful form of regularity proves to have been latent so long'. In contrast, Wallace argued that the attributed stable structure of order is suspect, given the creation of variation.
3. Gauss claimed in 1809 that he had used the OLS method since 1795.
4. Haavelmo also discussed the technical possibility of this approach: 'No necessity of independence of observations, it is necessary that the observations should be independent and that they should all follow the same one-dimensional probability law. It is sufficient to assume that the whole set of, say *n*, observations may be considered as one observation of *n* variables (or a "sample point") following an *n*-dimensional joint probability law, the existence of which may be purely hypothetical. Then, one can test hypotheses regarding this joint probability law, and draw inferences as to its possible form, by means of one sample point (in *n* dimensions)' (Preface to 1944, p. ii).
5. Ekeland concludes that the existence and relevance of chance does not necessarily lead to a probabilistic framework for modern statistics: 'The great discovery of these last years, in fact, is that statistics can function perfectly well without chance. The spread of computer techniques in management has led to the accumulation of enormous masses of data in all areas, and their simple classification, not to mention their interpretation, poses considerable problems. Traditional statistical methods such as factorial analysis are available to do this, but new methods of automatic classification and of data analysis have been developed which still call themselves statistics but do not rely on probabilistic models' (Ekeland 1993, p. 167).

REFERENCES

Aldrich, J. (1987), 'Jevons as a statistician: the role of probability', *The Manchester School of Economic and Social Studies*, **55**, 233–56.

Ekeland, I. (1993), *The Broken Dice – And Other Mathematical Tales of Chance*, Chicago: Chicago University Press.

Epstein, R. (1987), *A History of Econometrics*, Amsterdam: North-Holland.

Fisher, I. (1925), 'Our unstable dollar and the so-called business cycle', *Journal of the American Statistical Association*, **20**, 181–91.

Frisch, R. (1933), 'Propagation problems and impulse problems in dynamic economics', in K. Koch (ed.), *Economic Essays in Honour of Gustav Cassel*, London: Frank Cass, pp. 171–205.

Frisch, R. (1938), 'On Tinbergen', reprinted in D. Hendry and M. Morgan (eds), (1995).

Goldberger, A. (1991), *A Course in Econometrics*, Amsterdam: North-Holland.

Greene, W. (1993), *Econometric Analysis*, New York: Macmillan.

Griffiths, W., R. Carter Hill and G. Judge (1993), *Learning and Practicing Econometrics*, New York: Wiley.

Haavelmo, T. (1943), 'Statistical implications of a system of simultaneous equations', reprinted in D.F. Hendry and M.S. Morgan (eds), 1995, pp. 454–63.

Haavelmo, T. (1944), 'The probability approach in econometrics', *Econometrica*, **12**, supplement, 1–118.

Hendry, D. and M. Morgan (eds) (1995), *The Foundations of Econometric Analysis*, Cambridge: Cambridge University Press.

Johnston, J. (1987), *Econometric Methods*, New York: McGraw-Hill.

Judge, G., R. Carter Hill, W. Griffiths, H. Lutkepohl and T.-C. Lee (1988), *Introduction to the Theory and Practice of Econometrics*, New York: Wiley.

Klein, J. (1997), *Statistical Visions in Time – A History of Time Series Analysis, 1662–1938*, Cambridge: Cambridge University Press.

Koopmans, T.C. (1937), *Linear Regression of Economic Time Series*, Haarlem: Erven Bohn.

Koopmans, T.C. (1957), *Three Essays on the State of Economic Science*, New York: McGraw-Hill.

Legendre, A.-M. (1805), *Nouvelles Méthodes pour la détermination des orbites des comètes* (New Methods for the Determination of Orbits of Comets), Paris: Courcier.

Louçã, F. (1999), 'Intriguing pendula: founding metaphors in the analysis of economic fluctuations', *Cambridge Journal of Economics*, **25** (1), 25–55.

Maddala, G.S. (1992), *Introduction to Econometrics*, New York: Macmillan.

Maxwell, J.C. (1876), 'Does the progress of physical science tend to give any advantage to the opinion of necessity (or determinism) over that of contingency of events and the freedom of will', reprinted in W. Garnett (1882), *The Life of James Clark Maxwell*, London: Macmillan, pp. 434–44.

Morgan, M. (1990), *The History of Econometric Ideas*, Cambridge: Cambridge University Press.

Peters, E. (1994), *Fractal Market Analysis*, New York: Wiley.

Poincaré, H. (1908), *Science et méthode* (Science and Method), Paris: Flammarion.

Slutsky, E. [1927] (1937), 'The summation of random causes as the source of cyclic processes', *Econometrica*, **5**, 105–46.

Stigler, S. (1986), *The History of Statistics: The Measurement of Uncertainty Before 1900*, Cambridge, MA: Harvard University Press.

Tinbergen, J. (1939), *Statistical Testing of Business Cycle Theories*, Geneva: League of Nations, Economic Intelligence Service.

Tinbergen, J. (1990), 'The specification of error terms', in M. Velupillai (ed.), *Nonlinear and Multisectoral Macrodynamics*, Velupillai, NY: New York University Press, pp. 201–6.

Yule, U. (1927), 'On a method of investigating periodicities in disturbed series', *Philosophical Transactions of the Royal Society*, Series A, **226**, 267–98.

8. Technological and economic mobility in large German manufacturing firms

Uwe Cantner and Jens J. Krüger[1]

INTRODUCTION

The analyses reported in this chapter refer to the relationship between firm performance on the one hand and firm and industry evolution on the other. The empirical literature on this so-called industrial dynamics starts its analyses from a number of stylized facts related to structure and structural change (see Dosi et al. 1997). Among those structural factors, of considerable importance is the heterogeneity or asymmetry of firms which suggests a strongly idiosyncratic element in the technological performance of firms on the one hand and their economic performance on the other. The dynamics and evolution of an industry is then viewed as the result of these different heterogeneities over time.

There is some confusion in the recent literature on industrial dynamics about the amount of persistence or variability of certain variables like market shares or productivity measures over time. On the one hand, empirical studies such as those of Geroski and Toker (1996) on market shares or Jensen and McGuckin (1997) on relative labour productivity found considerable persistence of those measures. On the other hand, studies by Davies and Geroski (1997) or Mazzucato and Semmler (1999) concluded that market shares are rather unstable. Using patent data as measures of innovative activity in a statistical duration analysis, Geroski et al. (1997) conclude that very few firms innovate persistently over longer periods of time. The approach taken by Cefis and Orsenigo (2001) is most closely related to that used in this chapter. They estimate Markov chain transition matrices with patent data and find that the degree of persistence of innovative activities is not very high, but also point to the fact that there is considerable persistence in the sense that great innovators and non-innovators are likely to remain in their respective states.

Most of this empirical work either uses regression estimates to discover the determining factors of structural change or focuses completely on descriptive measures of the evolution of the shape of the distribution. In this chapter we adopt a different line of research in that we abstract from the shape of the distribution and the determinants of changes therein. We want to investigate the dynamics of differential changes that are present under the distribution (so-called intra-distribution dynamics) and therefore employ two methods that are capable of visualizing or quantifying the amount of such intra-distribution mobility. The first method relies on the concept of Salter curves, developed by Salter (1960). These represent the ranking of observations (characterizing the structure) and allow us to judge the extent of mobility within this ranking by comparing the Salter curves pertaining to different periods. The second method supplements the graphical Salter curve approach by quantifying the extent of mobility through the calculation of mobility indices which map the information of a Markov transition matrix into a scalar measure (Shorrocks 1978; Geweke et al. 1986). This approach also gives us the opportunity to test whether certain differences in mobility are significant in a statistical sense.

The plan of the chapter is as follows. In the next section, the data and the methodology used to measure total factor productivity are described. This is followed by a section containing the results on mobility obtained by Salter curves. As a quantitative measure of mobility, the following section introduces mobility indices based on Markov chains and reports the results we achieved using this method. Statistical significance of these results is explored through an application of bootstrapping in the penultimate section. Finally, the chapter concludes with some interpretations.

DATA AND PRODUCTIVITY MEASUREMENT

The data used in our analysis refer to a sample of large quoted German manufacturing firms observed over the 1981–93 period. Each firm is assigned to one of 11 industries: chemicals, electronics, precision mechanics/optics, plastics and rubber, machinery, automobiles, iron and steel, paper and board, construction, beverages and textiles. The data we use are all drawn from the balance sheets and the annual reports of the respective firms. For the determination of the productivity scores we use a model with a single output variable and the inputs labor, capital and material. Labour is measured in effective hours worked, capital is computed by the perpetual inventory method using data of investment and assuming a technical rate of depreciation, materials is the deflated gains-and-loss position 'raw materials and supply'. For the output the deflated sum of 'total sales', 'inventory changes' and 'internally used firm services' from the profit and loss accounts is computed. This output variable is also used to compute the firms' respective (real) output shares.

For the determination of the technological performance we apply a non-parametric measure of total factor productivity, a procedure discussed in much more detail in Cantner and Hanusch (2001). Applications of this approach can be found in a number of other papers (see, for example, Bernard et al. 1996; Cantner et al. 1996; Cantner and Westermann 1998; Krüger et al. 2000). Since a more detailed discussion of the procedure is contained in the above-cited papers we provide only a brief sketch in the following.

The approach attempts to determine the heterogeneous technological performances of firms that belong to the same industry. By applying linear programming, a so-called best-practice technology frontier function is determined. For this purpose data for the real input factors and the real outputs are used. The non-parametric nature of the method allows us to treat each firm as producing with a Leontief production function which may be quite different from the production functions of the other firms and is also permitted to change from year to year. The respective linear programme for a specific firm l can be compactly stated in matrix form:

$$\min \theta_l - \varepsilon \mathbf{e}^T \mathbf{s}^+ - \varepsilon \mathbf{e}^T \mathbf{s}^-$$

subject to:

$$\mathbf{Y}\boldsymbol{\lambda} - \mathbf{s}^- = \mathbf{y}_l$$
$$\theta_l \mathbf{x}_l - \mathbf{X}\boldsymbol{\lambda} - \mathbf{s}^+ = 0$$
$$\boldsymbol{\lambda}, \mathbf{s}^+, \mathbf{s}^- \geq 0$$

θ_l is the scalar productivity score of firm l with $\theta_l \in (0,1]$. A productivity score $\theta_l = 1$ is obtained if firm l is best practice and $\theta_l < 1$ indicates that the firm is below best practice. $\mathbf{s}^+$ and $\mathbf{s}^-$ are excess input and output slacks, respectively, $\mathbf{e}^T$ is a conforming vector of ones and ε is a so-called non-archimedian constant which is necessary to identify cases where firms are determined as best-practice although they obviously are not fully efficient.[2] $\mathbf{Y}$ and $\mathbf{X}$ denote the matrices of all n firms' outputs and inputs, respectively, in rows. $\mathbf{y}_l$ and $\mathbf{x}_l$ are the vectors of firm l's outputs and inputs. $\boldsymbol{\lambda}$ is a vector which contains the respective weights of the firms among the n that serve as the reference points against which the productivity of firm l is evaluated.

For measuring the economic performance of firms we refer to an output measure, the so-called output share which is the share of output of firm l

in the total output of the firms in the respective industry in a specific year. In order to make this measure comparable in construction to the measure of relative productivity we normalize it by dividing the output share of firm l by the largest output share in firm l's industry in the same period. Consequently, like the productivity scores the normalized output shares are bounded in the interval $(0,1]$ where the upper bound is secured to be realized by at least one firm.

Table 8.1 states for each industry some descriptive statistics with respect to the productivity scores and the normalized output shares. The last column gives information about the number of firms in each industry. From Table 8.1 we obtain the eye-catching result that the coefficient of variation (*CoeffVar* in the table, calculated as the standard deviation divided by the arithmetic mean) is substantially higher for the output shares of the different industries as compared with the productivity scores. This means that the distribution of the output shares is more dispersed than the distribution of the productivity scores, and this may be caused by higher fluctuations. But since the coefficient of variation (as a measure of dispersion) is more a measure of the shape of the distribution rather than a measure of intra-distributional change, a more dispersed distribution may also be the result of larger heterogeneity of the sample, which is totally consistent with a scenario of unaltered positions of the observations relative to one another. To abstract from the shape of the distribution and to focus on the amount of intra-distributional change we subsequently employ two different methods that are capable of visualizing

Table 8.1 Descriptive statistics

Industry	Productivity scores		Normalized output shares		#Firms
	Mean	*CoeffVar*	Mean	*CoeffVar*	
Chemicals	0.79	0.18	0.12	1.86	52
Electronics	0.77	0.18	0.07	2.46	36
Precision mechanics/optics	0.95	0.07	0.26	1.31	11
Plastics and rubber	0.88	0.13	0.21	1.28	21
Machinery	0.82	0.15	0.15	1.42	83
Automobiles	0.95	0.06	0.19	1.46	15
Iron and steel	0.85	0.12	0.17	1.44	37
Paper and board	0.90	0.11	0.39	0.82	13
Construction	0.93	0.07	0.22	1.30	22
Beverages	0.78	0.17	0.16	1.23	62
Textiles	0.81	0.16	0.26	1.03	40

or quantifying the amount of intra-distributional change, which we will simply call mobility.

SALTER CURVES

To visualize the amount of mobility in the productivity scores and the output shares we use the concept of Salter curves, named after their first use in a productivity context by Salter (1960). A Salter curve depicts the variable under examination after sorting the observations of this variable in a descending order. A visual impression of the heterogeneity in the sample can then easily be obtained from the slope of the Salter curve. A larger (negative) slope represents a more heterogeneous sample whereas complete homogeneity would result in a horizontal Salter curve. Salter curves of subsequent periods are plotted with the firms sorted in the same order as the firms of the first period so that regions of decreasing or increasing heterogeneity can be identified by looking where the Salter curve of a later period lies above or below the Salter curve of the first period.

In Figures 8.1 and 8.2 the first-period Salter curve is given by the solid line, where we take the mean of the productivity scores (respectively output shares) over the 1981–85 period as the variable under examination. The Salter curves for the means of the subsequent periods, 1985–89 and 1989–93, are drawn by the dashed and dotted lines, respectively. In both cases it is important to keep in mind that the observations are still sorted in the order of the first period (1981–85). Now we can easily see where heterogeneity increases and where it decreases compared to the first period. In regions of the plot where a Salter curve is below that of the preceding period firm heterogeneity has been increasing, and in regions where the Salter curve of the subsequent period lies above that of the preceding period heterogeneity has been decreasing. The magnitude of the deviations of subsequent period Salter curves can therefore be interpreted as a visualization of the amount of mobility in the sample with respect to the variable under consideration.

Figure 8.1 presents the Salter curves for the productivity scores. They show the development of the heterogeneity of the firms with respect to their technological performance. For the chemicals, electronics, paper and board, beverages and textiles industries we find that the technological heterogeneity of the firms has increased since the more recent Salter curves are (by and large) below the former ones. A contrariwise development is found for precision mechanics/optics, plastics and rubber, machinery, automobiles, iron and steel, and construction. In these cases, the Salter curves of the more recent periods are mainly above those of the later periods.

Figure 8.2 depicts the respective Salter curves for the output shares. First of all we recognize that the changes in the Salter curves here are of a much lower magnitude compared to the ones observed for the productivity scores. Thus, in general we find that the Salter curves in Figure 8.2 are much closer to one another than in Figure 8.1 which points to a more stable development of the normalized output shares than of the productivity scores. Concerning the development of heterogeneity in normalized output shares we see that for electronics, plastics and rubber, machinery, textiles and to a lesser degree for chemicals as well as iron and steel there is a tendency for an increase. Contrariwise for precision mechanics/optics, automobiles, paper and board, construction and beverages the heterogeneity in the output shares has decreased.

Besides the differences between industries, we can easily apprehend from Figures 8.1 and 8.2 that in our sample of large German manufacturing firms economic mobility (measured by the output shares) is substantially smaller than technological mobility (measured by the productivity scores). This central result is valid for every one of the 11 industries considered in this study and has also been established by Geroski (1998) for a sample of 280 large quoted UK companies over the 1972–82 period.

MOBILITY INDICES

Salter curves are a very useful instrument for visualizing the amount of mobility in a panel, but since they rely on the experience and discriminatory power of the viewer a comparison of the results with a more objective quantitative measure of mobility would be valuable. One class of such measures are mobility indices based on the estimated transition matrix of a Markov chain.[3]

The basis for the definition of a mobility index is the transition matrix of a Markov chain (see Norris (1998) for a book-length overview of Markov chains). The homogeneous first-order Markov chain we use in this chapter is a stochastic process in discrete time $\{x_t\}_{t=1,2,\ldots}$ which can assume n different states $x_t \in I = \{1, \ldots, n\}$ and where the movements between the states are controlled by a $n \times n$ transition matrix $\mathbf{P}$ with elements defined by:

$$p_{ij} = \Pr(x_t = j | x_{t-1} = i); \; i, j \in I \quad \text{where} \quad \sum_{j \in I} p_{ij} = 1 \quad \forall i \in I.$$

To understand how a mobility index works it is essential to recall that large elements on the main diagonal of the transition matrix are equivalent to a high propensity of staying in a certain state in the next period, whereas large off-diagonal elements indicate a high propensity of moving from

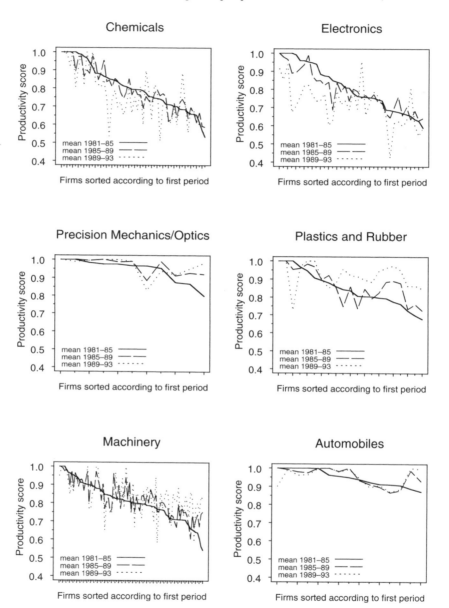

Figure 8.1   Salter curves for productivity scores

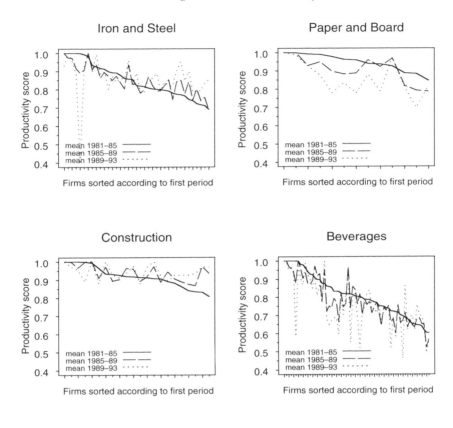

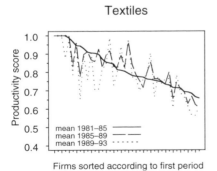

Figure 8.1 (continued)

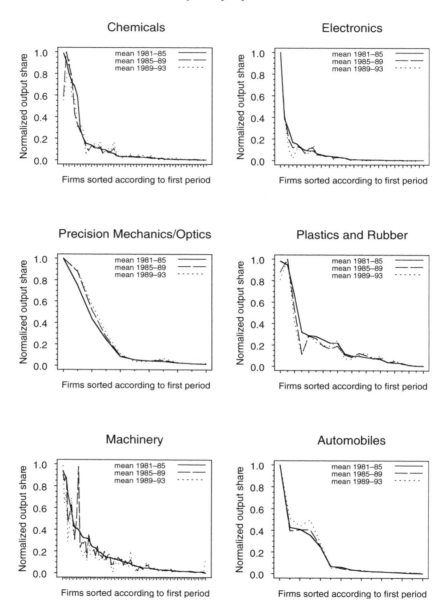

Figure 8.2   Salter curves for normalized output shares

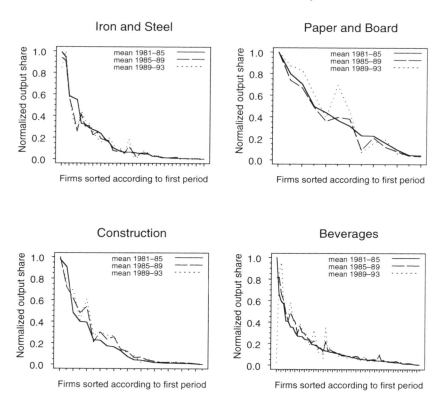

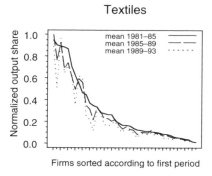

Figure 8.2 (continued)

one state to another between two periods. The aim of mobility indices (see Shorrocks 1978; Geweke et al. 1986) is to weigh the magnitude of the off-diagonal elements of a transition matrix against the magnitude of the diagonal elements in a consistent manner. Precisely, mobility indices are continuous real scalar valued functions $M(\cdot) \in [0,1]$ over the set of transition matrices that provide a ranking of transition matrices with respect to mobility in that $\mathbf{P}_1$ is said to be more mobile than $\mathbf{P}_2$ if $M(\mathbf{P}_1) > M(\mathbf{P}_2)$.

One natural requirement which is imposed on mobility indices is that the identity matrix will be ranked lower than any other transition matrix, $M(\mathbf{I}) = 0$, since it represents a Markov chain that is characterized by complete immobility (in this case the probability of staying in a certain state is exactly equal to one for all states). Additional criteria that a mobility index should fulfil are stated in Shorrocks (1978, pp. 1014f.). Before we describe the particular examples of mobility indices we use in this chapter it should be noted that 'no single mobility statistic has the minimum requirements regarded as essential' (ibid., p. 1023). Following this advice we consider various mobility indices simultaneously in order to obtain a valid summary picture of what is going on in the data with respect to the specific aims of our analysis.

The particular mobility indices we use in this chapter are stated in the notation of Geweke et al. (1986, pp. 1409f.) and discussed subsequently:

$$M_B(\mathbf{P}) = \sum_{i \in I} \pi_i \sum_{j \in I} p_{ij} |i - j|$$

$$M_U(\mathbf{P}) = n \sum_{i \in I} \pi_i (1 - p_{ii}) / (n - 1)$$

$$M_P(\mathbf{P}) = [n - \text{trace}(\mathbf{P})] / (n - 1)$$

$$M_E(\mathbf{P}) = \left[n - \sum_{i \in I} |\lambda_i(\mathbf{P})| \right] / (n - 1)$$

$$M_2(\mathbf{P}) = 1 - |\lambda_2(\mathbf{P})|$$

$$M_D(\mathbf{P}) = 1 - |\det(\mathbf{P})|.$$

$M_B(\cdot)$ is called Bartholomew's index and has the feature of giving larger changes a higher weight than smaller changes. For its calculation the vector of stationary probabilites $\boldsymbol{\pi} = (\pi_1, \ldots, \pi_n)'$ with $\boldsymbol{\pi} = \mathbf{P}\boldsymbol{\pi}$ is needed. Also based on stationary probabilites is the index $M_U(\cdot)$ which is simply defined as the unconditional probability of leaving the current state, scaled by $n/(n-1) \cdot M_P(\cdot)$ is the trace index introduced by Shorrocks (1978, p. 1017). It is the inverse of the harmonic mean of expected durations of remaining in each state, scaled by $n/(n-1)$. The eigenvalue index $M_E(\cdot)$, where $\lambda_i(\mathbf{P})$ is the ith largest eigenvalue of $\mathbf{P}$ and $|\lambda_i(\mathbf{P})|$ is its modulus, is positively related to the average rate of convergence of the chain towards its ergodic limit. It is identical to the trace index in the case of all eigenvalues positive and real since the trace of a matrix is the sum of its eigenvalues. Since Markov transition matrices always have one eigenvalue equal to unity and all other eigenvalues not larger than one in modulus, the second largest eigenvalue dominates the asymptotic rate of convergence of the chain and this fact is captured by the second eigenvalue index $M_2(\cdot)$. Finally, the determinant index $M_D(\cdot)$ is related to the average magnitude of the moduli of the eigenvalues originating from the equality of the determinant and the product of all eigenvalues.

Tables 8.2 and 8.3 report the results of the mobility index calculations for output share and productivity measures, respectively. All mobility indices are based on transition matrices estimated consistently by maximum likelihood which calculates each transition probability estimate $\hat{p}_{ij}$ by the number of transitions from state i to state j divided by the number of times the chain leaves state i (Norris 1998, p. 56). The results are given for a four-state Markov chain where the states are determined by fractiles so that the observations of the initial period are uniformly distributed across the states.

In Table 8.2 we see that the rankings of the industries according to the different mobility indices with respect to the productivity scores are quite consistent with one another. Industries that show consistently low productivity mobility are chemicals, electronics and beverages. In contrast, machinery, iron and steel, paper and board, and construction, are characterized by relatively high productivity mobility, irrespective of the choice of

Table 8.2 Mobility indices for productivity scores

Industry	M_B	M_U	M_P	M_E	M_2	M_D	#Firms
Chemicals	0.27	0.34	0.35	0.35	0.11	0.77	52
Electronics	0.29	0.35	0.35	0.35	0.18	0.76	36
Precision mechanics/optics	0.27	0.27	0.68	0.65	0.33	0.99	11
Plastics and rubber	0.38	0.46	0.47	0.47	0.20	0.91	21
Machinery	0.49	0.55	0.55	0.55	0.30	0.93	83
Automobiles	0.29	0.35	0.64	0.64	0.23	1.00	15
Iron and steel	0.47	0.54	0.59	0.59	0.25	0.99	37
Paper and board	0.44	0.41	0.66	0.63	0.24	0.99	13
Construction	0.75	0.69	0.76	0.76	0.42	1.00	22
Beverages	0.27	0.32	0.40	0.40	0.12	0.84	62
Textiles	0.32	0.39	0.40	0.40	0.15	0.83	40

Empirical perspectives

Table 8.3   Mobility indices for normalized output shares

Industry	M_B	M_U	M_P	M_E	M_2	M_D	#Firms
Chemicals	0.05	0.07	0.09	0.09	0.04	0.24	52
Electronics	0.03	0.04	0.08	0.08	0.02	0.24	36
Precision mechanics/optics	0.07	0.09	0.12	0.12	0.02	0.33	11
Plastics and rubber	0.14	0.17	0.17	0.17	0.07	0.44	21
Machinery	0.12	0.16	0.16	0.16	0.05	0.42	83
Automobiles	0.08	0.11	0.16	0.16	0.03	0.43	15
Iron and steel	0.11	0.15	0.15	0.15	0.05	0.40	37
Paper and board	0.05	0.07	0.13	0.13	0.02	0.36	13
Construction	0.08	0.09	0.13	0.13	0.04	0.35	22
Beverages	0.07	0.09	0.10	0.10	0.02	0.27	62
Textiles	0.10	0.13	0.17	0.17	0.04	0.43	40

the mobility index. The remaining industries are in between, with contradictory results from different mobility indices in some cases. Consistent with the findings of Cefis and Orsenigo (2001) which are based on patent data, we also find that persistence is slightly higher (because mobility is slightly lower) in chemicals than in electronics and considerably higher in chemicals than in machinery.

Turning to the results for the output shares in Table 8.3 we also find a similar agreement of the different mobility indices with respect to the ranking of the industries. Here plastics and rubber, machinery, paper and board, and construction are the industries with the largest amount of mobility. At the lower end we find chemicals, electronics, precision mechanics/ optics and beverages which are quite immobile, although we have to admit that the mobility differences across the industries are substantially lower than they are in the case of the productivity scores.

Directly comparing the magnitudes of the mobility indices in Tables 8.2 and 8.3, we find that the mobility indices of the productivity scores are at least twice as high as the respective mobility indices of the normalized output shares. Thus, consistent with the results of the Salter curves, technological mobility is much higher than economic mobility across all the industries considered.

The calculations of the mobility indices are robust in various respects. First, results obtained using a five-state Markov chain instead of the four-state chain show no qualitative differences. Second, using a fractile Markov chain where the states are determined separately in every period according to the rule we employed for the initial period (see Quah 1996, pp. 150f.) even strengthens the central result of a much larger magnitude of mobility in productivity scores as compared to mobility in output shares. Third, using labour productivity instead of total factor productivity again leads – with one exception – to the same conclusion. Fourth, we are not able to control for mergers of firms in our balanced panel with outside firms. We do not think that mergers affect our conclusions significantly since mergers tend to bias output share mobility upward and have an uncertain (but possibly increasing) effect on productivity mobility.

DIFFERENCE-OF-MEANS TESTS

One weakness of the above comparisons is that uncertainty in the estimation is not considered and therefore the differences between the mobility indices of the productivity indices and the output shares may be due to estimation error. Schluter (1998) derives the asymptotic distribution of the trace index M_P on which statistical tests can be based. This distribution is normal with mean $\mu = (n - \Sigma_{i \in I} p_{ii})/(n - 1)$ and variance $\sigma^2 = (n - 1)^{-2} \cdot \Sigma_{i \in I} p_{ii}(1 - p_{ii})/n_i$ where n denotes again the number of states, p_{ii} are the diagonal elements of the transition matrix and n_i denotes the number of times the chain leaves state i. By the properties of the normal distribution the asymptotic density of the difference of trace index of the productivity scores of an industry, M_P^p, and the trace index of the output shares of the same industry, M_P^o, is given by:

$$M_P^p - M_P^o \sim N(\mu_p - \mu_o, \sigma_p^2 + \sigma_o^2 - 2\rho\sigma_p\sigma_o)$$

where $M_P^p \sim N(\mu_p, \sigma_p^2)$, $M_P^o \sim N(\mu_o, \sigma_o^2)$ and ρ denotes the Bravais–Pearson correlation coefficient of M_P^p and M_P^o. Based on this result it is evident that the statistic:

$$s = \frac{\hat{M}_P^p - \hat{M}_P^o}{\sqrt{\hat{\sigma}_p^2 + \hat{\sigma}_o^2 - 2\hat{\rho}\hat{\sigma}_p\hat{\sigma}_o}}$$

is a standard normal variate under the null hypothesis $H_0: M_P^p = M_P^o$. Estimates for the means and variances of the trace indices are easily calculated, but the remaining difficulty with this result is that no estimate for the correlation coefficient ρ of the trace indices is available. A possible way to proceed is to assume independence and simply set $\hat{\rho} = 0$ which leads to a test statistic:

$$s_0 = \frac{\hat{M}_P^p - \hat{M}_P^o}{\sqrt{\hat{\sigma}_p^2 + \hat{\sigma}_o^2}}.$$

Since we really want to test the hypothesis $H_0 : M_P^p \leq M_P^o$ which is rejected if s is larger than the $1 - \alpha$ quantile of the standard normal distribution, a superior solution is to assume the value of ρ that leads to the smallest value of s, all other things constant. In the present case this amounts to assuming that the trace indices are perfectly negatively correlated, that is $\hat{\rho} = -1$, and basing the difference-of-means test on the statistic:

$$s' = \frac{\hat{M}_P^p - \hat{M}_P^o}{\sqrt{\hat{\sigma}_p^2 + \hat{\sigma}_o^2 + 2\hat{\sigma}_p\hat{\sigma}_o}}.$$

Thus, the null hypothesis $H_0 : M_P^p \leq M_P^o$ is rejected in favour of $H_1 : M_P^p > M_P^o$ if s' is larger than the $1 - \alpha$ quantile of the standard normal distribution. This procedure assumes the most unfavourable case and therefore secures that if the null is rejected based on the test statistic s' it would also be rejected if we were able to compute s, since $s' \geq s$ irrespective of which value $\hat{\rho}$ takes on in its range $[-1,1]$.

Applying the procedure outlined above to the differences of the trace indices for the productivity score and the output shares of each industry separately, we obtain the results that are summarized in Table 8.4. Columns two to four contain the differences of the trace indices, the test statistic s_0 under the independence assumption and the test statistics s'. Comparison of the statistics s_0 and s' shows clearly that $s_0 \geq s'$ holds in any case. The p-values of the difference-of-means tests in the fifth column are based on

Table 8.4 Difference-of-means tests for the trace index M_P

Industry	$M_P^p - M_P^o$	s_0	s'	p-value	#Firms
Chemicals	0.2623	9.8479	7.1917	0.0000	52
Electronics	0.2697	8.3445	6.1282	0.0000	36
Precision mechanics/optics	0.5637	6.1638	4.7311	0.0000	11
Plastics and rubber	0.3047	6.3932	4.5883	0.0000	21
Machinery	0.3884	15.4455	11.1556	0.0000	83
Automobiles	0.4777	9.8958	7.0028	0.0000	15
Iron and steel	0.4416	11.4899	8.3678	0.0000	37
Paper and board	0.5286	8.5145	6.0958	0.0000	13
Construction	0.6268	13.0429	9.3394	0.0000	22
Beverages	0.3017	11.6831	8.5819	0.0000	62
Textiles	0.2378	7.0232	5.0201	0.0000	40

Note: The p-values are the marginal significance levels of a rejection of $H_0 : M_P^p \leq M_P^o$ in favour of $H_1 : M_P^p > M_P^o$ based on the test statistic s'.

the test statistic s'. Large values of s' correspond to low p-values and lead to a rejection of the null hypothesis. The results in the table show that for all industries, the null hypothesis that the mobility of the productivity scores is not larger than the mobility of the normalized output shares, is strongly rejected with p-values that are essentially zero. We also observe that the test statistics are larger for those industries where the trace indices are farther apart from one another and also for those with a larger number of firms. The same statement holds true for the eigenvalue index M_E which is identical to the trace index in all industries because all eigenvalues are real and positive so that the sum of the moduli of the eigenvalues is equal to the trace of the transition matrix.

Thus, we find that the differences of the mobility indices for the productivity scores and the output shares are not only quite large in magnitude but also significant in a formal statistical sense. This provides a further piece of evidence in favour of the hypothesis that the technological sphere is considerably more turbulent than the economic sphere and sharpens the conclusions obtained from the other mobility indices and the Salter curves.

INTERPRETATION AND FURTHER RESEARCH

To summarize, using two different approaches we have found a pattern of a much higher technological mobility (measured by the mobility of total factor productivity scores) as compared to economic mobility (measured by the mobility of output shares normalized by maximum output share in the respective industry) that is consistent across the large quoted firms of 11 industries in the German manufacturing sector. The differences between technological and economic mobility are large in magnitude although they are not significant in a statistical sense in all of the industries.

Two opposing forces are at work with respect to technological mobility. On the one hand we have the notion of success-breeds-success which implies a low degree of mobility. On the other, we have the notion of catching-up fuelled by the exploitation of advantages of relative backwardness and the notions of falling behind and of leapfrogging whose effects point to a high degree of mobility. Thus, if we interpret technological mobility as the result of the differential success of firms in the implementation of technological innovations our findings suggest that the tendency towards success-breeds-success is dominated by the other forces that promote turbulence with respect to productivity. With respect to economic mobility we can hypothesize mobility-reducing effects of the success-breeds-success phenomenon, possibly supported by the working of dynamic economies of scale, and mobility-enhancing effects of market competition. In that case we find a domination of the former bundle of forces.

Equally interesting is a classification of industries according to increasing/decreasing technological and economic heterogeneity based on the Salter curves. Although at the present stage of our analysis this is rather tentative, we can identify precision mechanics/optics, automobiles and construction as industries characterized by decreasing economic as well as technological heterogeneity. At the other extreme, chemicals, electronics and textiles can be identified as industries in which both economic and technological heterogeneity is increasing. The mixed cases comprise machinery, plastics and rubber, and iron and steel with increasing economic heterogeneity and decreasing technological heterogeneity, and paper and board, and beverages as cases with decreasing economic heterogeneity and increasing technological heterogeneity.

A theoretical model that may have the potential to explain these differential dynamics of technological and economic heterogeneity is the replicator dynamics model (see Metcalfe 1994). So one promising avenue for further research is to integrate the purely empirical findings regarding mobility reported in this chapter into the theoretical framework provided by the replicator dynamics model and its extensions. Such a connection of the technological sphere to the economic sphere would be extremely valuable, but this endeavour may prove quite difficult since the two spheres are very different with respect to the changes of heterogeneity. The technological sphere is characterized by a low coefficient of variation combined with high mobility and in the economic sphere matters are exactly reversed. Another line of research could focus on the differences in technological and economic mobility between the industries. Here, the bootstrapping approach might find another fruitful field of application.

NOTES

1. We thank the participants of the Economic Transformation in Europe (ETE) workshop in Jena (February 2002), the International Schumpeter Society Conference in Gainsville/Florida (March 2002) and the Brisbane Club meeting in Manchester (July 2002) for valuable suggestions on an earlier draft of the chapter.
2. On this issue see Cantner et al. (1996).
3. Applications of mobility indices in economics include among others Mancusi (2000) for quantifying mobility in technological specialization, Proudman and Redding (1998) and Redding (2001) for measuring mobility in international trade specialization and Quah (1996) for analysing regional output fluctuations in the US states.

REFERENCES

Bernard, J., U. Cantner and G. Westermann (1996), 'Technological leadership and variety – a data envelopment analysis for the French machinery industry', *Annals of Operations Research*, **68**, 361–77.

Cantner, U. and H. Hanusch (2001), 'Heterogeneity and evolutionary dynamics – empirical conception, findings and unresolved issues', in J. Foster and J.S. Metcalfe (eds), *Frontiers of Evolutionary Economics: Competition, Self-Organization and Innovation Policy*, Cheltenham, UK and Northampton, MA, USA: Edward Elgar, pp. 228–77.

Cantner, U. and G. Westermann (1998), 'Localized technological progress and industrial dynamics – an empirical approach', *Economics of Innovation and New Technology*, **6**, 121–45.

Cantner, U., H. Hanusch and G. Westermann (1996), 'Detecting technological performance and variety – an empirical approach to technological efficiency and dynamics', in E. Helmstädter and M. Perlman (eds), *Economic Dynamism: Analysis and Policy*, Ann Arbor, MI: University of Michigan Press, pp. 223–46.

Cefis, E. and L. Orsenigo (2001), 'The persistence of innovative activities: a cross-country and cross-sectors comparative analysis', *Research Policy*, **30**, 1139–58.

Davies, S.W. and P.A. Geroski (1997), 'Changes in concentration, turbulence, and the dynamics of market shares', *Review of Economics and Statistics*, **79**, 383–91.

Dosi, G., F. Malerba, O. Marsili and L. Orsenigo (1997), 'Industrial structures and dynamics: evidence, interpretations and puzzles', *Industrial and Corporate Change*, **6**, 3–24.

Geroski, P.A. (1998), 'An applied econometrician's view of large company performance', *Review of Industrial Organization*, **13**, 271–93.

Geroski, P.A. and S. Toker (1996), 'The turnover of market leaders in UK manufacturing industry, 1979–86', *International Journal of Industrial Organization*, **14**, 141–58.

Geroski, P.A., J. van Reenen and C.F. Walters (1997), 'How persistently do firms innovate?', *Research Policy*, **26**, 33–48.

Geweke, J., R.C. Marshall and G.A. Zarkin (1986), 'Mobility indices in continuous time Markov chains', *Econometrica*, **54**, 1407–23.

Jensen, J.B. and R.H. McGuckin (1997), 'Firm performance and evolution: empirical regularities in the US microdata', *Industrial and Corporate Change*, **6**, 25–47.

Krüger, J.J., U. Cantner and H. Hanusch (2000), 'Total factor productivity, the East Asian miracle and the world production frontier', *Weltwirtschaftliches Archiv*, **136**, 111–36.

Mancusi, M.L. (2000), 'The dynamics of technology in industrial countries', Working Paper no. 118, Centre for Research on Innovation and Internationalisation Processes (CESPRI).

Mazzucato, M. and W. Semmler (1999), 'Market share instability and stock price volatility during the industry life cycle: the US automobile industry', *Journal of Evolutionary Economics*, **9**, 67–96.

Metcalfe, J.S. (1994), 'Competition, Fisher's principle and increasing returns in the selection process', *Journal of Evolutionary Economics*, **4**, 327–46.

Norris, J.R. (1998), *Markov Chains*, Cambridge, MA: Cambridge University Press.

Proudman, J. and S. Redding (1998), 'Persistence and mobility in international trade', in J. Proudman and S. Redding (eds), *Openness and Growth*, London: Bank of England, ch. 2.

Quah, D. (1996), 'Aggregate and regional disaggregate fluctuations', *Empirical Economics*, **21**, 137–59.

Redding, S. (2001), 'Specialization dynamics', Working Paper, London School of Economics.

Salter, W.E.G. (1960), *Productivity and Technical Change*, Cambridge, MA: Cambridge University Press.

Schluter, C. (1998), 'Statistical inference with mobility indices', *Economics Letters*, **59**, 157–62.

Shorrocks, A.F. (1978), 'The measurement of mobility', *Econometrica*, **46**, 1013–24.

9. A conceptual framework to model long-run qualitative change in the energy system

Andreas Pyka, Bernd Ebersberger and Horst Hanusch[1]

INTRODUCTION

The energy-related industries are sectors where, compared to many other industries, extremely long time horizons are relevant for the strategic planning of the actors. On the one hand, the investment costs are extremely high and most often irreversible, that is, the power plants cannot be used for other purposes; on the other, the investment time for constructing new power plants and complementary activities such as the construction of distribution networks is also extremely protracted. Additionally, the influence of regulatory authorities as well as political actors is strong due to the specific industry history (that is, energy is considered to be of decisive national importance) and the strong interrelation with other economic and social activities (for example, environmental issues, transport and so on). Finally, technological development is often extremely costly as well as uncertain, which makes joint efforts between public and private actors necessary. Bearing in mind these specific industry characteristics, the energy sector seems to be of particular interest when it comes to the analysis of the long-run and technological-driven evolution of industries.

Although there is a rather long tradition in economics for studying the transformation of industries, starting at the beginning of the twentieth century with Joseph Schumpeter, Simon Kuznets and J.B. Clark, since the late 1950s this long-term view has been lost in the industrial economics literature. There are basically two reasons for this.

On the one hand, industrial economics was mainly embedded in the dominating neoclassical framework and its so-called structure–conduct–performance–paradigm (for example, Bain 1956). Due to the specific assumptions necessary for an analysis within the neoclassical framework, a process perspective including qualitative change and development was ignored. Instead, only the quantitative dimension of potential equilibrium states and its comparative static were considered. On the sector level this means that the analysis is restricted to long-run equilibria structures describing, for example, the number of firms in a particular industry without putting emphasis on those factors driving the emergence and maturation of industries. By restricting the analysis on the quantitative dimension, industrial economics implicitly confines itself to the analysis of a system characterized by a constant set of activities and proportional development, basically neglecting innovation processes and technological development.

On the other hand, since the early 1980s, the developing evolutionary strand within economics is responsible for a so-called 'Schumpeterian Renaissance' (for example, Giersch 1984). Within the evolutionary economics approach, it is argued that only by relaxing the strong assumptions of neoclassical economics can an understanding of long-run transformation processes within economies and, with this, of the sources of economic growth and qualitative change, be developed. Basically, instead of homogeneous and well-informed actors optimizing their profits, in evolutionary economics the analysis draws on heterogeneous populations of bounded rational actors which experimentally try to improve their situation or at least maintain the status quo. However, the respective tools allowing the consideration of these constitutive elements were not available from the beginning and first have to be developed.

In evolutionary economics, analysis is heavily supported by the tremendous development of and easy access to computational power within the last 30 years which has led to the widespread use of numerical approaches in almost all scientific disciplines. Nevertheless, while, for example, the engineering sciences focused on the applied use of simulation techniques from the very beginning, in the social sciences most of the early examples of numerical approaches were purely theoretical.

There are two reasons for this. First, since the middle of the twentieth century, starting with economics, equilibrium-oriented analytical techniques flourished and were developed to a highly sophisticated level. This led to the widely shared view that within the elegant and formal framework of linear analysis offered by neoclassical economics, the social sciences could reach a level of accuracy not previously thought to be possible.

Second, within the same period, new phenomena of structural change exerted a strong influence on the social and economic realms. Despite the mainstream neoclassical successes in shifting the social sciences to a more mathematical foundation, an increasing dissatisfaction with this approach emerged. For example, by the 1960s the benchmark of atomistic competition in neoclassical economics had already been replaced by the idea of monopolistic and oligopolistic structures under the heading of workable competition (for example, Scherer and Ross, 1990). A similar development emphasizing positive feedback effects and increasing returns to scale caused by innovation led to the attribute 'new' in macroeconomic growth theory in the 1980s (Romer 1990).

In addition to these stepwise renewals of mainstream methodology, an increasingly larger group is claiming that the general toolbox of economic theory, emphasizing rational behaviour and equilibrium, is no longer suitable for the analysis of complex social and economic changes. In a speech at the International Conference on Complex Systems organized by the New England Complex Systems Institute in 2000, Kenneth Arrow stated that until the 1980s the 'sea of truth' in economics lay in simplicity, whereas since then it has become recognized that the 'sea of truth lies in complexity'. Adequate tools have therefore to include the heterogeneous composition of agents (for example, Saviotti 1996), the possibility of multi-level feedback effects (for example, Cantner and Pyka 1998) and a realistic representation of dynamic processes in historical time (for example, Arthur 1988). These requirements are congruent with the possibilities offered by simulation approaches. Accordingly, it is not surprising that within economics the first numerical exercises were within evolutionary economics.

The first-generation simulation models were highly stylized and did not focus on empirical phenomena. Instead, they were designed to analyse the logic of dynamic economic and social processes, exploring the possibilities of complex systems behaviour. However, since the end of the 1990s, more and more specific simulation models that aim at particular empirically observed phenomena have been developed, focusing on the interaction of heterogeneous actors responsible for qualitative change and development processes. Modellers have had to wrestle with an unavoidable trade-off between the demands of a general theoretical approach and the descriptive accuracy required to model a particular phenomenon. A new class of simulation models has shown to be well adapted to this challenge, basically by shifting this trade-off outwards: so-called agent-based models are increasingly used for the modelling of socioeconomic developments.

Agent-based models in an evolutionary setting seems to be the adequate tool for the analysis of long-term qualitative developments as we can observe them in the energy-related industries. Our chapter deals with the design of a conceptual framework for such a model.[2] The next section is concerned with the importance of an analysis of qualitative development in general and it is shown that evolutionary economics offers an adequate framework for this. The following section then focuses on agent-based modelling as 'the' tool allowing endogenously caused development processes to be incorporated. The subsequent section deals with particular phenomena of qualitative change in the energy-related industries. In the penultimate section, the constitutive elements of an agent-based model of qualitative change in the energy sector are introduced. The final section closes the chapter with some conclusions and an outlook on further research.

QUALITATIVE CHANGE IN AN EVOLUTIONARY ECONOMICS PERSPECTIVE

When examining change and development processes within industrialized economies, economists usually focus their attention on the movement of certain variables that they consider to be a good description of the basic effects of economic growth and development. In mainstream economics the phenomenon of economic development is, for example, empirically analysed on the macroeconomic level as the improvement of total factor productivity in time which lowers prices and leads to the growth of incomes. Accordingly, most often the GDP per capita is used as an indicator describing economic development in a quantitative fashion. Although it is impressive to observe the growth of income in economies over a long time span (Figure 9.1), this indicator, due to its quantitative nature only, does not tell us about the structural and qualitative dimensions underlying

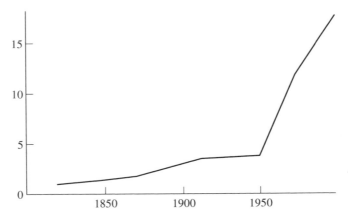

Figure 9.1   Germany's GDP over the last 200 years

economic development. This becomes even more obvious on the sectoral level where the analysis is most often restricted to a long-run equilibria structure describing, for example, the number of firms in a particular industry without putting emphasis on those factors driving the emergence and maturation of industries. By restricting their analysis on the quantitative dimension, the economic mainstream implicitly confines itself to the analysis of a system characterized by a constant set of activities, basically neglecting innovation processes.

However, in less orthodox economic approaches it is argued, and it is indeed also one of Schumpeter's major contributions, that economic development also includes prominently qualitative changes not only as an outcome but also as an essential ingredient which justifies us speaking of ongoing transformation processes. Qualitative change manifests itself basically via innovation of different categories (for example, social, legal, organizational) of which technological innovation very likely is among the most important ones. Qualitative change is the transformation of an economic system, characterized by a set of components and interactions, into another system with different components and different interrelationships (for example, Saviotti 1996). An analysis of qualitative change therefore necessarily has to include the actors, their activities and objects which are responsible for the ongoing economic development.

An example of the significance of qualitative changes can be found in Figure 9.2, which displays the development of employment shares of the primary, secondary and tertiary sectors in Germany for the same time interval as GDP per capita above. What strikes us immediately is that everything except a proportional growth of all sectors is taking place

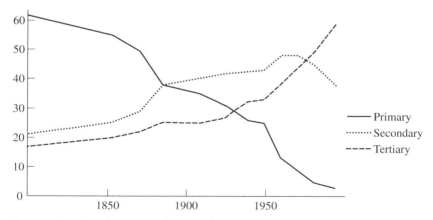

Figure 9.2   Development of sectoral employment in Germany

from 1800 to the 1990s. Instead, severe and radical changes underlie the transformation of the economic system observed in Figure 9.1. Of course there are many other variables, for example, the emergence of new industries, the increasing variety of different commodities available or the rate of introduction of new technologies, which also reflect the importance of the qualitative dimensions of economic development. By its very nature, the transformation of an economic system is a multi-faceted phenomenon. Accordingly, it is misleading to focus only on quantitative changes of the economy when analysing the driving factors of the transformation of economic systems over time. To better understand the mechanisms and dynamics behind the observed developments, one has to explicitly include the qualitative dimensions. To achieve this, in addition to the prevailing cost orientation, economic analysis also has to consider an important knowledge and learning orientation. The following subsections are concerned with the implications of this knowledge orientation, which can also be considered as the heart of the matter of evolutionary economics.

Knowledge-based Approach of Evolutionary Economics

It is beyond the scope of this contribution to discuss in detail the criticism brought forth by evolutionary economics with respect to assumptions underlying the mainstream economic reasoning. Extensive discussions can be found in, among others, Clark and Juma (1987), Silverberg (1988) and Dopfer (2001). For our purposes it is sufficient to mention three major points that evolutionary economists claim to be of outstanding importance in the discussion of economic development processes and which are incompatible with traditional economic approaches. These points are also constitutive for that strand of literature within evolutionary economics which is concerned with industry evolution and technological progress, namely the neo-Schumpeterian approach. Here, instead of the incentive orientation of neoclassical industrial economics, a knowledge orientation underlies the investigation of industries and innovation processes in particular. First of all, neo-Schumpeterian theory seeks to explain how innovations emerge and diffuse over time. A specific feature of these processes is uncertainty, which cannot be treated adequately by drawing on stochastic distributions referring to the concept of risk. Therefore, the assumption of perfect rationality, underlying traditional models cannot be maintained; instead the concepts of bounded and procedural rationality are invoked. Consequently, actors in neo-Schumpeterian models are characterized by incomplete knowledge bases and capabilities. Closely connected, the second point concerns the important role played by heterogeneity and variety. Due to the assumption of perfect rationality, in traditional models homogeneous actors and technologies are analysed. Heterogeneity as a source of learning and novelty is by and large neglected, or treated as a temporary deviation. Finally, the third point deals with the time dimension in which learning and the emergence of novelties take place. By their very nature, these processes are truly dynamic, meaning that they occur in historical time. The possibility of irreversibility, however, does not exist in the mainstream approaches, which rely on linearity and equilibrium.

Thus, traditional economic theories, summarized under the heading of incentive-based approaches, with their focus on cost-based and rational decisions only, exclude crucial aspects of actors' behaviours and interactions, which are influenced by a couple of factors lying by their very nature beyond the scope of these approaches. Although, of course cost–benefit calculations (with respect to innovation, itself a problematic activity) play an important role, the actors' behaviour is also influenced by several other factors such as learning, individual and collective motivation, trust and so on. It is the role of these factors that the knowledge-based approach of evolutionary economics explicitly takes into account.

By switching from the incentive-based perspective to the knowledge-based perspective, the neo-Schumpeterian approaches have realized a decisive change in the analysis of the transformation of economic systems. In this light the introduction of novelties mutate from optimal cost–benefit considerations to collective experimental and problem-solving processes (Eliasson 1991). The knowledge base of the actors is no longer perfect; instead, a gap opens up between the competences and the difficulties which are to be mastered (Heiner 1983) (C–D gap). There are two reasons for this C–D gap when it comes to innovation. On the one hand, technological uncertainty introduces errors and surprises; on the other, the very nature of knowledge avoids an unrestricted access. Knowledge in general, and new technological know-how in particular, are no longer considered as freely available, but as local (technology specific), tacit (firm specific), and complex (based on a variety of technology and scientific fields). To understand and use the respective know-how, specific competences are necessary, which have to be built up in a cumulative process in the course of time. Following this, knowledge and the underlying learning processes are important sources for the observed heterogeneity among agents.

Challenges for Analysing Qualitative Change

From the discussion above we can identify two major challenges for an analysis of qualitative change.

The first challenge is that a theoretical framework adequately displaying our notion of qualitative change has to incorporate concepts that comply with the notion of development of evolutionary economics in the sense discussed by Nelson (2001). Basically he refers to path-dependencies, dynamic returns and their interaction as constitutive ingredients for evolutionary processes in the socioeconomic realm.

The second challenge is that we generally have to focus on both the micro and meso levels of the economy, since our understanding of the term 'qualitative change' refers to a changing composition of components and interaction of and in the economic system. In doing so we can identify some stylized facts that are considered of crucial importance when qualitative change in an economy is considered. The most obvious ones are as follows.

First, an increasing importance of knowledge-generation and diffusion activities is observed at least in the sectors of the economy that are considered to be the most dynamic and innovative ones. This coins the notion of a transformation of the economy into a knowledge-based economy. Second, this is accompanied by a continuously increasing specialization and, related to this, an increasing variety of products and services coexisting simultaneously. Third, specialization and differentiation go hand in hand with an increasing importance of (market and non-market) interactions between the agents. Fourth, behind this increasing variety we observe innovation processes that at the same time improve efficiency of the production process and the quality of the products. Fifth, this innovation process is driven by competition selecting between different technological alternatives. Finally, the environmental constraints can be considered as filter and focusing devices in this selection process, either supporting or suppressing the diffusion of new technologies.

Once the relevance of these facts for the transformation of an economy is accepted, the research has to account adequately for those developments.

Micro and Meso Perspectives

Obviously this aim can only be accomplished by abandoning an aggregate perspective but instead focusing on a micro- or meso-level population approach (Metcalfe 2001). This allows for examining diverse agents, their interaction and the knowledge-induced transformation of both. By doing this, modelling openly has to take into account the importance of micro–macro–micro feedback effects (for example, Silverberg 1988). In their decisions actors obviously consider macro (-economic) constraints, but they also exert a significant influence on the altering of these constraints (Dopfer 2001). The interrelated inspection of the meso and micro levels reflects the idea that analysis on the aggregated meso level relies on description, whereas analysis on the micro level focuses on explanation of the phenomena found on the meso level (ibid.).

Knowledge

Considering this will lead to a revision of standard economic models as analysis here closely follows reality. Traditional 'production functions' include labour, capital, materials and energy. Knowledge and technology are only external influences on production. However, recent analytical approaches have been developed allowing the explicit consideration of knowledge as well as learning of actors as a means of acquiring new knowledge. Improvements in the knowledge base are likely not only to increase the productive capacity of the other contributing factors of production and to lead to the introduction of new products, as a visible outcome of the transformation process, but also to alter the organizational processes of knowledge creation, namely the interrelationships between the actors. Thus, transformation relates to result and process dimensions similar to the terminology elaborated in Herrmann-Pillath (2001).

Consequently, it cannot be assumed that there exists a fixed set of activities and relationships in the social and economic spheres, especially when it comes to knowledge generation and learning. But this by no means implies that no such set exists at all. It does exist, although by its very nature it is evolving continuously. In this respect transformation not only refers to the feedback processes, but it also and with major relevance refers to the change of the set itself during the process. This is evolution, and evolution is the very reason for not using static equilibrium theories or dynamic models to analyse qualitative developments, as they are based on the notion of reversibility. The notion of evolution demands that we resort to ideas of irreversibility and path-dependence.

THEORETICAL AND CONCEPTUAL CONSIDERATIONS

An exploration of settings fulfilling the above requirements very likely needs numerical techniques, which are regarded as a major tool in evolutionary economics (Kwásnicki 1998; Aruka 2001). Although simulation analysis comes in various flavours, most of them reflect Boulding's view that we need to develop 'mathematics which is suitable to social systems, which the sort of eighteenth century mathematics which we use is not' (Boulding 1991). An increasing literature is now concerned with the application of so-called agent-based models. This approach consists of a decentralized collection of agents acting autonomously in various contexts. The massively parallel and local interactions can give rise to path-dependencies, dynamic returns and their interaction. In such an environment, global phenomena such as the development and diffusion of technologies, the emergence of networks, herd behaviour and so on, which cause the transformation of the observed system, can be modelled adequately. This modelling approach focuses on depicting the agents, their relationships and the processes governing the transformation. Very broadly, the application of an *agent-based modelling approach* offers two major advantages with respect to knowledge and learning orientations.

The first advantage of agent-based modelling is the capability to show how collective phenomena came about and how the interaction of the autonomous and heterogeneous agents leads to the genesis of these phenomena. Furthermore, agent-based modelling aims at the isolation of critical behaviour in order to identify agents that more than others drive the collective result of the system. It also endeavours to identify points of time where the system exhibits qualitative rather than sheer quantitative change (Tesfatsion 2001). In this light it becomes clear why agent-based modelling conforms with the principles of evolutionary economics (Lane 1993a, 1993b). It is 'the' modelling approach to be pursued in evolutionary settings.

The second advantage of agent-based modelling, which is complementary to the first, is a more normative one. Agent-based models are not only used to obtain a deeper understanding of the inherent forces that drive a system and influence the characteristics of a system. Agent-based modellers also use their models as computational laboratories to explore various institutional arrangements, various potential paths of development so as to assist and guide, for example, firms, policy makers and so on, in their particular decision context.

Agent-based modelling thus uses methods and insights from diverse disciplines such as evolutionary economics, cognitive science and computer science in its attempt to model the bottom-up emergence of phenomena and the top-down influence of the collective phenomena on individual behaviour.

The recent developments in new techniques, in particular the advent of powerful tools of computation such as evolutionary computation (for a summary of the use of evolutionary computation and genetic programming in particular, see Ebersberger 2002), opens up the opportunity for economists to model economic systems on a more realistic, that is, more complex basis (Tesfatsion 2001).

Any entity that has no actors cannot exert an influence on the current state of the system or the development of the system. To illustrate this point, bits of information have nil influence on the system as long as they are not put into the appropriate context by a capable individual, influencing its activities. A resource cannot change the system as long as it is not used for carrying out certain activities that change the nature and the structure of the system. Hence in the centre of the stage there is the actor and its activities.

REASONS FOR STUDYING THE ENERGY SYSTEM

There are two reasons why the energy sector seems to be an example *par excellence* for our purposes as outlined above. Firstly, the energy sector is relevant for the entire economy. In Figure 9.3 we see the development of the world energy demand for the last 150 years continuously increasing over the whole time span with an increasing rate after the Second World War.

Regarding the development of primary energy resources in Figure 9.4, it becomes obvious that the importance of different energy sources diverges over time and that new energy sources enter the scene from time to time. We observe the development of the share of different energy sources over the same time interval. Whereas the importance of wood is decreasing over time and coal had reached its peak in the early twentieth century, natural gas had not entered the scene by then, and nuclear energy technologies were not available before the 1960s.

Secondly, compared to other sectors, qualitative change proceeds in - relatively long time periods. Accordingly, different mechanisms and effects are comparatively easier to separate as not too many overlapping develop-

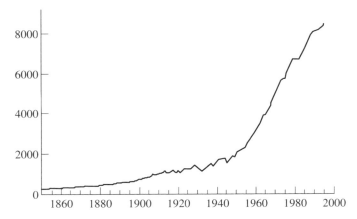

Figure 9.3   Development of world energy demand within the last 200 years

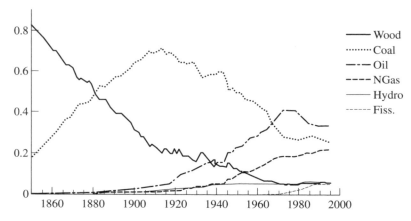

Figure 9.4   Development of the share of primary energy resources

ments are to be expected, which would make the discrimination of causes and effects more difficult. Related to this, it is not invention that is of particular importance, but the first commercial application, that is, innovation, as well as the spreading of the new technologies, that is, diffusion. This means that in the analysis, when it comes to incremental innovation in the diffusion process, technological uncertainty is less severe. Most often the relevant technologies already exist as blueprints and the transformation process basically deals with the application and improvement of these technologies.

In this respect, the political system exerts crucial influence on the transformation process, demanding the applied population perspective including the interactions between economic and political actors. Finally, the transformation in the economic system very likely leads to qualitative changes in the energy demand, such as the most recent decoupling of economic growth and energy demand. Here, on the one hand, political efforts such as, for example, the Kyoto Protocol, again shape this development. On the other hand, however, it is very likely that within the bundle of goods and services in the demand function, the degree of knowledge intensity increases and the degree of energy intensity decreases parallel with the emergence of the knowledge-based economies. Whereas, as already mentioned above, the creation of knowledge is accompanied by positive external effects, due to thermodynamic principles the use of energy goes hand in hand with negative externalities. In this respect, an increasing knowledge intensity in production and demand is very likely to lead to a changing energy intensity of economic growth. Figure 9.5 illustrates the interesting

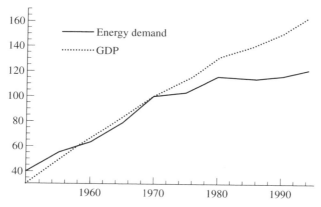

Figure 9.5   Development of world energy demand and GDP (index)

decoupling of the world energy demand from the development of the GDP since the 1970s.

BUILDING BLOCKS OF THE MODEL

In accordance with the principles elaborated in the previous section, the techno-economic model of the energy system utilizes the agent-based approach (Gilbert and Troitzsch 1999; Tesfatsion 2001). A conceptual framework for the analysis of long-run qualitative change can be composed of the following building blocks: in particular we consider actors, actions, endowments, interactions and evaluation, and decision processes as the decisive ones for such a model. The building blocks discussed here are not separate and unrelated entities. Rather, they are the result of a systematization process. They represent our conceptual view on the issue developed to clarify the analytical concepts and to facilitate implementation of the simulation model in the second step. In the following subsections we sketch the building blocks.

Actors

We consider actors as being the major driving force in the evolution of the energy sector. As such, we regard them as the reason for the manifestation of qualitative change in the system. They are the crucial components of the system. The model requires a multi-agent approach, which assumes that agents populating the model can be divided into various categories according to their activities, resources, routines and relations.

On an aggregate level we have to distinguish different groups (popula-tions) of actors that share common features, discriminating one population of actors from the others. However, underneath the surface of the group we find a heterogeneous population of individual actors each being character-ized by individual features.

Accordingly, a central issue is the general design of the actors. Actors are represented as a code that has the standard attributes of intelligent agents (Wooldridge and Jennings 1995):

- *autonomy*, which means that agents operate without other agents having direct control of their actions and internal states. This is a necessary condition for implementing inter- and most importantly intra-population heterogeneity;
- *social ability*, that is, agents are able to interact with other agents not only in terms of competition but also in terms of cooperation. This includes the possibility of modelling agents that show various forms of interaction blended from competition and cooperation;
- *reactivity*, agents are able to perceive their environment and respond to it; and finally,
- *proactivity* enables the agents to take the initiative. This means that not only are they adapting to changing circumstances, but they are also engaged in goal-directed behaviour.

The above points indicate that the actors in the simulation are not only able to adapt their behaviour to a given set of circumstances, but in a neo-Schumpeterian sense they are also able to learn from their own experience and to modify their behaviour creatively so as to change the circumstances themselves.

When modelling the features and characteristics of the artificial agents the above-mentioned standard attributes have to be implemented. As the agents in our conceptual framework can be characterized by their actions, endow-ments, interactions and their evaluation, and decision processes, these con-ceptual building blocks have to be designed so as to reflect the attributes.

Actions

The different actions performed by different actors enable us to classify certain groups of actors. Actions are not the only feature that we use to dis-tinguish different groups of actors – their endowment might be another cri-terion for differentiation – but they are one of the most striking ones and are connected to others such as endowments, interactions and so on, which will be discussed below. At a first glance, we could distinguish between firms and households by saying that the former produce commodities and the latter consume them. However, we shall discuss below that the grouping of households and firms cannot be sustained in the context of the energy system.

Energy-producing actors

With regard to the population of firms, the actions of some firms might complement one another as most firms only account for a small fraction of the total production chain necessary for the energy sector's final energy production. The activities involved range from the mining and refining of resources to production and distribution of the final energy. On these grounds we differentiate the groups of actors according to their actions.

The actions carried out by the firms producing and distributing the final energy are constrained by the available and, most of the time, by the already-installed technology. Of course new technology can also be sought by the individual firm, but this contributes only a minor part. The major part of the 'new technology' can be regarded as a given and the firms are able – given that they acquire the respective competences and capabilities – to choose a specific technology. Their research and development activities are then basically concentrated on the improvement of the application of the different technologies.

Energy-consuming actors

Concerning energy consumption, we can distinguish two main populations of consumers according to the activity that the energy is used for.

First, firms use energy as a factor of production. Energy enters the production function in the same way that capital, labour and knowledge do. By a combination of the factors, firms produce commodities endowed with characteristics which give positive utility to the final users of the goods. In mainstream economics, firms are usually seen as optimizing the amount and kind of goods produced, subject to some constraints.

Households consume energy not because of the direct utility gained from energy consumption but as a factor of household production. Energy has to be moderated by a process of factor combination to yield goods or services with characteristics that deliver utility to the household. Other factors of production such as capital and labour influence the efficiency of energy use in the household. The goods and services produced in the household range from meals, which need household appliances as capital goods, and human labour and the ingredients and energy as factor inputs, to mobility, which needs cars as capital goods, and human labour and gasoline as inputs. Hence, the household's energy use can be modelled by a household production function.

Regulatory authorities
With reference to the conceptual framework of an industrial system
(Mathews 2001) it becomes obvious that for our purposes we have to
broaden the view. We have to add actors other than firms to the description
of the system. Policy actors shape the energy system in a decisive way by
designing the overall framework within which the other actors operate.
Consequently, our analysis must include this particular group of actors
that are responsible for the rules of the game. Furthermore, and particularly important when it comes to the analysis of long-run transformation
processes, policy actors also bridge the gap between basic and applied
research. This means that the technological strands that are developed to a
commercial application are most often the ones that have survived a polit-
ically guided selection process.

To summarize, we consider the following populations of actors: agents
responsible for the production and distribution of energy, commodity-
producing agents who use energy as a factor of production, as well as energy-
and commodity-consuming agents, and policy-making and -regulating
agents. By this, we acknowledge the role of the energy-producing and
-consuming entities as well as the regulatory entities in shaping the energy
sector. However, as already mentioned, the actors within one population do
not exhibit homogeneous behaviour; rather they are differentiated in terms
of their performing certain actions.

Routines
Each of the basic categories of actors is modelled not by a representative
agent but by a population of heterogeneous agents. For any of those subpopulations, rules and routines can be derived which govern the particular
actions of the agents, and the interaction and the interrelation of the agents
within and among the subpopulations. Actions and routines are conceptu-
ally closely related. Take, for example, an electricity-producing firm. The
production of energy is the action of this particular firm. However, the way
electricity is produced is governed by routines. Hence routines are realizations of actions and it is through routines that actors manipulate reality.
Not only does the endowment with resources shape the nature of the
actors, but also their individual routines make up a large part of the actors'
heterogeneity. Nelson and Winter (1982) relate routines to the satisficing
behaviour and the bounded rationality of actors. Routinized behaviour
causes some stickiness and some inertia of the system, which results in
some stability of the system – stability, at least to a certain degree.

Households, for example, do not optimize their heating behaviour; they
rather want to keep the room at a comfortable temperature, which might
vary by several degrees centigrade. This behaviour translates into their

energy demand, be it the immediate demand for natural gas or electricity or the amount of oil being kept in stock for the winter.

Large integrated energy suppliers, for example, maintain a simple rule based on the difference between the wholesale or retail price of gas for deciding whether to stock gas, to resell it or to use it for electricity production.

Routines for commercial actors can be thought of as business processes and standard operating procedures. For households, routines can be thought of as habitualized or automated procedures and activities. Routines are repeated on a regular basis as long as they lead to a sufficient result, then they are modified. Repetition of the routines results in a certain degree of stability of the system without requiring the agents to be fully rational and informed. In the context of the energy system it becomes obvious that the assumption of fully rational individuals cannot reasonably be sustained. How many consumers, for example, know precisely how a nuclear power plant works, or what inputs are necessary to create how much electricity?

As indicated, actors manipulate reality through their routines. Hence routines are not only focused on internal procedures of the actors, but they also govern external relationships with actors of the same basic group and with actors of other groups. However, routines of one group can only be replicated by actors of the same group. For simplicity we assume that routines cannot transcend the boundaries of the specific groups of actors.[3] Households may replicate successful routines of other households by imitation and learning; firms may imitate successful routines of competitors and collaborators often moderated and facilitated by business consulting companies.[4] The actors, however, are not constrained to pick the most suitable one from a given set of routines, as would be the case for purely reactive agents. Furthermore, proactive agents can create routines themselves, try them out, and discard them if the routines do not obtain the desired results. They can also continue using them once they are deemed to be successful. When creating new routines, the actors do not have to design them from scratch, most often, agents adopt routines and modify them so as to customize them to their particular needs. Hence, building proactive agents for the simulation hinges on the implementation of routines, their modification and their updating.

Endowments

Access to material and immaterial resources, and their availability together with the competences, make up the endowment of the actors. They combine components of the endowment in production processes. Accordingly, the endowments are the crucial assets of agents in accomplishing their tasks, be it production or consumption. Following Matthews (2001), what makes the difference between the evolutionary perspective and more conventional economic perspectives, is that resources are also the decisive factor which allows for heterogeneity between the firms. This becomes even more important, since a specific resource endowment does not completely determine the output of a firm. The range of possible outputs follows only from the actor's specific combination of its resources with its routines (see above).

All actors are characterized by different sets of endowments. This is true not only for the different populations of actors, but also for the actors within the single populations identified above. For example, energy-producing firms differ considerably with respect to their capital stocks, which are not only of different age but also restricted to very specific technologies, for example, nuclear power stations or wind turbines. Furthermore, the access to primary energy resources on the one hand as well as to distribution networks on the other makes a decisive difference between single actors. Of course, the commodity-producing firms also differ considerably in their energy dependence (for example, steel versus consulting companies) as well as on specific energy sources (for example, oil versus natural gas). In the same way, households cannot simply switch between alternative energy sources (for example, natural gas versus solar energy) but are dependent on distribution networks (for example, gas pipelines), their specific income situation and so on. Finally, different regulatory actors have rather specific possibilities for influencing the energy markets which range from the fostering of certain technologies (technology policy) to the design of general contracts between the energy supply and demand side (regulation).

With regard to the standard attributes of agents, it is obvious that agent autonomy can only be achieved with the notion of personal and individual endowments of certain factors. It is the idea of individual property rights on production factors or income that enables us to model actors acting with their own set of endowments. There is no governing entity to rule the spending or the use of endowments as long as the agents obey the rules set up by the regulatory authority.

Interactions

Concerning the relevant interaction between the different actors in our model, we have to consider a rather broad set of relationships ranging from competitive to cooperative, from bilateral to multilateral as well as from decentralized to hierarchical relations. Furthermore, a technological as well as an economic realm has to be considered. For example, the qualitative development of the energy system is shaped not only by technological competition (for example, coal versus nuclear power), but also by the exploitation of complementary relationships between different demand needs (for example, combined heat and power systems) or synergies between capital goods producers and energy suppliers. Also, economic competition can go hand in hand with cooperation between different actors, for example, in market-consolidating periods when networks of actors bundle their efforts (for example, via mergers) and competition no longer takes place between different individual actors but between different networks (for example, recent developments in the German electricity market). Cooperative relationships can also be found in user–producer relationships when, for example, transactions are characterized by long-term contracts or technological specificities. Very prominently, network externalities shape the relationships in most of the energy markets, where the supply is pipeline bounded. Additionally, hierarchical interaction is central for the regulatory authorities which on the one hand design the rules of transactions and on the other play a moderating role between different actors or populations of actors.

Evaluation and Decision Processes

The discussion up to this point reveals that we have to cope with a heterogeneous set of actors. Some actors produce energy, some consume it or use it for household production; some actors regulate, some actors maximize utility, others satisfice.

The question here is how to unify the decision process of such a diverse set of actors while preserving the possibility for heterogeneity.

If we resort to imagining the decision process as a competition of several possibilities and the selection of one of the possibilities we can use an evolutionary terminology to describe the process. Let us use the term 'fitness function'[5] for the device that evaluates the possibilities and let us furthermore use the term 'selection' for picking one or several of the possibilities. We model the prototype of the decision process in two stages.

First, a real-world actor can only decide on the actions and routines he/she carries out on the basis of his/her perception of reality. The perception of reality by a real-world actor is a mental representation of the world. Hence, by its very nature it is a model. A modelled actor contains models of the (modelled) reality. The actors' mental modelling of the current state of the reality, however, is not a bijective mapping of the reality into the symbolic representation. Rather there are several models that are compatible with the observations available to the actor. In addition to the current state of the reality, the actors condense possible future states of the reality into scenarios. To have a basis upon which the actor can decide, the most likely one has to be selected from the set of the competing mental models of reality. A fitness function, for example, representing the likelihood of each model, does the job. A mental representation of this type can be modelled, for example, by genetic algorithms or genetic programming as can be seen in Dosi et al. (1999) or Edmonds (1999).

Second, on the basis of his perception of the real world the actor decides on which actions to perform. As any situation can be handled by various actions and routines, the actor has to choose which one to take. Here again we can think of a fitness function ruling the choice process. By focusing on certain features of the actions and routines and ignoring other characteristics, the fitness functions in this stage implicitly include the aims of the actor.

The use of the metaphor fitness function requires the notion of selection as a subsequent step. The selection process performed after the fitness evaluation of the activities represents the type of behaviour the actor is assumed to perform.

The building blocks introduced above constitute the dynamics of a socioeconomic model which in a further step have to be connected with the technological realm in order to combine the socioeconomic dynamics with real-world phenomena. This ensures that the model is realistic.

Technology

To model the interaction of the agents, the model needs a technological background that is strongly determined by the characteristics of the already- or soon-to-be-available technologies of energy transformation, transport and distribution. This background of the model consists of a flow model of the energy system that incorporates the energy resources and the technologies to transform and distribute the energy. As we model this by a directed graph we can easily track and manipulate the flow of energy from the resources to the end-user. Manipulation of the flow model is necessary, as the introduction of a new technology such as fuel or photovoltaic cells changes the structure of the model and changes the background for the interaction of the agents. The agents, however, can change the structure and the content of the flow model according to their preferences, too. Again, here we have a component of the model that causes mutual interaction with other components.

OUTLOOK

The agent-based model offers a possibility for investigating the socio-economic interrelationships in the energy system, whereas the energy flow model incorporates the technological and environmental aspects of the energy system. Hence, each model has its particular and therefore restricted problem domain. We argued above that the energy system is characterized by strong socioeconomic and technoeconomic interdependencies. Those cannot be analysed in either the agent-based model or the energy-flow model in their stand-alone version. The valuable insights on the mutual dependency of the socioeconomic and the technological spheres can only be gained by a fusion of both models, which will allow for the analysis of socioeconomic and technoeconomic characteristics of the system and will enable us to shed new light on various transition processes.

In particular, we shall apply the merged framework to two recent transitions in the German energy system. First, we shall try to reconstruct the transition of central heating systems from oil to natural gas. The second transition to be modelled will be the emergence and diffusion of technologies that exploit renewable energy sources, and the effects on this of liberalization and carbon dioxide taxes.

On the one hand, those two applications of the general framework will be of particular interest to real-world agents such as energy suppliers and policy makers, while on the other, they will serve as a tool to validate the methodological approach undertaken by this project.

An extension of our investigation of the energy system raises the question whether historical developments such as the large-scale transition from wood to coal and from coal to oil could also be handled using the proposed methodological and instrumental framework.

NOTES

1. The authors would like to thank Thomas Hamacher and Markus Biberacher from the Max Planck Institut for Plasmaphysics, Garching for their helpful assistance.
2. Recently Mathews (2001) has developed a conceptual framework for the analysis of an industrial market system, which is quite close to our building blocks. However, the building blocks introduced here take account of the broader research programme.
3. This assumption is in contrast to the idea of benchmarking in the business literature, where key features of 'best' routines of units from other and unrelated sectors are the bases of improvement.
4. Here again the hierarchical composition of the model enables us to structure and stress the relevant features and to unify the building blocks and their relation so as to facilitate setting up an appropriate simulation model. The hierarchical composition in the context of routines refers to the micro–meso analysis laid out in the exposition above.
5. Again we use a notion also found in Mathews (2001). However, we substantiate the idea and depict the decisions as a two-stage process.

REFERENCES

Arthur, W.B. (1988), 'Competing technologies: an overview' in G. Dosi, C. Freeman, R. Nelson, G. Silverberg and L. Soete (eds), *Technical Change and Economic Theory*, London, New York: Pinter, pp. 590–607.

Aruka, Y. (2001), *Evolutionary Controversies in Economics: A New Transdisciplinary Approach*, Tokyo, Berlin: Springer.

Bain, J.S. (1956), *Barriers to New Competition: Their character and Consequences in Manufacturing Industries*, Cambridge, MA: Harvard University Press.

Boulding, K.E. (1991), 'What is evolutionary economics?', *Journal of Evolutionary Economics*, **1**, 9–17.

Cantner, U. and A. Pyka (1998), 'Technological evolution – an analysis within the knowledge-based approach', *Structural Change and Economic Dynamics*, **9**, 85–108.

Clark, N. and C. Juma (1987), *Long Run Economics – An Evolutionary Approach to Economic Growth*, London: Pinter.

Dopfer, K. (2001), 'Evolutionary economics: framework for analysis', ch. 1 in Dopfer (ed.), *Evolutionary Economics: Program and Scope*, Boston, MA, Dordrecht, London: Kluwer Academic, pp. 1–44.

Dosi, G., L. Marengo, A. Bassanini and M. Valente (1999), 'Norms as emergent properties of adaptive learning: the case of economic routines, *Journal of Evolutionary Economics*, **9**, 5–26.

Ebersberger, B. (2002), *Genetische Programmierung: Ein Instrument zur empirischen Fundierung ökonomischer Modelle* (Genetic Programming: An Instrument for the Empirical Foundation of Economic Model(s)), Wiesbaden: Deutscher Universitätsverlag.

Edmonds, B. (1999), 'Modelling bounded rationality in agent-based simulations using the evolution of mental models', in T. Brenner (ed.), *Computational Techniques for Modelling Learning in Economics, Advances in Computational Economics*, Dordrecht: Kluwer Academic, pp. 305–32.

Eliasson, G. (1991), 'Modelling the experimentally organized economy', *Journal of Economic Behaviour and Organization*, **16** (1–2), 153–82.

Giersch, H. (1984), 'The age of Schumpeter', *American Economic Review*, May, **74** (2), 103–109.

Gilbert, N. and K. Troitzsch (1999), *Simulation for the Social Scientist*, Milton Keynes: Open University Press.

Heiner, R.A. (1983), 'The origin of predictable behaviour', *American Economic Review*, **73**, 560–95.

Herrmann-Pillath, C. (2001), 'On the ontological foundation of evolutionary economics', ch. 1 in K. Dopfer (ed.), *Evolutionary Economics: Program and Scope*, Boston, MA, Dordrecht, London: Kluwer Academic, pp. 89–139.

Kwásnicki, W. (1998), 'Simulation methodology in evolutionary economics', in F. Schweitzer and G. Silverberg (eds), *Evolution und Selbstorganisation in der Ökonomie (Evolution and Self-Organisation in Economics), Selbstorganisation: Jahrbuch für Komplexität in den Natur-, Sozial- und Geisteswissenschaften*, **9**, Berlin: Duncker & Humblot, 161–86.

Lane, D. (1993a), 'Artificial worlds and economics: Part I', *Journal of Evolutionary Economics*, **3**, 89–107.

Lane, D. (1993b), 'Artificial worlds and economics: Part II', *Journal of Evolutionary Economics*, **3**, 177–97.

Mathews, J.A. (2001), 'Competitive interfirm dynamics within an industrial market system', *Industry and Innovation*, **8**, 79–107.

Metcalfe, J.S. (2001), 'Evolutionary approaches to population thinking and the problem of growth and development', in K. Dopfer (ed.), *Evolutionary Economics: Program and Scope*, Boston, MA, Dordrecht, London: Kluwer Academic, pp. 141–64.

Nelson, R.R. (2001), 'Evolutionary perspectives on economic growth', ch. 5 in K. Dopfer (ed.), *Evolutionary Economics: Program and Scope*, Boston, MA, Dordrecht, London: Kluwer Academic, pp. 165–94.

Nelson, R.R. and S.G. Winter (1982), *An Evolutionary Theory of Economic Change*, Cambridge, MA: Harvard University Press.

Romer, P.M. (1990), 'Endogenous technological change', *Journal of Political Economy*, **98**, 77–102.

Saviotti, P.P. (1996), *Technological Evolution: Variety and the Economy*, Cheltenham, UK and Brookfield, USA: Edward Elgar.

Scherer, F.M. and D. Ross (1990), *Industrial Market Structure and Economic Performance*, Boston, MA: Houghton Mifflin.

Silverberg, G. (1988), 'Modelling economic dynamics and technical change: mathematical approaches to self-organization and evolution', in G. Dosi, C. Freeman, R. Nelson, G. Silverberg and L. Soete (eds), *Technical Change and Economic Theory*, London, New York: Pinter, pp. 531–59.

Tesfatsion, L. (2001), 'Agent-based modelling of evolutionary economic systems', *IEEE Transactions on Evolutionary Computation*, **5**, 1–6.

Wooldridge, M. and N.R. Jennings (1995), 'Intelligent agents: theory and practice', *Knowledge Engineering Review*, **10**, 115–52.

Index